Local Vino

HEARTLAND FOODWAYS

The Heartland Foodways series seeks to encourage and
publish book-length works that define and celebrate
midwestern food traditions and practices. The series
is open to foods from seed to plate and to foodways
that have found a home in the Midwest.

Series Editor
Bruce Kraig, Roosevelt University

Editorial Board
Gary Fine, Northwestern University
Robert Launay, Northwestern University
Yvonne Lockwood, Michigan State University Museum
Lucy Long, Bowling Green State University
Rachelle H. Saltzman, Iowa Arts Council

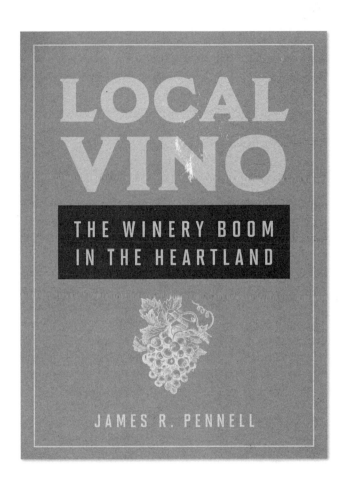

LOCAL VINO

THE WINERY BOOM IN THE HEARTLAND

JAMES R. PENNELL

UNIVERSITY OF ILLINOIS PRESS
Urbana, Chicago, and Springfield

Library of Congress Control Number: 2016949268
ISBN 978-0-252-04074-0 (hardcover)
ISBN 978-0-252-08225-2 (paperback)
ISBN 978-0-252-09919-9 (e-book)

Contents

Illustrations

Figures

Tables

Acknowledgments

A book project such as this about real people in real places is dependent on the kindness of so many people. I am most indebted to all the people who spent an hour or two sharing the stories of their lives and work with me. I could not begin to capture all the interesting things they shared. For the winery owners, hopefully my biggest gift in return will be that more people will appreciate the challenges of the work you are doing, will visit your wineries, experience your hospitality and fine work, and hear some of your stories I didn't include. For the university and industry organization folks who have been so helpful, I hope that those thinking about getting into the winery business will take advantage of your wisdom earlier rather than later and take it to heart. Although the primary focus of this book is winery owners and their work, I thank Butch Fennema and Dianna Hamilton for sharing their experiences as customers who appreciate what Midwestern wines and wineries offer. Sadly, Dianna's husband Steve, who also talked with me, passed away before I could finish the book and share it with him.

I would not have had the firsthand experience picking and crushing grapes and bottling wine without the support and generosity of John, Bill, and Laura Richardson at Mallow Run Winery. In addition to allowing me to pry into their lives, John and Bill graciously responded to my questions for almost five years when I was trying to understand various things about the business. John also read an early version of the manuscript. These three and their infectious enthusiasm for what they are doing got me thinking about this project, and I really can't thank them enough. They are masters at making a good time for everyone.

I am deeply indebted to Bill Regier, former executive director of the University of Illinois Press and acquisitions editor for the Heartland Foodways series, for seeing some promise in this work and encouraging me to include additional Midwestern states in my project. The added states helped to confirm the many things I had learned in Indiana while broadening my understanding of some of the differences across states that impact what winery owners can do. Although I could not address all the states I would have liked on my out-of-pocket budget, I had the opportunity to meet many more wonderful people by crossing state lines, and I developed a much richer perspective. I hope you enjoy retirement, Bill. I couldn't have asked for a better replacement when Assistant Acquisitions Editor Marika Christofides took over the project. She was a pleasure to work with, calming my fears about the transition and ably helping me bring the project to completion. The entire University of Illinois Press staff I have worked with have been wonderful—Michael Roux, Kevin Cunningham, Steve Fast, Roberta Sparenberg, and Jennifer Comeau. Jane Lyle copyedited the manuscript, deftly smoothing my prose and making it a much better read than it would have been otherwise.

I owe my friends and University of Indianapolis colleagues many thanks for putting up with me the last four years as I talked incessantly about "the book." My brother Don frequently joked that "there is no book." He's also kept me informed about Texas wines, as a good brother should do. My bandmates in Acoustic Catfish, Rob Gobetz and Scott Morgan, are owed an apology for my inattention to our "business" as the book project stretched across and consumed so much time. They are both good friends who understand that sometimes we listen to and follow different drummers in our lives.

I am thankful for the support and encouragement of my department colleagues Tim Maher, Kevin Whiteacre, Amanda Miller, and Bobby Potters; my dean, Jen Drake; and the university's director of public information, Scott Hall, and provost, Deb Balogh. I am especially grateful to the university and our sabbatical and grants committee for giving me the opportunity to take a sabbatical during the 2011–12 academic year to spend time in the field and conduct interviews. It provided some of the time I needed to get the project well off the ground while also allowing me to pay my bills. Thanks also go to UIndy sociology graduate student Heather Coyle, who helped me out with some transcription and did a nice job for someone unfamiliar with wine terms. Our administrative assistant Gwen Thomas helped me out so many times in so many ways, especially while I was department chair, that I won't list them.

I also owe many thanks to Ken Colburn, my undergraduate mentor, who helped me understand how everyday life was sociologically interesting. He and his wife, Mary Moore, my friend and colleague at the University of Indianapolis, were companions in conviviality at the time when my interest in wine was developing and helped me understand it as a pleasant supplement to a social occasion. I am also deeply indebted to Bill Firestone, my dissertation supervisor at Rutgers University, who gave me the opportunity to further develop my interviewing and analytical skills studying teacher networks in California and Vermont.

The person to whom I owe the most thanks is my wife and closest colleague, Greta. She took trips to wineries with me, shot photos (some of which appear in this book), observed or heard things I sometimes overlooked, talked with me constantly about what I was thinking, gave skillful, detailed feedback on each manuscript draft, transcribed parts of interviews when I was running out of time, and enthusiastically shared in the contemplation of many bottles of wine. She tolerated a number of vacations when I mostly sat at the computer and worked. I could not have seen this project through to the end without her love and support. This kind of work takes over a person's life, and I deeply appreciate that she willingly shared the pains and pleasures of it.

The final caveat is that I am ultimately responsible for the sentences you will be reading. I had a massive amount of information to sift through, and growing grapes, making wine, and owning a winery are not simple subjects. I draw heavily on what people told me, as evidenced by the many quotations. But ultimately, this is my account of what I learned, and there could be many others. I hope your understanding of what it takes to get the grapes in the bottle is enriched by what I have written. That was my goal. Whether I succeed or not, I'm quite sure your reading will be enhanced by a bottle of wine.

1

Getting Together
at the Local Winery

It's a warm May evening, the first pizza night of the year at Mallow Run Winery in Bargersville, Indiana. My band, Acoustic Catfish, is performing at the event, and as we prepare to start our second set, more than three hundred people are gathered on the patio and spread across the hillside that gradually descends to the creek for which the winery is named. It doesn't take my sociologically trained eye to know that something is going on here, and my band is only a very small piece of it. I had noticed that wineries were starting to pop up around Indiana and throughout the Midwest, and I wondered how variations on this scene were playing out in those different places. So I set out to learn why people were flocking to wineries on weekends and holidays, to visit tasting rooms and attend barbecues, concerts, and other events, or simply to hang out with friends and family. What was attracting them, who were the masterminds behind this phenomenon, and were these little oases in the hustle and bustle of everyday life as idyllic as they seemed for their creators? I was starting to think that maybe I should get a little piece of this life myself. This book reflects what I discovered over four years of in-depth exploration.

I was especially interested in states, like my home state of Indiana, that are not typically associated with wine in the minds of most people—not just East and West Coasters, but Midwesterners as well. Michigan has a bit of a reputation for wine, and so does Missouri. Their recent commercials put out by their state departments of tourism to attract folks like me make that pretty clear, with images of vineyards and clinking wineglasses. But the boom has hit the corn and soybean states, and the growth has been phenomenal over the last two decades. The number of wineries in Indiana, for example, has more than quadrupled from the seventeen in 2003. A regional marketing report by Timothy Woods and Matthew Ernst listed fifty-seven wineries in Indiana in early 2011; the Indiana Wine Grape Council reported a total of sixty-one wineries later that year, and by December 2015 the number stood at eighty (Woods and Ernst 2011; Indiana Wine Grape Council, n.d.). The number of

Figure 1.1. Concert crowd at Mallow Run Winery in Bargersville, Indiana, September 14, 2013. Photo by Greta Pennell.

wineries in Iowa has grown even more during that time period, with twenty more than Indiana. Illinois has over one hundred wineries, and Ohio has over two hundred.

The winery boom is not just a Midwestern phenomenon; it is a national phenomenon. I am not talking about the well-known wineries of California, Oregon, and Washington, which were once locals themselves and harbingers of things to come. Wineries are popping up in every state. They have grown in number and output at an astounding rate during the last two decades, even during economic recessions. From 2000 to 2012, the number of California wineries grew by 259 percent, but the corresponding figure for the rest of the United States was 347 percent (Wine Institute 2013). Most all wineries outside the West Coast are small family operations.

In this book, I examine the local winery phenomenon in the Midwest, focusing heavily on the industries in Ohio, Indiana, Illinois, and Iowa. This is a story with three interdependent parts. One part focuses on wineries as places that bring people together to informally socialize with others. Wineries are fun places to be—merry, festive, convivial. They are gathering places that lure people out of their houses and away from their televisions and computers. (I am not including here those little computers known as cell phones that have become so pervasive. Unlike coffee shops, where individuals often hang out to work on their laptops, wineries don't seem to be used for this purpose at present.) The experience of getting together with friends and making new acquaintances gives customers the opportunity to be a part of something beyond themselves. This sense of group membership is often labeled "community." That "we-feeling" can be generated by a friendship, a club membership, a commitment to one's country, or some momentary experience of common humanity. Community can also mean a shared connection to the land or a particular place. Local wineries are successful to a great extent because they produce this feeling of being involved in something with others in a special place.

The second part of this story involves having an inspiration, doing good work, and being rewarded for that effort. This is part of the mythos of our society often referred to as the American dream. Newman (1999, 76) labeled it "meritocratic individualism," the shared belief that rewards are commensurate with our individual talents and efforts. Wineries take a tremendous amount of work to start and successfully operate. My central argument is that well-made wines and the wineries that produce and serve them unite two things: the need for community and the desire to pursue and be rewarded for good work. Local wineries bring producers and consumers together, not in some anonymous marketplace, but in a setting where they can get to know each other, celebrate life, and share a local product and place. This experience serves as an oasis in a world increasingly dominated by global production and distribution through international corporations—corporations that primarily measure their value in profits as they attempt to manufacture meaningful connections to their products and/or services through marketing.

The third part of this story considers local wineries in the context of this larger world. Local wineries have created a successful niche by distinguishing themselves from the global wine industry. They are big players in the burgeoning "buy local" movement. However, they are not islands in the global market, but connect with it in a number of ways. They have thrived in part due to the success of the international wine industry and the expanding market for wine. The international industry occasionally pushes back to maintain economic dominance and make sure it gets what it considers its due. The survival of local wineries is also shaped by the groups they enter into relationships with, including each other in professional associations, educational institutions, and government regulatory and promotional agencies. They have been successful because they have negotiated their organizational environments fairly well, pushing back against constraints and expanding their opportunities. However, they must continually monitor the political terrain and work to speak with one voice. This is easier said than done in the face of the heavy time demands of a labor-intensive business.

I want to make clear up front that I am not an expert on viticulture, tending vineyards and growing grapes, or winemaking and enology, the science (and art) of making wine. I am a sociologist who was interested in learning more about this economic and social phenomenon I was witnessing. I enjoy wine and know quite a bit about it, supplemented by many visits to wineries in California, as well as Oregon and trips abroad, and much reading on the subject. The experiences I had while visiting and performing at Indiana wineries focused my interest on learning more about these establishments as social and economic entities. I was fortunate to receive a sabbatical for the 2011–12 academic year. During that time I visited about half the wineries across Indiana, tasting wines and interviewing the owners or talking informally with them or their employees. I also interviewed members of the Purdue Wine Grape Team, a group of specialists who do research, offer workshops, and provide technical assistance on wine and grape production. I volunteered a couple days a week during the fall at Mallow Run Winery, and I also spent time there in February 2012 pruning the vines. I wanted to get firsthand experience with the work involved in producing wine. Little did I know how much there was to learn. I also started making some forays into other states, visiting some of the wineries in the Shawnee Hills region of southern Illinois for the first time in the spring of 2012. I visited wineries in Kentucky, Tennessee, and Alabama during a vacation. Then I was asked if I could consider this phenomenon more regionally. During 2014 and 2015, I interviewed winery owners in Ohio, Illinois, and Iowa, interviewed or corresponded with state-level industry specialists, and visited many other wineries in those states. In what follows, I try to share the knowledge and insights of the owners through the lens of an interested observer and wine drinker.

Local wineries are becoming important places for building community, pursuing the American dream, and negotiating between local communities and larger institutional contexts and actors. I will briefly introduce each of these three parts of the local winery story, then expand on them in the following chapters.

Creating Community

A growing body of work suggests that people across the United States are seeking out opportunities to get together informally in community gathering places such as farmers' markets, coffeehouses, independent bookstores, and taverns (Oldenburg 2001; Tiemann 2008). Ray Oldenburg championed these "third places" in his seminal work *The Great Good Place* (1989, 2nd ed. 1999). Third places fulfill a number of functions beyond what is offered by home (first places) or work (second places). They bring neighbors together and serve everyone. They also assimilate newcomers into the community, in part because anyone can freely come and go; there are no formal barriers to admission. While they bring people together, they allow for some social sorting to occur, the kind that helps community members know "who can do what." They serve as staging areas for events, including during times of crisis. They make possible "public characters" who know everyone and their business and keep a watchful eye over the community's welfare. They bring different generations of people together. Third places are fun; they give community members an opportunity to entertain each other, primarily through conversation. They provide informal forums where different opinions can be expressed on the concerns of the day that require civil responses whether one agrees or not. And regulars in third places help each other out (Oldenburg 1999, xvii–xxv).

Oldenburg and other writers (e.g., Putnam 2000), note a decline in third places over the last half-century as the American population shifted from cities and small towns to suburbs, and corporate chains such as Starbucks and big-box stores such as Walmart closed down mom-and-pop stores, standardizing products as well as social roles and customer experiences in the process. Another factor in the decline of third places was the shift from entertainment involving face-to-face relations in community settings to home-based entertainment mediated by televisions and computers (Putnam 2000; Turkle 2011). These standardized and mediated experiences can be pleasant, but they are often predictable. Corporate-dominated media provide simplified story lines mixed with product bombardment. We are pushed to judge ourselves by the things we have or, more commonly, don't have and want to purchase (Schor 1998, 79–83). The popular media hinder the development of our creative capacities and skills in engaging others, especially those who are different from us.

In contrast, local wineries provide a sense of connection to the producers of the products they sell and the places where they are purchased and often consumed. It is not unusual to have the winemaker serve you at the tasting bar or stop by your table for a chat. Customers can talk about their preferences and be heard. They can notice changes in what is served or the décor and compliment or complain. However, unlike internet "flames" sent by anonymous writers, comments are met by a face in a place. Customers and owners can get to know each other in ways that promote friendly banter, even on points of disagreement.

Local wineries also give customers the opportunity to contribute to the social scene. People come to wineries for birthdays and anniversaries, or more commonly just to get together with family, old friends, or new acquaintances. They come looking for some conversation over a bottle of wine or two and a cheese plate or a barbecue sandwich. Unlike bars in some states that require patrons to be twenty-one to enter, there is no law barring parents from bringing their children to local wineries. Some wineries even allow customers to bring their dogs. Perhaps somewhat surprising, customers can volunteer to help with the work at some wineries. I will say more about this in chapters 3 and 5.

Local wineries are deeply embedded in their local communities and become part of the identity of the places where they are located. Not only do they provide a convivial setting in which to get together with others, but they give back. They hold benefits, donate money or product, and rally other businesses to give back to the community. They also use or partner with other local businesses and encourage customers to buy locally. Some wineries preserve and repurpose historic farms and farm buildings, maintaining important parts of their community's history and culture while inventing new uses and practices.

Pursuing the American Dream

Americans pass down from generation to generation the idea that we are all free to pursue our hopes and dreams and become successful. There is no promise of success, only the freedom to pursue it. However, there is a strong suggestion that the rewards of those pursuits will be commensurate with the talent and hard work invested. Some sociologists refer to this belief as "meritocratic individualism" (Hargreaves 1980; Newman 1999). Studies show that while this belief is widespread, one's family's wealth or social class is a better predictor of life outcomes than one's talents and hard work (Hertz 2006). But for most Americans, these findings don't much matter. The belief in the possibility of success is drilled into us, as is the likelihood of failure if we don't make an effort.

For many, the ultimate success story is becoming your own boss of a successful business. Some don't care what business they go into as long as it is successful. The proliferation of franchises selling prepackaged operations suggests that there are legions who fit this description (Gibson 2003; U.S. Census Bureau 2010). But others want a business that means something more—that is a reflection of some aspect of their personal talents and interests.

From the Old World aspirations of Chateau Thomas Winery or Markko Vineyard, to the urban chic of Hopwood Cellars or Quail Crossing Cellars, to the family-farm feel of John Ernest Vineyard and Winery or Galena Cellars, local wineries and their products become extensions of their owners' identities. Some start as weekend endeavors—an expensive hobby that at some point requires the owners to either make a bigger commitment or put the project on the shelf. Many develop from a family farm. Some owners are "foodies" who emphasize food as much as their wines. They may have a soft spot for certain types of animals (yes, the former Grateful Goat Vineyard and Winery had goats; Whyte Horse Winery was named after a beloved white horse). They often feature certain wine varieties favored by the owners, or the winemaker becomes known for certain wines that are popular with customers. Wineries and their owners' identities are not simply asserted, but reflect a process of negotiation between owners and customers. Although wine is generally associated in popular culture with a certain sophistication, the winemaker who over-promotes that identity may be viewed as snobby by customers, who then share that interpretation with others. Wine may have been an emblem of elite life in the past, but its consumption has been "democratized" to some extent as a result of mass production and marketing (Howland 2013).

Unlike purchasing a franchised business, starting a winery usually means starting from scratch. Like any small business, a winery is no sure thing. Many plans for wineries are never executed. If they do get off the ground, they take much care and nurturing. Winery entrepreneurs who want to make a living from their creations are typically committing to a seven-day work week for the foreseeable future.

Still, seeing positive results from one's own vision and hard work is attractive. Go to a local winery on a weekend in the U.S. heartland and you are usually witnessing a success story. People have gathered, wine is being poured, food is being passed, and conversations are lively. The proprietor moves between taking care of business and talking with customers. Running a winery looks like fun. Successful wineries can be shared with partners and family and passed on to succeeding generations as well. At this historical moment, a winery seems to be a good investment of time and money.

The Institutional Contexts of Local Wineries

Bringing communities together while at the same time realizing the American dream sounds like the basis for a great B movie script. Of course, movies leave out most of the struggles and complications of real-world stories. Local wineries and the people who make them successful on an everyday basis are a great story, and I will share some of their accounts. But winery owners have gotten some help from the pioneers who labored to reestablish the wine industries in each state and from sympathetic politicians. They have also benefited from the global wine industry's efforts to make wine a popular beverage.

One reason sociologists and other social scientists pursue their studies is that they want to help people see how things that are not so evident contribute to life outcomes. In the United States, we tend to see the world from the perspective of individuals cooperating and competing with other individuals. However, there are larger dimensions of the social world that act on us as we use them in our own actions, or as we struggle against them. Sociologists use the term "institution" to represent sets of beliefs and practices that are patterned or structured, shape our thoughts and actions, and are often taken for granted as right and appropriate. These institutionalized beliefs and practices are formally organized as businesses, governments, schools, families, and religious institutions (to name some of the big categories). When someone in everyday conversation refers to economic institutions or educational institutions, they are often talking about particular business or school organizations where people engage in these sets of practices guided by certain beliefs. But the term "institution" is used by sociologists in a more general way to reflect the categories of organizations or groups and their beliefs and practices. Particular organizations or groups typically associated with one domain often act across and are impacted by other institutions. To be successful, people associated with a certain organization and institution often must understand and be able to effectively act within other institutional domains that shape their opportunities and constraints. In contemporary society, this also means being able to adapt to or take advantage of institutional changes. Changes can be unpredictable and far-reaching in relationships that have gone global.

I will say more about local wineries and their relationship to other organizations and institutions in later chapters. My point here is that these wineries and their owners are not solely responsible for their successes but have realized successes or suffered failures within institutional contexts. It is reasonable to think that they succeed or fail in relation to their local communities. This is only partly the case. I think local wineries are interesting because they are located at a nexus where different institutions and processes come together: global and local businesses and economic processes; local, state, and national government bodies and legal processes; and local communities and their various institutions. A few examples will have to suffice here.

Local wineries may contribute to the widespread customer interest in wine, but they did not create it. The larger wine industry did. Costs related to entering the business are lower compared to earlier times when production technology and materials were more expensive and less readily available. Again, the expansion of the wine industry has reduced these costs.

The availability of capital for starting a small winery has also changed. Bankers in the heartland would have viewed an application for a winery startup loan with much skepticism forty years ago. Not so today, as a number of winery owners I interviewed reported.

Wineries also operate within the purview of a set of local, state, and national political institutions that structure opportunities and constraints. During Prohibition, wineries would have been violating the law if they made and sold wine, unless it was for religious purposes. Now, instead of being illegal, wine and other types of alcohol are heavily regulated. For example, local winery owners are restricted in how much wine they can sell. Yet they are not powerless in relation to these laws. Their allowable gallonage continues to be raised as a result of the pressure that they individually and collectively bring to bear on state legislators. Indiana wineries also pushed legislators to pass a tax of five cents per gallon on all wine sold in the state, which goes directly to the Indiana Wine Grape Council, housed at Purdue University. Those funds are used for wine industry marketing, promotion, and research. Ohio has a tax for the same purposes, which is also currently five cents per gallon: three cents as a permanent tax, with the additional two cents as a renewable tax. Illinois had a similar tax at one time that assisted the wine industry, although it was dropped. Iowa provides some funds from its excise tax for wine grape research and promotion. Variations on these arrangements have been implemented in other states to aid wineries with startup, marketing, and technical problems. This "institutional isomorphism," or copying of organizational arrangements and practices from other places, is a common strategy pursued by potential beneficiaries in various types of industries. Your parents might not have bought that logic when you were a kid and you asked to do something because your friends were doing it, but when it involves neighboring states in a competitive environment, it is a persuasive argument for politicians and the public.

Changes in the related institutional arrangements have contributed to the growing number of wineries in the Midwest, as well as the amount of wine they produce. These changes didn't just happen; they were actively pursued by pioneers in some states who paved the way and whose successes served as examples for others inside and outside their states. In the following chapters, I examine different dimensions of this success story. In chapter 2 I trace the growth of local wineries. This growth is largely attributable to their attractive qualities for customers, which I describe in chapter 3. Chapter 4 explores various points of entry into the business and owners' differing rationales. The kinds of work and working conditions involved in local winery operation and how these are experienced by owners and employees are the focus of chapter 5. Chapter 6 examines collaboration among winery owners, including their efforts to deal with the political terrain and the common problems they face there. Problems winery owners share in each of the states I examine are discussed in chapter 7, such as forming a collective identity in the face of much variation and producing high-quality wines. Midwestern wineries' various connections to and ability to compete with the global wine industry are considered in chapter 8. I conclude by arguing that community-oriented businesses such as local wineries are important to our social and economic well-being, and they cannot be produced or replicated on a mass scale and still achieve the same results. Their strength is their diversity, which is a product of their responsiveness to their local contexts and their owners' and employees' ingenuity.

A few short comments are in order about the purpose and style of what I am presenting here. I did not write this book for other sociologists to advance disciplinary theory or knowledge in some manner, although perhaps some lessons will be drawn from my efforts by others in the field (or perhaps my academic peers will shake their heads in horror). I am not suggesting that some of the often esoteric work in my discipline is unimportant. But I think the account I provide here best fits where the academic and popular worlds occasionally intersect. I wrote this account for a general educated audience with an interest in knowing more about local wineries, their owners, and the work that goes into making them a success. More specifically, I wrote it for all those people who regularly frequent local wineries and help make them the success story they are, as well as people who might be interested but have not yet discovered these pleasures in their own backyards. Hopefully it will provide readers with some insights into the creation and operation of these well-loved places that they hadn't considered or didn't know previously, and also sober some readers up a bit should the wine and conviviality get them to thinking about opening their own place.

2

The Long Road to the
Midwestern Winery Boom

When Indiana became a state in 1816, it already had a burgeoning wine industry. The big wine states of today, California, Oregon, and Washington, were mostly wilderness with some missions and outposts developing up the coast. Commerce between the Eastern states and the Midwestern territories and states was growing. The U.S. wine industry grew throughout the nineteenth century, but a number of obstacles, most notably vine diseases and poor quality, limited growth. Prohibition and inhospitable state laws post-Prohibition restricted production and kept demand low until the late 1960s and early 1970s.

The shipment of high-quality European wine was quite expensive in the first three centuries of European immigration to America. Elites who traveled to Europe, including Thomas Jefferson, developed an interest in and taste for fine French wine. Jefferson also experimented with grape growing and winemaking (Barr 1999, 84–85; Pinney 1989, 126–29). The wine available in the colonial period and the first century of nationhood, commonly referred to as Madeira, was often of poor quality and fortified to extend its shelf life. Consequently, hard apple cider, whiskey made from corn, and inexpensive imported rum were more popular (Butler and Butler 2001, 4–5). However, French settlers in the colonial period, German and Swiss immigrants in the early to mid-nineteenth century, and Southern and Eastern European immigrants in the late nineteenth and early twentieth centuries brought their cultures with them to the United States, which included growing grapes and making and drinking wine.

Early Commercial Wine Production in the Midwest

As James L. Butler, owner with his wife Susan of Butler Winery and Vineyards in Bloomington, Indiana, and his historian son John J. Butler note in their history of wine production and grape growing in Indiana, wine was made from wild grapes by French settlers in the Vincennes area during the last half of the seventeenth century. Their efforts to grow European grapes that would make higher-quality wine were a failure due to diseases that would stymie efforts to grow European grapes in most of the United States for the next two centuries (Butler and Butler 2001, 5–6).

The Ohio wine industry's promotional materials commonly claim that Ohio was the home of the first successful commercial wine producers, pointing to Nicholas Longworth, a wealthy businessman and attorney, who began his first commercial wine efforts in 1923. Although Cincinnati became the early center of the wine trade, to a great extent due to Longworth's efforts, the first successful commercial vineyards were established in the Indiana Territory along the Ohio River, at Vevay, by Swiss settlers. They harvested their first crop in 1806 or 1807 (Butler and Butler 2001, 47). The grapes, known as Cape and Madeira grapes, were hybrids of European and American grapes that were resistant to phylloxera (a type of louse) and the molds and mildews that proliferated in the hot, humid summers (ibid., 38–40, 74). In 1815, the Harmonists, a German religious group led by George Rapp, planted a vineyard at New Harmony, on the Wabash River in the southwestern portion of the Indiana Territory. They had some success with American and French hybrid grape varieties, most notably the Cape and Madeira, but failed in their attempts to grow German varieties because of their susceptibility to disease (Pinney 1989, 131–32). As wine historian Thomas Pinney observes, "For the decade of their flourishing, roughly 1815–25, the two centers of wine production at New Harmony and at Vevay made Indiana the unchallenged leader of the first period of commercial wine production in the United States" (1989, 131).

By the 1850s, the Ohio River Valley was recognized as America's Rhine Region. The area was concentrated around Cincinnati, but included wineries in the southeastern area of Indiana known as New Switzerland. In 1859, Ohio was the biggest wine-producing state, with 35 percent of the total produced in the nation (Butler and Butler 2001, 123). In 1860, Indiana vintners produced 102,895 gallons of wine, less than one-fifth of Ohio's output. However, the labor shortage caused by the Civil War and the preference for planting Catawba grapes, which were more susceptible to mold and mildew, led to a decline in the Ohio Valley production of wine (ibid., 126). Wine production in Ohio shifted from the Cincinnati area in the southern part of the state to the northeast around Cleveland and the northwest around Sandusky. The amount of wine produced in Indiana remained fairly constant through the 1870s and 1880s, but production there shifted from the Ohio River Valley to Terre Haute and the northern part of the state near Lake Michigan (ibid., 128–29).

Pinney refers to Missouri after the Civil War as "the center of winemaking in the Midwest" (1989, 390). By the 1870s, California and Missouri were the biggest wine-producing states. Missouri had some of the leading experts in viticulture in the country; it was the state's first entomologist who identified the phylloxera louse, which was ravaging the vines in France. But diseases such as black rot, a common Midwestern fungal infection, limited expansion in Missouri and throughout the Midwest (ibid., 391–93). By 1890, New York was the second-leading grape-growing and wine-producing state, although it was still well behind California (ibid., 374).

Commercial wine production came somewhat late to Illinois and Iowa as well as Michigan and the other Midwestern states. The first commercial winery in Illinois was founded in 1857 in the Mississippi river town of Nauvoo. Despite its relatively late start, by 1900 Illinois was the fourth-largest producer of wine in the United States. In Iowa, the Amana Colony was founded in 1854, with the wine made mostly for local consumption. By 1868, grape growing and wine-making were reported in sixteen different Iowa counties (Pinney 1989, 396, 403). Despite Michigan's reputation as a fruit producing state, especially in the southwestern part of the state near Lake Michigan, the wine industry did not take off there until the end of Prohibition (ibid., 382).

The temperance movement limited the growth of wineries across the Midwest during the late nineteenth and early twentieth centuries. Kansas was the bellwether, constitutionally banning alcoholic beverages in 1880 after establishing what Pinney (1989, 397) refers to as a "promising" industry there. Prohibition effectively destroyed most of the wine industry. No wineries continued to exist in the Midwest except in Ohio and Missouri. As Pinney (2005, 8–18) notes, a few large winemakers were able to stay in business by making wine for sacramental purposes. Some products containing alcohol were allowed for medicinal use or as food and tobacco flavoring, but production for these purposes was modest. Grapes were used for nonalcoholic products such as juice, jelly, and vinegar, as well as for making wine at home, which the Supreme Court determined was legal under the law. Home winemaking boomed, with a federal estimate that more than 100 million gallons were being produced annually by 1930 (Barr 1999, 171). It was still illegal, however, to make, transport, or sell wine for commercial purposes other than the permitted ones already noted.

The mishmash of restrictive state laws that followed the end of Prohibition continued to make it difficult to produce wine in most states. In 1937, Ohio and Missouri were the only Midwestern states with wineries. Ohio had 130 licensed wineries, second to California's 630, but produced very little wine. Missouri had only 12 wineries. Of the 122 million gallons of wine produced that year, California produced 115 million. In Indiana, the Liquor Control Act of 1935 restricted the ability of potential winemakers to sell directly to customers or retail establishments. Instead, they had to sell their wine to wholesalers, who would then sell it to retailers, who would in turn sell it to customers. As the Butlers note,

This three-tiered system was not conducive to restarting the Indiana wine industry. It would have been nearly impossible for an Indiana winery to be large enough at the start to offer the volume and pricing necessary to enter its wines into the distribution system. The only reasonable option for a vintner under the 1935 law would have been to bring bulk wine from California and bottle it for sale to a wholesaler; and in fact this was done. However, this would not have been a true "Indiana wine" because no Indiana grapes were used and no regional wine character developed. It is obvious that in 1935 the state legislators were not concerned with restarting the Indiana wine industry. Until the restrictive laws of 1935 were changed, there would be no rebirth of the Indiana wine industry. (2001, 136)

Making Wine Popular: Marketing Sophistication with Some Sweetness to the Masses

My first memory related to wine and wine drinking is of my mother buying a square-bottomed bottle of Taylor New York State Red, probably in the mid- to late 1960s. Wine ads were also sprinkled through the popular media. I remember pastoral images of the countryside that seemed to promote the earthy, beautiful origins of the wine alternating with well-heeled couples enjoying themselves over a bottle of wine and the romance it evidently promoted.

Prior to Prohibition, Americans drank more dry table wine than wine fortified with additional alcohol and sugar. After Prohibition, from 1934 until 1966, fortified wines far surpassed the production of table wines. In 1967, American wine tastes shifted, and the consumption of fortified wines went into a rapid decline (Pinney 2005, 57, 225, 227). The U.S. wine industry really started heating up in the 1970s. As recounted in the book *Judgment of Paris* by George M. Taber (2005), and more loosely in the film *Bottle Shock*, released in 2008, a 1973 California Cabernet Sauvignon and a 1973 California Chardonnay took first place against elite French wines in a blind tasting in France in 1976, lending legitimacy to wines produced in the United States. However, most Americans were not drinking wines of this quality, especially in the Midwest.

The first "wine" I tasted was in 1972, when my brother and one of his friends came to visit, and we somehow went out and illegally purchased a bottle of Boone's Farm Strawberry Hill—wine in the loosest sense of very generic stuff with strawberry flavoring added. We thought of it as hippie wine, and we felt pretty "cool." (Note that there is no wine in Boone's Farm today; it's now a flavored malt beverage.) Boone's Farm led to Mateus and Lancers, what we thought of as "real" wines that satisfied our undeveloped palates and gave us a little buzz, with bottles that doubled as candleholders and indicated our good bohemian taste. During the mid-1970s, what I somewhat jokingly refer to as "gateway wines" proliferated. Lambrusco and Liebfraumilch were sweet, but seemed a bit more sophisticated. Liebfraumilch led me to explore other German wines, which came in tall, sophisticated-looking bottles and had a taste profile that first-time wine drinkers could handle as long as the wine did not have an overly musty taste or smell, which occasionally was the case. I started to learn some of the German varieties and their quality designations.

The big gateway wine bomb that was dropped on the public was the result of an accident. White Zinfandel was the result of an effort to make a dry white Zinfandel from the red-grape varietal at Sutter Home Winery in St. Helena, California, in 1975. An unintended short fermentation and some skin contact resulted in a pinkish, rather sweet wine (Kushman and Beal 2007, 290–91). Sales boomed in the early 1980s. As Pinney observes, White Zinfandel seemed to be "the wine equivalent of the American soft drink" (2005, 341). Inexpensive, even immature grapes and concentrate could be used to sweeten it, and it required no aging, so it could be sold immediately (ibid.). Other California wineries followed suit, and the pinkish wine attracted a popular following, including in Indiana.

By the time White Zinfandel came along, I was exploring somewhat more refined but still relatively inexpensive California, French, Spanish, and Eastern European wines, the latter of which started to creep in as the Soviet Union and the countries it dominated began to open up to the West and fall apart politically and economically. These offered a more challenging "taste profile," or range of flavors and nuances. Some of my fellow Hoosiers were with me on this, but most of them stuck with the soda-pop wines. This preference has held throughout much of the Midwest and South, and shapes what is sold in these states today. It also influences the perceptions of East and West Coasters and those in other wine-drinking countries about the undiscerning tastes of Midwesterners. However, the popularity of this style of wine played an important role in the growth of the Midwest wine industry.

The Slow Development of the Midwest
Wine Industry after Prohibition

Of the few Midwestern states that had wineries at the end of Prohibition, Ohio was clearly the leader, but its production was very limited. New York produced the most wine outside of California, with fewer wineries than Ohio (123 to Ohio's 138) but more than three times as much production (Butler and Butler 2001, 135). Missouri and Michigan also had wine industries, "though only in Michigan did it seem to have much economic life," according to Pinney (2005, 271). It would take some "nouveau pioneers" to end the stagnation—or in the case of Indiana, to even make commercial winemaking and sales legal.

Most of Ohio's wineries in those years were located in the northern part of the state along Lake Erie. Some had survived through Prohibition, including Heineman's Winery on South Bass Island, which is still in operation today. Klingshirn Winery opened in 1935 between Cleveland and Sandusky, and it continues to produce wine. In 1937, Anna and Nicholas Ferrante opened a winery in Cleveland. Their sons Peter and Anthony moved the operation to Harpersfield Township in 1979, near Geneva, where the family owned vineyards (Cattell 2014, 294).

In the Cincinnati area, Meier's Wine Cellars started as the John C. Meier Grape Juice Company in the late 1800s. It survived Prohibition through its grape juice trade, and realized steady growth after repeal. Renamed in 1938, Meier's Wine Cellars developed into the largest winery in the state with regional distribution. Located in Silverton, a suburb northeast of Cincinnati, it began sourcing most of its grapes from North Bass Island in Lake Erie, beginning in the 1940s. Primarily a producer of sweet and fortified wines using mostly Ohio grapes, it was purchased in 1976 by Paramount Distillers in Cleveland (Meier's Wine Cellars n.d.). As part of Paramount, Meier's purchased three other wineries in the Sandusky area in the northern part of the state (Cattell 2014, 294). Paramount sold some of its winery holdings in 2002 to Lonz Inc., and Meier's in 2011 to a St. Louis company, Luxco Inc. (Firelands Winery 2016; Suttell 2011).

Despite the presence of wineries in Ohio in the early 1960s, the industry was in decline. Just as people were predicting its demise, the Ohio Agricultural Research and Development Center (OARDC) established a research vineyard along the Ohio River, then set up a research winery at its Wooster campus. A viticulturist was hired in 1963, and an enologist not long thereafter. Small research plots were then established at various points along the Ohio River, from one end of the state to the other. These developments led to a renewed interest in wine in the southern part of the state, and a new winery, Tarula Farms, opened in Clarksville in 1967. Others followed, yet the wineries in northern and central Ohio continued to dominate (Pinney 2005, 271).

In 1968, Arnie Esterer planted nine acres of *vinifera* grapes in Conneaut, in the far northeastern corner of the state near Lake Erie. *Vitis vinifera* grapes (*Vitis* is the genus name for grape) are the European varieties that include those most wine drinkers are familiar with, including Cabernet Sauvignon, Cabernet Franc, Pinot Noir, Syrah, and Chardonnay. They tend to be less cold tolerant than the American *labrusca* and French-American hybrid varieties, the latter of which have been bred in part for greater cold tolerance. Esterer was inspired by Dr. Konstantin Frank, who had raised *vinifera* grapes in the cold of the Ukraine before relocating to the Finger Lakes region of New York. While on vacation from his job as an engineer, Esterer spent a week with Frank in October 1967 and was convinced from that experience that with the proper location and care, *vinifera* varieties such as Chardonnay, Cabernet Sauvignon, and Pinot Noir could be grown in the Lake Erie area. Esterer told Dr. Frank he wanted to purchase a few acres to plant some vines, but Frank insisted he needed at least 100 acres. Partnering with Tim Hubbard, they purchased 130 acres for $15,000. In 1972, Esterer left his job to tend his vineyard and make wine full time.

Illinois

According to Internal Revenue Service records cited by Butler and Butler (2001, 135), Illinois had ten wineries in 1938. One of those businesses produced the majority of the state's wine. Mogen David Winery used New York grapes to make "several million gallons" of sweet kosher wines in downtown Chicago (Pinney 2005, 279). A much smaller operation, Gem City Vineland Company in Nauvoo, was licensed in 1936 by some descendants of Emile and Annette Baxter and continued to operate on the same property the Baxters had purchased in 1866 for their own vineyard and winery. The business had survived by selling grapes and other fruit during Prohibition (History of Baxter's Vineyards, n.d.).

Other developments prior to the 1980s included the founding of the Ramey and Allen Champagne Vineyards winery in 1966 in the village of Monee, south of Chicago. Bern Ramey and Joseph Allen made sparkling wines from French hybrid grapes that Pinney (2005) notes were reportedly quite good. Their vines were wiped out two years later by weed killer used in the surrounding cornfields (ibid., 279–80), a problem that continues for Midwestern wineries to this day. The vineyard and winery were sold and became Thompson Winery Company in 1970, which closed in the mid-1980s (Cattell 2014, 274; "Old Depot Gets Timely Face Lift" 2003).

In 1976 a law was passed that permitted wineries to sell onsite directly to customers, thereby enabling them to avoid the three-tier system. Gem City Vineland Company opened a tasting room in 1977 (Cattell 2014, 274). Lynfred Winery was founded by Fred and Lynn Koehler in 1979 in Roselle, a western suburb of Chicago, when Fred's hobby "got out of hand" and they "had to go commercial" (Lynfred Winery 2014). Unlike most small wineries in Illinois at the time, Koehler started using grapes shipped from California to make some of his wines, a common practice today, in addition to producing fruit wines from Midwest fruit. The winery's location near Chicago provided a large population on which to draw.

The Illinois wine industry began to slowly show some signs of life in the 1980s. The establishment of a more affordable Limited Wine Manufacturers License in the early 1980s allowed for production of up to forty thousand gallons as long as it was made from Illinois-grown grapes. Christine Lawlor, with the assistance of her parents, Robert and Joyce Lawlor, her brother, Scott, and his wife, Karen, opened Galena Cellars Vineyard and Winery in 1985 in downtown Galena, located in northwestern Illinois in the Mississippi River Valley. It was Christine's third winery. She opened Christina Wine Cellars in McGregor, Iowa, in 1976, after studying enology at Fresno State University. She then opened a second winery in La Crosse, Wisconsin, in 1978. The family closed the Iowa and Wisconsin wineries in 1990, then purchased a farm outside Galena, planted vines, and moved their winery production there (Galena Cellars Vineyard & Winery 2013).

Kelly Logan, a fifth-generation Baxter, and his wife, Brenda, took over the operation of Gem City Vineland Company in 1987 and renamed it Baxter's Vineyards. According to Brenda, Kelly began working at the winery in 1979, and she started later. After purchasing the business, she became the winemaker "by default," while Kelly cared for the vineyard and worked another job. As will be discussed in more detail later, the operation of small wineries in the Midwest often requires at least one owner to keep a full-time job for income and benefits such as health insurance.

In 1980, Guy Renzaglia, a psychology professor at Southern Illinois University, purchased some land with Ted Wichman and Mark Cosgrove in the small Union County town of Alto Pass. (Wichman already had a small vineyard at what is now Owl Creek Vineyard in Cobden, Illinois.) They planted ten acres of French hybrid grapes on the property in 1982, but the town was "dry" by law, so they struggled to find a market for their grapes, selling to Lynfred Winery and a small winery in Iowa. Guy's son Paul, a special educator who had returned home to do graduate work, joined the operation in 1985. A special referendum passed in 1987 allowing retail alcohol sales in the community, which enabled Alto Vineyards to begin selling wine in December 1988. According to Paul, they produced twelve hundred gallons and sold out in two days.

Illinois had a handful of small wineries by 1988, with the addition in 1985 of Chateau Ra-Ha in Grafton, just north of St. Louis, Missouri, and Waterloo Winery in Waterloo, just south of St. Louis. Spread thinly in three corners of the state, and with little support from the state government for the industry, the prospects in Illinois looked rather gloomy. To prod the state legislature and improve on their practice, winery and vineyard owners founded the Illinois Grape Growers and Vintners Association in 1987. It would take another ten years to get any support from the state (Pinney 2005, 280).

As wine gained a following in the late 1960s and early 1970s, home winemaking began to regain some of the popularity it had enjoyed during its Prohibition heyday. Wine Art stores selling wine- and beer-making supplies popped up throughout much of the country (Pinney 2005, 249). Some home winemakers in Indiana grew bored with the middling wines they were making from Wine Art's concentrate and started to experiment and share information. The result was the reestablishment of the Indiana wine industry.

A handful of wine enthusiasts and makers were integral in bringing the industry back to life. Dr. Donald MacDaniel, an optometrist in Connersville; William Oliver, an Indiana University law professor from Bloomington; Jack Easley, an attorney, and his wife, Joan, from Indianapolis; and Ben Sparks, a retired navy aviator and commander from Brown County, were producing wine in quantities they could not consume or give away. MacDaniel had been growing French hybrid grapes since 1958 and using them to make wine. Oliver began planting grapes in 1966, the Easleys in 1971, and Sparks about that same time (Butler and Butler 2001, 140–41). All were interested in starting wineries, but they knew the laws were prohibitive. MacDaniel had legislation drawn up to allow the production and sale of wine based on Ohio laws, and Oliver worked with some of his former law students to author some legislation based on Pennsylvania law. Oliver's version was submitted, and the result was Public Law 77, more commonly known as the Small Winery Law, which was passed April 8, 1971. The law limited production to no more than fifty thousand gallons per year, with no more than 14 percent alcohol. Although it required that any fruit or honey used in making the wine be produced in the state, wineries could apply for a permit to import those ingredients if they could not obtain them in-state (Butler and Butler 2001, 141).

Four months later, MacDaniel opened Treaty Line Winery outside Connersville. Oliver Winery opened just north of Bloomington in May 1973. By the end of 1974, seven wineries were operating in Indiana, including Easley Winery in Indianapolis, which had a vineyard on the Ohio River (Butler and Butler 2001, 141–42). The fledgling industry founded the Indiana Winegrowers Guild in July 1975, as a result of the efforts of Sparks and his wife, Lee, to promote the industry and assist with improving viticulture in the state.

The growth in the number of wineries was steady, but rather modest through the 1980s. By 1979, according to the Butlers (2001, 214–16), ten wineries had been bonded by the state, and one bond had been terminated. At the time of publication of their book in 2001, the Butlers noted that twenty-eight bonded wineries were in operation, with twenty-four open to the public for retail sales, so some of the bonds were active but not in use. The startups tended to come in spurts, with multiple wineries opening in some years and none in others; but between 1971, when the Small Winery Law was passed, and 2001, the rate of growth was about one winery a year.

Iowa

As already noted, Christine Lawlor started a winery in Iowa in 1976, before relocating to Wisconsin and then Illinois, but others had blazed the trail in the state before that, although on a rather small scale compared to the other states. The descendants of the German settlers who founded the Amana Colony, now known as the Amana Colonies, gave up their elders' communal lifestyle and developed independent commercial enterprises, including wineries, in 1932 (Pinney 2005, 178). Pinney observes that they did not maintain vineyards, making wine instead "from purchased grapes as well as from a variety of other fruits, vegetables, and greens, including wild grapes, dandelions, and red clover" (ibid.). Both Pinney (ibid.) and Cattell (2014, 264) claim that rhubarb wine is the signature wine of the Amana wineries.

Western Iowa also had vineyards and commercial winemaking after repeal. A cooperative in Council Bluffs produced wine mostly from local Concord grapes (Pinney 2005, 179). The vineyards were destroyed in 1977 by the herbicide 2,4-D, used in corn and soybean production, and wine production ceased. According to Cattell (2014, 276), by 2000, only thirteen wineries operated in the state, eleven in the Amana Colonies. Ron Mark started Summerset Winery in 1997 in Indianola, a small town south of Des Moines. That same year, Dr. Paul Tabor started Tabor Home Vineyards and Winery near the very small town of Baldwin, in eastern Iowa. Prospects did not look bright, but Mark and Tabor, along with Bill Brown, who opened Timberhill Winery in 2001 (since closed), formed the Iowa Grape Growers Association in 2000. They began soliciting the support of the Iowa Department of Agriculture and Iowa State University with much success (ibid., 276).

The Midwestern Wine Boom

It took about six decades after the end of Prohibition before interest in local wineries really began heating up in the Midwest, especially in the "non-wine" states I'm examining here. The number of wineries started accelerating in the mid-1990s, with phenomenal growth in the first decade of the twenty-first century. In the second decade, there were clear signs that the rate was tapering off.

There are two ways to think about the growth of the wine industry in the Midwest. One is in terms of the increase in the number of wineries. In general, the view of Midwestern winery owners has been the more, the merrier. If there were many wineries struggling to make ends meet and more starting up, that would not be a good thing, but that generally has not been the case. The other indicator of growth is the output or volume of wine produced. How much wine is being made each year, and is the amount going up? If output is increasing for most wineries in a state, that is usually a good thing economically as long as it is being sold at a profit. A wine glut or too much wine sitting in tanks, barrels, or bottles on shelves may drive prices down. But state output numbers are also not sufficient by themselves, because the numbers may be driven by the growth of a few bigger wineries while the rest struggle.

Identifying the number of operating wineries in a state would seem to be a rather simple task, but such is not the case. The U.S Alcohol and Tobacco Tax and Trade Bureau (TTB), which is part of the U.S. Department of Treasury, is tasked with issuing permits and collecting federal taxes on wineries and other alcoholic beverage producers. However, not every permit holder is necessarily operating a winery. Obtaining a permit is one of the first steps in becoming a winery, and some permit holders never get beyond that step or take a long time before actually opening for business and selling wine. For example, Downing Vineyard and Winery LLC in Fairmount was on the TTB list for Indiana but was not yet open when I talked to the owner in June 2015. He was hoping to open within a few months, but there were no signs of operation in January 2016.

Also, in any given year, wineries likely go out of business even though their federal permit is still active. So, for example, the TTB showed the D'Avella Family Winery in Granger, Indiana, as a permit holder, but the winery was closed. The same was true for four other Indiana wineries: Ferrin's Fruit Winery and Grape Inspirations Winery, both in Carmel; Grateful Goat Vineyard and Winery in Palmyra; and Kauffman Winery in Mt. Vernon. Last, firms that are not really operating wineries may have a winery license. For example, Proximo Distillers LLC has a TTB permit for Indiana but is a liquor distributor of well-known brands. The corporation has no operating winery that I could identify. Similarly, Pri-Pak Inc. is a contract beverage manufacturer, making products, including alcoholic beverages, for other businesses. The alcoholic beverage licensing structure in Ohio also results in some establishments getting state and federal permits that make them appear to be wineries when in fact they make little or no wine. In addition, as Midwest Wine Press founder and editor Mark Ganchiff notes, "The Federal TTB does not take into consideration where wine is made or where wine grapes are sourced from. For example, according to the TTB, a winery located in Illinois that imports finished wine from California is an Illinois winery" (Ganchiff 2013).

The state wine organizations seem to be a somewhat more accurate source of information than the TTB for identifying operating wineries, but they aren't always totally comprehensive because the rules for being included on lists vary by state. As Ganchiff (2013) points out, the Michigan Grape and Wine Industry Council list includes only wineries that source at least half their grapes from Michigan. In Indiana, Legacy Lane Vineyard in Brookville was on the May 24, 2015, TTB list, but it was not on the Indiana Wine Grape Council's list at indianawines.org and showed no signs of being open on the internet. Legacy Lane was in the process of making and selling wine as of late 2015, according to the winery's Facebook page, but it was still not listed in the indianawines .org directory of Indiana wineries in January 2016. Ironhand Vineyard in South Bend also did not appear on indianawines.org when I checked in June 2015, yet the winery existed, was making wine from its own grapes, and could be visited by appointment. It had been added to the list when I checked in January 2016.

Getting a detailed picture of how much wine is being produced by which wineries is an even bigger challenge. Production output is reported by the TTB for each state, but not for each winery, since this is considered private information. Occasionally researchers at the state or national level collect data and request production numbers from individual wineries. I won't go into the difficulties of collecting that data and reporting accurate numbers, but it is a daunting and expensive undertaking. So it doesn't happen very often, and the numbers tend to be aggregated or combined in a manner that doesn't reveal which wineries are producing how much. I did ask the winery owners I interviewed about the growth of their wineries generally in terms of production and percentage growth in income over the last few years, but I did not conduct a study of wine production by every winery in each state.

Although the wine industry has grown across the board, the increase in the number of wineries in Midwestern states that are not usually viewed as "wine states" has been rather spectacular in the last two decades. Table 1 shows the number of wineries in the four states I am examining for selected years where data was available, as well as Michigan and Missouri, which have a bit more of a wine reputation outside their state lines. I was unable to find data on Iowa and Michigan for some of the years selected. By 2015, Ohio was the winner by my count in terms of the sheer number of wineries, with Michigan second and Missouri third. Ganchiff (2015), relying on TTB data, put Michigan first in 2015 and Ohio second. So he has probably overcounted Michigan wineries and I have undercounted them. Suffice it to say that Ohio and Michigan have the most wineries, and Missouri is third, with a couple dozen more wineries than Illinois. Of the states listed, only Indiana has failed to break the hundred-winery mark.

Table 1. Growth of Midwestern Wineries in Selected States, 1993–2015

State	1993	2003	2007	2011	2014	2015
Illinois	7	23	83	101	104	104
Indiana	5	17	40	61	70	80
Iowa	—	18	65	—	101	101
Michigan	—	—	112	129	143	141
Missouri	10	22	86	125	132	129
Ohio	7	26	114	159	217	233

Note: No nonproprietary data were available for Iowa and Michigan in the years indicated. Figures indicate the number of wineries in operation by the end of the year.

Sources: Matt Mullins, Ohio Department of Commerce, personal communication, January 12, 2016; Bradley Beam, Illinois Grape Growers and Vintners Association, personal communication, January 6, 2016; Jeanette Merritt, Purdue University, personal communication, July 2, 2015; Ganchiff 2015; *Wines and Vines* 2015; Turdoon, Clause, and Holz-Clause 2003; Woods and Ernst 2011.

Table 2 shows the percentage of growth in the number of wineries that occurred between 2003 and 2015 in four-year increments and overall. Overall growth ranged from a whopping 352 percent in Illinois to a phenomenal 796 percent in Ohio from 2003 to 2015. Perhaps somewhat surprising, in Iowa, the biggest producer of corn and hogs in the United States and home to many more pigs than people, wineries grew at a quicker rate than in Illinois and Indiana during this time frame, nearly catching up to Illinois while far outpacing Indiana. I will discuss this more in chapter 6, but Pinney (2005, 281) probably underestimated how quickly the resources brought to bear in Iowa, as well as in Illinois, Indiana, and Ohio, could rapidly improve Midwestern wines and advance the industry. I think there is more to the story than this, as I will discuss in the next two chapters. It also has to do with the winery experience itself and what needs that experience satisfies for customers and owners.

The growth in wineries appears to have leveled off in the last few years (see table 2), although Ohio and Indiana have continued to experience substantial

Table 2. Percentage Growth of Midwestern Wineries in Selected States, 2003–2015

State	2003–07	2007–11	2011–15	2003–15
Illinois	261	22.0	3.0	352
Indiana	135	52.5	31.0	371
Iowa	261	—	—	461
Michigan	—	15.0	8.5	—
Missouri	291	45.0	3.0	486
Ohio	338	39.0	46.5	796

Source: Calculated by the author from the figures in Table 1.

increases. Ganchiff (2015), using TTB data, would add Michigan in the continued growth category, but my source (*Wines and Vines* 2015) did not indicate that. This leveling off could mean that the industries are approaching maturation, or it could indicate that potential business owners' and customers' interests have shifted to craft breweries and distilleries. Even some wineries have added breweries and distilleries—I will have more to say about that later. Only a few winery owners I spoke with thought the number of wineries in their state had peaked. The large majority felt there was still substantial room for growth. Most owners are savvy businesspeople who read the trade literature. They talked to me about local wineries' market share relative to global brands and the gallons of wine drunk in their state per capita as areas for growth. But they also had noticed the slowdown, especially in Illinois, and talked about the problem of people getting in without sufficient capitalization or commitment to the work necessary to make high-quality wine.

Growth is also evident in the volume of wine being produced in Midwestern states. The TTB maintains easily accessed records on the amount of wine produced by each state (www.ttb.gov/statistics/). Table 3 indicates the percentage growth in wine production every other year from 2007 to 2013, as well as total percentage growth over that time frame for six Midwestern states, California, and the entire United States. Growth from 2007 to 2009 was modest for some states and declined in Illinois, Missouri, and Ohio. California's production, which drives U.S. production figures, was the same as the national increase. But for the six-year period from 2007 to 2013, wine production grew at a faster rate in all the Midwestern states in table 3 except Illinois and Missouri than in California or the United States overall. The numbers that really jump out are Ohio's, which show the state's "exploding" growth, as one industry person put it (Flannigan 2012). From a decline in the first two years, production in Ohio increased from just over 1.2 million gallons to almost 3.6 million gallons, or nearly 194 percent, from 2007 to 2013. Michigan also had a sizable jump of 72.8 percent, and Indiana's and Iowa's production increased at a faster rate than California's and the nation's overall. Gains in Illinois and Missouri were modest and substantially below the U.S. increase. I set the table up as every other year so that it would be easier to look at, but that hid some of the up or down years in some states. Every state on the list experienced at least one downturn in an even year.

Of course, wine production in the Midwest is a drop in the bucket compared to California and the nation as a whole. California's wine industry produced 85.4 percent of the wine in the United States in 2014 (see table 4). Midwestern wineries are not going to take over or dominate the industry, and I am not trying to suggest in any way that they will. The point is that they are growing, with wine production increasing at a more rapid pace than in California, and

Table 3. Percentage Growth in Wine Production for Selected
Midwestern States, California, and the United States, 2007–2013

	2007–09	2009–11	2011–13	2007–13
Illinois	−2.3	6.2	18.6	23.0
Indiana	4.9	38.0	−2.0	41.9
Iowa	6.9	16.2	10.7	36.6
Michigan	2.2	21.8	38.8	72.8
Missouri	−4.3	11.8	6.8	14.2
Ohio	−7.0	40.1	125.3	193.6
California	10.0	−2.2	18.9	27.8
U.S. Total	10.0	−2.2	20.8	29.9

Source: Calculated from Alcohol and Tobacco Tax and Trade Bureau, U.S. Department of the Treasury, "Wine Statistics," http://www.ttb.gov/wine/wine-stats.shtml.

Table 4. Percentage of U.S. Wine Produced by California, Ohio,
and Selected Midwestern States, 2009–2014

	2009	2010	2011	2012	2013	2014
California	89.3	89.7	89.0	88.9	87.6	85.4
Ohio	0.15	0.15	0.21	0.38	0.4	0.56
Illinois, Indiana, Iowa, Michigan, Missouri, Ohio	0.65	0.65	0.83	0.91	1.0	1.1

Source: Calculated from Alcohol and Tobacco Tax and Trade Bureau, U.S. Department of the Treasury, "Wine Statistics," http://www.ttb.gov/wine/wine-stats.shtml.

that drop in the bucket they produce is gradually gaining as a percentage of the U.S. total, as indicated in table 4. Collectively the Midwestern states indicated have increased their production from .65 percent of U.S. production in 2009 to to 1.1 percent in 2014, representing almost 10 million gallons of wine. Ohio's share of U.S. wine production has nearly quadrupled (from .15 to .56) in that time. Its share of the wine produced by the Midwestern states discussed here has grown from just under one-fourth of the total to just over half.

I asked the winery owners I interviewed about the growth of their wineries, and their responses were generally quite similar: they showed gains each year. A number of them reported a healthy 10 to 20 percent annual increase in sales. Those who did not report those levels of growth tended to be in locations that were less accessible to population centers or well-traveled routes, or they had been open for many years and their business had leveled off. In 2012, Larry Satek, owner with his wife, Pam, of Satek Winery, described their business's growth as "very solid, very solid. Just year after year, we have been growing at a phenomenal rate. The best way to explain it is that in 2011 we sold ten times as much wine as in 2001. That's pretty expansive." Jeff Quint, owner of Cedar Ridge Winery and Distillery in eastern Iowa, said they had been doing 30 percent annual growth in sales after opening and were still at about 14 percent a decade later. Paul Renzaglia, at Alto Vineyards, reported a 15 to 20 percent bump in sales after opening a new tasting room and event facility.

It was common for wineries to open and do quite well in the first few years, sometimes struggling to keep up with demand. Blue Sky Vineyard, in the southern Illinois village of Makanda, opened in 2005. When I asked co-owner and general manager Jim Ewers about the winery's growth, he said, "When we first started, it was exponential." His winery had difficulty keeping up with the demand for red wine, partly because it takes much more time to produce than white wine, and production has to be planned at least two years out. John Richardson at Mallow Run said their production and sales doubled each year in their first three years of operation before slowing some.

Older wineries tended to have slower but steady growth. Van Creasap, the owner of Shamrock Vineyard in rural north-central Ohio, reported "pretty darn consistent" annual growth of 5 to 10 percent. Nick Ferrante said his winery was growing by roughly two percentage points per year after a decade of faster growth that began in 1995. He said the winery was about as big as he wanted it to be. Some others had leveled off. Chris Lawlor-White said that production at Galena Cellars had peaked and leveled off about a decade ago. Joe Henke, at Henke Winery in Cincinnati, said his production leveled off in 2013. Arnie Esterer, at Markko Vineyards, said his production had been about the same for some time, and he had just raised his prices.

Oliver Winery and Easley Winery have staked their continued growth on retail sales. Their products can be easily found in grocery stores, pharmacies, and liquor stores in Indiana and surrounding states. I asked Bill Oliver about his winery's growth in 2011, and he simply said, "Ridiculous." Oliver Winery is now the largest winery east of the Mississippi River. I had taken a tour of the winery three weeks before interviewing Bill, and our tour guide noted that Oliver wines were distributed in fifteen states. Early in our interview, Bill told me that Oliver wines were distributed in nineteen states. When I asked about the discrepancy, he smiled and pointed to the success of their recently released fruit ciders in opening up new markets. When I mentioned some winery owners' complaint that wholesale distributors were lousy salespeople, he replied that Oliver had its own sales staff.

Size clearly matters if a winery wants to enter and succeed in the three-tier wholesale distribution stream. Small wineries typically find it difficult to produce enough product to satisfy distributors' demands and cannot make sufficient profits if wholesalers take a chunk of their potential income. Some small wineries have set themselves up as micro-distributors to serve retail outlets and restaurants. This can range from a few outlets in the case of small Indiana wineries to a hundred or so for some Iowa wineries. Where and how a winery can distribute is heavily dependent on what state law allows. I will examine the issues related to distribution in more depth in chapters 6 and 8.

The growth of wineries would not be sustainable without adequate compensation for winery owners to both stay in and grow their businesses. In my interviews, I did not ask winery owners about their income or profits directly, but I did ask whether they were able to support themselves and their families from their winery incomes, or if they had other income sources. Some were supporting themselves and their families as well as other employees through winery income, but others were using the profits from their wineries to invest in the business and expand production, paying themselves little or nothing. As might be expected, newer wineries seeking to rapidly expand production and sales tended to be in the second camp. Since wineries tend to be family operations owned by couples, parents and children, or siblings, someone on the ownership team often held a full-time job to make ends meet until the winery was sufficiently profitable.

As someone interested in the intersection of social and economic activity, I think that a combination of factors has driven growth. Growth requires demand. Midwestern wineries would not be booming without strong and growing customer demand. What is going on in the national and regional popular cultures helps drive that demand. Demand has gone up due to the proclaimed health benefits of moderate wine drinking, which have been heavily publicized in the press and even by doctors, as well as the "buy local" and "local food" movements. And with wine having been successfully associated through marketing with romance and sophistication, wineries are typically nice places for people to gather. Demand has also been driven by increasing ease of access—the growing availability of wineries in more areas offering a place to hang out—and the development of wine trails and wine tourism. The next chapter explores in more detail the attraction local wineries and their wines hold for their customers.

3

More than Marketplaces

The Attraction of Local Wineries

My wife and I had cabin fever one cold Sunday in February 2007 and decided to take a drive in the snow-covered countryside southeast of Indianapolis. We meandered on country roads through eastern Johnson County, then cut west to I-65 at Franklin. Heading back north toward Indianapolis, we noticed a blue informational sign just before the Whiteland exit that said "Mallow Run Winery." We were a bit surprised that a winery had popped up in Whiteland without our knowing about it. So we exited and took Whiteland Road through Whiteland. We continued well past the town for six or seven miles, crossing U.S. 31 and a couple of state highways. We were thinking we had somehow missed the winery when we saw the entrance at the western edge of Bargersville.

As we drove up the long gravel driveway, we saw grapevines to the right and a snow-covered field to the left. The tasting room was in a barn at the top of a ridge that dropped off on the north side to Mallow Run, a small creek that winds its way through the countryside to the White River a few miles to the west. The barn was glossy white with a bright red metal roof and had clearly been recently renovated. As we stepped inside the entrance, we were greeted with beautiful unfinished barn-wood walls, heavy hand-cut beams, and newly finished wide-plank floors that gave the place a rustic, homey feel. A four-sided tasting bar was in the middle of the room, with three of the sides raised so that customers could stand comfortably and taste wine. The fourth side displayed goods and served as a checkout station for purchases. There was a substantial stone fireplace on the back wall. Large windows to the north looked out over the creek and let in plenty of natural light. We struck up a conversation with John Richardson, who told us he was a retired high school English teacher and, with an impish smile, said the winery was his "retirement project."

John grew up on the farm. He studied English at Purdue University, then took a job teaching English at New Albany High School, where he worked for thirty-two years. John had been making wine at home for years, and he and his son Bill, a stockbroker with a degree in agriculture from Purdue, started raising and selling grapes on the property prior to deciding to open the winery. John told us about the renovation of the barn and how he and Bill had decided to start the winery as a way to keep the farm in the family. The farm had been in John's family—the Mallows, Frys, and Richardsons—since 1835, and it was recognized by the State of Indiana as a Hoosier Homestead farm, meaning that descendants of the original family had been living there for at least a hundred years.

I thought the tasting room looked like a great space to hear some music and asked John if they were planning to have any. He said they had tried a few things, but it was either too loud for people to talk or not loud enough to hear. I told him I thought I could get the volume right. My band had been playing at the Chateau Thomas tasting room in the Brown County town of Nashville without a problem for several years. He said they might try having music out on their large wooden deck in the summer, and I gave him my business card.

Bill's wife, Laura, handled the events at the winery. My band started playing on their deck the first summer they were open, then played inside the tasting room during the winter. The next summer, they had us play on a concrete patio they had previously been using for crushing and pressing grapes. The winery quickly became a weekend attraction for locals. After a bit of a rocky start, they improved their ability to serve the masses of people who showed up most Saturday and Sunday afternoons from two to five o'clock for music, wine, and food. They did an occasional pizza night from five to eight and had special events such as a performance by the Carmel Symphony Orchestra. Later they covered the patio, added removable walls, and installed gas heaters so the space could be used in the winter months. They also added restrooms to the small building they had constructed to serve food and wine during the spring, summer, and fall.

Bill and Laura Richardson first met when they were playing in the Carmel Symphony Orchestra, she on clarinet and he on French horn. John also sang in a local vocal group, the Castlewood Singers, who occasionally performed for special events at the winery such as a Valentine's Day dinner. As musicians themselves, Bill, Laura, and John seemed to have a special affection for music. Laura came up with changing menus of soups in the winter and made or brought in barbecue, pizza, and other simple, tasty dishes in the warmer months, along with a dessert. On weekdays they had what has become a common feature at many Midwestern wineries, a cheese and fruit tray, as well as hummus and crackers.

We started to see a lot of the same faces at many of our performances, including some of our band's regular following who took a liking to the winery. Mallow Run is located just a few minutes from Center Grove, a part of Greenwood with mostly middle- and upper-middle-class families, the prime wine-

Figure 3.1. John, Laura, and Bill Richardson (*left to right*), the owners of Mallow Run Winery. Photo courtesy of Josh Marshall/AIM Media Indiana, used by permission.

drinking demographic group. It is also about two miles east of State Road 37, the major highway between Indianapolis and Bloomington, and only fifteen minutes south of I-465, the beltway that circles Indianapolis. Another major north-south state highway (135) is only a few miles to the east, and an east-west state highway (144) is just north of the winery and jogs south a bit to cross Whiteland Road. So the winery is easily accessible from all directions, a short drive from the major population center of the state, and close to the homes of a demographic group that tends to frequent wineries. The combination of location and a quality experience—good wine, good food, interesting events, and a friendly, service-oriented, family-run business—resulted in fast growth.

Wineries as Community Gathering Places

Like any other business, wineries have a profit motive for their production and sales. Most sell their wine by the glass or bottle, to be drunk onsite. And all winery owners like to see bottles and cases go out the door with customers or, in some circumstances, to wholesalers and on to retail establishments. Some states allow wineries to distribute their wines directly to retailers and restaurants up to a certain limit, and all the wineries in Midwestern states can ship wine directly to in-state customers under certain conditions. Shipping out of state is more difficult. I will talk much more about this in chapter 6. Many also sell food and wine-related merchandise such as wineglasses, corkscrews, gifts, T-shirts, and other items that customers like to purchase as mementos of their visit. Joel Kopsa of John Ernest Vineyard and Winery in Tama, Iowa, told me that gift shops are an expected part of the winery experience.

In a smaller town, a local winery may be the economic center of the community. Wineries provide jobs, attract customers to other local businesses, and pay taxes that come back to the community directly or indirectly. This economic activity is important to the community, and especially so in smaller communities. But wineries are more than a business: they fill a need for places where people can experience community. They provide opportunities to make connections with and informal commitments to a group of people and a place. So what are the features of wineries that create this quality? Why do people flock to them?

First is the wine itself. A common theme among Midwestern winery owners is that wine is not just a beverage; it is a shared experience. Tasting and drinking wine provides a ready-made topic and occasion for conversation. There is a culture to wine, a set of beliefs, practices, and language that can be learned and shared. In addition to grape varieties, there are styles of wine, styles of glassware, pouring and tasting procedures, production methods, and terminology that captures this culture. To be successful, winery owners see part of their task as educating customers about wine, especially those who are new to wine, or at least new to Midwestern varieties. All offer tastings of their products either for free or, as is becoming more common, for a small fee. They are quick to note that there is no correct opinion about wine. Taste preferences vary, so people are free to express their opinions without hard feelings. Servers often ask customers what kind of wine they like: sweet, semi-sweet, or dry. The vocabulary of wine can seem intimidating to a novice, so servers typically keep the conversation simple and let the customers ask questions and comment on the wine. Winery owners often provide descriptions or tasting notes on their wine lists to suggest particular qualities they and other experienced wine drinkers may discern. These descriptions can offer an introduction to some of the language and can also prompt conversation.

Midwestern wine comes in a range of varieties, blends, and styles. Those who are new to Midwestern wines but are familiar with common *vinifera* varieties such as Chardonnay, Cabernet Sauvignon, or Syrah will discover dozens of different *labrusca* and hybridized (human-produced, genetically crossed or blended) strains with unfamiliar names. Some wineries' lists are relatively short, while older wineries such as Ferrante and Debonne in Ohio; Oliver, Huber's, Chateau Thomas, and Turtle Run in Indiana; Galena Cellars and Lynfred in Illinois; and Tassel Ridge in Iowa can have long lists of varietals. Some emphasize sweeter styles, but most provide a range of "flavor profiles" or "taste profiles." New vintages offer changes each year, some better, some not. But this variation and complexity provides a nearly endless source of conversation and new experiences.

Some researchers have linked the attraction of wines and wine culture to their historical association with elites. They argue that with the growth of the middle class and its members' desire to distinguish themselves from the masses, wine has become a tool for pursuing those social class pretensions. The result has been a "democratization" of wine consumption (Howland 2013). There is probably some truth to these claims. Wine drinking certainly offers "cultural capital" that can be useful in some social relationships, as is the case with any interest or activity. Enological advances have also raised the quality of cheaper, mass-produced wines and made it harder to distinguish between them and more expensive wines. These technological advances have also benefited the wine produced by small Midwestern wineries in the last couple of decades, improving quality and allowing them to compete with the mass-produced wines with which most customers may be more familiar. Some Midwestern wineries are also beginning to produce more complex, higher-priced "fine" wines for connoisseurs.

My interviews with winery owners suggest that most are careful to avoid coming off as pretentious, probably because of their economically and experientially diverse customers. As Joel Kopsa explained, "Some of the other wineries around, they want to be . . . they're in a bigger town, they want to get the little more upper crust. We want the upper crust and the people who are just down to earth, too . . . that's what we want and what we try to do." I will discuss the different choices winery owners make about their wines in more detail later, but Kopsa's approach of making wines of various flavors and styles to appeal to a wide range of taste preferences was most common. Some of the individual preferences that customers exhibit are likely associated with social class as well as regional differences, but I don't think class aspirations or distinctions are the primary motive for hanging out at Midwestern wineries. Rather, the appeal lies in the opportunity to kick back and enjoy some informal socializing while sharing, enjoying, and discussing the merits of a range of beverages that appeal to diverse palates.

The second attraction of wineries is the place. A place is both a physical and a social setting. Wineries throughout the Midwest are typically located in areas that have unique natural and built features. As Jeanette Merritt, marketing specialist for the Purdue Wine Grape Team when I interviewed her in November 2011, told me, "I think our wineries have opened to fit their communities. That's what makes them successful. You fit where you are surrounded by." Each winery takes on some of the unique qualities of the place where it is located. Most in the Midwest are in rural areas with pastoral scenery and a variety of buildings, some classic, others quirky. These settings give people the opportunity to connect with nature and a little part of the rural heritage of the United States. Mary Hofmann of White Oak Vineyards in Carlock, Illinois, talked about being only ten minutes from Bloomington-Normal, yet in a rural setting that gives city dwellers a place "to chill out" where they can "hear themselves again and watch the birds fly by." Some wineries are in urban areas and can have a more contemporary feel. They may be in a repurposed structure, a strip mall, or a new building built to the owners' specifications. Some are on or near major highways, and others are in what seems to be the middle of nowhere. Whatever the geographical setting, winery owners typically put much thought into creating a comfortable, inviting place for their customers that takes advantage of attractive and unique features.

Wine intimately connects product with place, especially at wineries that use their own or locally produced grapes. The connection between product and place has received renewed interest as part of the more general emphasis on "going local." The winery owners I interviewed noted that they had benefited from the local food movement and the growing emphasis on locally grown food and local products. Wineries offer opportunities for customers to learn and see how their products are made.

Wineries are also social settings that promote hanging out and enjoying some friendly conversation. The wine itself commonly serves as a topic of discussion. Most wineries in the Midwest are family friendly. It is common to see three generations of family members gathering for an afternoon together, whether to celebrate a birthday or anniversary, or just to spend some family time. Couples on afternoon dates and groups of friends, neighbors, and coworkers frequent wineries to share a bottle and chat, sometimes accompanied by some entertainment, but other times left to their own devices. Unlike religious institutions, which also serve as gathering places in communities, wineries bring together people with diverse beliefs—except perhaps those religious teetotalers who avoid any setting where alcohol is served. John Richardson noted that the church down the road from Mallow Run initially had reservations about the winery opening so close by, but now many of its members are regulars. Mary and Rudi Hofmann, the owners of White Oak Vineyards, gradually gained more acceptance after having to petition for a referendum in their "dry" township, which barely passed, 167 to 164.

Wineries with outdoor space offer some of the amenities of local parks. They often have wildlife, picnic tables, water features such as ponds or creeks (the "run" in Mallow Run), flower gardens, trees, and grassy areas that invite people to linger and children to romp or roll down a hill. At a winery, however, it's possible to share an alcoholic beverage with your friends and family, something

Figure 3.2. Jonathan Keiser and Leslie Tucker celebrate the anniversary of their first date by revisiting Mallow Run Winery's tasting room, August 17, 2015. Photo by Greta Pennell.

that is banned in most other public settings. The combination of wine and place, a combination of physical and social qualities, creates an experience that people seek out because it is enjoyable on many levels.

Getting into Wines and Wineries

In July 2012 at Mallow Run Winery, I interviewed Steve and Dianna Hamilton, a couple I had become acquainted with during my band's performances there. Steve had recently retired as a special education teacher, and his wife, also a teacher, was nearing retirement. They often met up with another couple or two at the winery. They told me they had primarily been beer drinkers until they started coming to Mallow Run. Their first visit was on the last day of the school year. Their principal was retiring and urged them to come along to see the winery and celebrate the occasion.

> STEVE: So he [the principal] said, "You need to come out and see this," and it was a neat place. I didn't know it was out here. So we started coming out just once in a while.

DIANNA: Yeah, and I knew Ken and Debbie were playing out here, so we started coming out and hearing them, and then we just got . . .

STEVE: We got caught up with crazy people [grinning].

DIANNA: And then we got hooked [laughing].

Steve and Dianna both agreed that they were not very knowledgeable about wine, noting that one of their friends was more of an expert. I asked them what they liked about drinking wine:

DIANNA: Well it's not like drinking beer, where you drink it usually a little faster. This is more a sip, you know, you sip and it's just a longer process, more enjoyable. You enjoy the wine more because you're not just gulping it down.

STEVE: And sometimes, like beer, it's either really light beer or really dark, and you can tell the difference between those. But a lot of times you can try ten different kinds of beer, and if you really haven't tried all those a lot, you can't tell the difference. You can try ten different kinds of wines here, and you are going to know that they are all different. If you don't know what they are, you can find out. But you can tell a real difference.

DIANNA: You could take Bud Light and Coors Light, you know, unless you are a beer connoisseur, you are not really going to know the difference much.

STEVE: Yeah, I remember that first day [with his principal] and they had us try different things. And so they said, well, try that, and it was real dry . . . I had heard of dry wines, but I'd never really had one. And I thought, huh, that's interesting, because I don't think I could swallow because it was . . . because it was dry, it wasn't like this [the wine we were drinking during the interview]. They said, "That was dry wine," and it sure was [laughing].

DIANNA: And who would think rhubarb wine would be their big seller, you know?

I asked them which wines they preferred. Dianna mentioned liking Riesling, but Steve said he didn't care for it. Steve mentioned Seyval Blanc, and they both talked about Mallow Run's Vino Rosso, a close-to-dry (and sometimes dry, depending on the year) red wine made from Sangiovese grapes from California. Dianna mentioned that they both liked the Traminette, the sweeter one, not the drier. I asked which was their favorite Indiana wine:

DIANNA: I think the Seyval Blanc, probably.

STEVE: It's a little more pricey, but we still get that one.

DIANNA: It's refreshing.

STEVE: Yeah, it is. It's sweet and kind of sour.

DIANNA: It's kind of like lemonade, you know, there's a sweet and then there's that little thing where you want to smack your lips a little.

In contrast to Steve and Dianna, who saw themselves as less experienced wine drinkers, my friend and former university colleague William "Butch" Fennema began to develop his wine knowledge on a visit to California with one of his brothers, who was already into finer wines. Since then, he had visited every major wine region in California, as well as wineries in Oregon, Washington, New York, Virginia, Michigan, Missouri, and other states. He had also been to wineries in Australia and Canada. He named more than a dozen Indiana wineries he had visited, and noted that he was probably leaving out a number of others. He also cellared wine and figured he had about six cases at the time I interviewed him. In November 2015, he became an adult beverage specialist at a local store that was part of a large grocery chain. I asked Butch what wines were his favorites:

Place of origin doesn't really matter to me. I have some that, how would I say it, I don't care for as much as others. Chilean wines tend to have a dust in them. I horrified Joseph [a local chef] when I made the comment. A lot of the Chilean wines, and I like wines generally with dust in it, but there's something in the Chilean, in many of the Chilean wines. But in terms of place of origin, I really don't have favorites. It's the wine itself. And it's . . . again, it would not be related to Cab or Zin, but to a more full-bodied, more tannic—I like the stronger wines. Let me rephrase that. I shouldn't say stronger—heavier wines, more tannic. Although particularly in the summer when it's hot, a nice little White Riesling is wonderful, a crisp kind of thing, but generally speaking, more Cabs, Zins, more tannins. And again, I say that with the caveat that I've had some aged Pinots from Oregon, ohhhh!

I asked Butch which Indiana wine is his favorite, and he said:

Hmmm. I'm going to have to start with our [favorite] winery first—Thomas Family. And again, it's part of the experience. Cassie [his girlfriend] and I have gone in there and done lunch, and you can do three ounces of this cheese and four ounces of that. They've got loaves of bread they'll heat. Pepperoni, salami, and, you know, it's just kind of the right atmosphere. That said, I have had some of the best Indiana wine there. I would say one of the best because as much as anything, not only was it just incredibly fabulous, it surprised me. I had a Chardonnay at Charlie Thomas's place [Chateau Thomas Winery] in Plainfield that was about twenty years old. I didn't know that could be done. And that was just a golden nectar of the gods kind of thing.

I told Butch that Dr. Thomas had said he still had some of that Chardonnay left, and he replied:

I know. He told us that night. He said, "This is from my private collection"—a "Don't ask, you can't get any" kind of thing. But those two stick out in my mind. I've had other really good reds, the Cab that I mentioned at Paoli Peaks down there. [JP: French Lick?] Right—stands out as being wonderful.

Butch is nearing retirement age, and as noted, Steve was retired and Dianna was nearing retirement when I interviewed them in 2012. From its rise in popularity through the 1990s, wine was most popular with middle-class professionals over the age of thirty. However, Larry Satek of Satek Winery told me he had observed a demographic shift at the beginning of the new century.

> And when you talk about your cultural revolution, it is happening right now. And it started happening, I would say in real seriousness, probably around 2000, 2002. I did a very detailed study of what the demographics of wine drinkers were about at that point, and the people were still primarily older, college-educated, upper-class wine drinkers. And one of the questions that a lot of people said is: Where are the rest of the wine drinkers coming from? What happens when these guys move on and don't drink wine anymore? And as soon as we opened, I started to realize that our demographics, at least, we started having a lot of twenty-somethings—twenty-one-somethings, I'd say twenty-one-somethings [laughing, referring to the drinking age]—coming and trying to learn about wine. And there were a lot. They were way disproportionate to the thirty-to-forty-year-olds. Fifty-and-sixty-year-olds, they came in because that was our demographics primarily. But, and this has just been growing, I guess there are a lot of millennials at this point. This is a real phenomenon, and you know, they look at the world a little differently, and that's perfectly fine. I'm just glad that wine is part of their world [laughing].

Market researchers also began to note this trend. In a national survey conducted in 2002, Scarborough Research found that while nearly half of wine drinkers were between the ages of thirty-five and fifty-four, one-fourth were younger and also substantially "[more] likely than the average purchaser to spend $20 or more on a bottle of wine" (Scarborough Research 2003, 1). The study also found that the ethnicity of wine drinkers mirrored their percentages in the general population, and that Hispanics and African Americans were also more likely to purchase higher-priced wines.

In addition to the flavors people enjoy and the role of wine as part of a social experience, it gained another attribute in the 1990s. Research that found drinking red wine produced health benefits made its way into the popular consciousness in 1991 through outlets such as the CBS television news show *60 Minutes*. Andrew Barr does a nice job of describing the genesis and explaining the pros and cons of this claim in *Drink: A Social History of America* (1999). As Barr observes (233–34), the relationship between wine and a reduced rate of heart disease and, perhaps, cancer may be chemical, due to its being drunk regularly and more slowly than other alcoholic beverages, and commonly with food. It may be that the antioxidants in wine, and/or alcohol in modest amounts, reduce heart disease. It may also be that those who lead a healthier lifestyle gravitate toward wine. Last, it may be that drinking wine adds enjoyment to life, reducing stress and making wine drinkers happier than non–wine drinkers.

The idea that red wine is good for people comes up frequently in conversation at the wineries, though usually as a joke about why people are drinking it. In Somerset, Kentucky, I observed a stark example of the impact of this research on both the popular and medical consciousness. My wife and I visited wineries in states in other areas of the country so I could compare and contrast their wines and settings with my observations of Midwestern wineries. We were in Somerset sampling wine at Sinking Valley Winery's tasting room when an older, heavy-set gentleman in overalls came in with his wife. He asked our server, the wife of the couple who owned the winery, if he could sample some wine. He told her he didn't really like wine, but his doctor had told him he should start drinking a glass or two a day for his heart. He sampled one and asked her if he could "cut the wine" with grape juice, and would it still have the medical benefit. She told him he could do that, and he walked out the door with two bottles of a sweet red. She didn't mention that red grape juice has most of the antioxidant benefits that wine provides.

My observations suggest that an appreciation for wine can lead wine drinkers to hang out in enjoyable places such as local wineries, and those enjoyable places prompt socializing over local wines. Whatever the physiological effects, socially people are having a good time with friends and family. And while some people's enjoyment of wine may prompt them to frequent local wineries, it is common to find customers such as Dianna and Steve who are introduced to wine as a result of visiting and then frequenting a local winery.

The Role of Place in the Wine Experience

Good wine is important to the success of wineries. But just as important for wineries that are heavily dependent on selling wine on location for survival is the setting and the people who work there. Butch noted a number of times during our interview that it isn't just the wine, but "the experience"—the setting, the people, and the moment—that makes a wine special. He recalled some early experiences in California that combined wine with beautiful settings:

> There's a winery, Dynamite Winery [in Sonoma, California]—what they make is dynamite, they call it—and Cassie and I missed the tasting in the morning. We called them and told them we were really sorry, we're not going to make it, but we wanted to call in case you could put somebody else on. They said, "Well, we've got a tasting this afternoon if you would like to come." Oh, yes! You know, 'cause it's really a very good wine. It's not great, but it's very good. We got there, we had bought a sandwich and we were going to sit out there and have something. So I went in and I said, "You know, we wanted to let you know we are not stalking the

place," and they said, "Oh, would you like a glass of wine?" And they gave both of us this nice big pour of Dynamite, and we sat on their back porch deck at the picnic table, overlooking the vineyards that went up the hills. And I'm not sure if I've ever had a better glass of wine than that . . .

But again, to me, the wine is part of the experience. I've had better wines, but not necessarily better experiences. One of the best bottles of wine I had was with [my brother]. We were camping in Yosemite, and I couldn't even tell you what it was. It was a really outrageously good red wine because that's what we took camping. We're laying there in the middle of this field looking at one of the best places to watch the stars, out in the middle of the Yosemite drinking this outrageous bottle of red. So to me, it's as much the experience, the people around me, as it is the bottle.

Butch compared his experiences at Indiana wineries favorably to the other places he had been, including Tasmania:

Again, our better ones will stack up against any time, any place. That's again why Tasmania comes to mind. Cassie says when you drive up the lane, you see the tractor coming to the tasting house because the farmer planted the grapes, harvested the grapes, made the wine, bottled the wine, and is driving the tractor. And that, to me, also adds to the experience. So I want to say, it's Butler, down in Bloomington, it's almost always the owner when I've been there . . . and he is very conversational, a wonderful person, and it just makes such a great experience. Which is why Thomas Family is wonderful, because it's one of the Thomases that's doing it. They do have a bigger staff now that takes care of you. I pretty much know all of them, too. But it's often Steve. If you are going to talk about wine, you can be talking to the winemaker, if the winemaker is conversational. We do have some winemakers who should stay in the winery, not in the tasting room [laughing].

Wineries are often local hangouts, frequented by regular customers. Customers become loyal to these establishments. They know the people who work there, the wine they sell, and the events and routines of the place. I asked Steve and Dianna which Indiana winery they liked the best, and as Mallow Run regulars, they responded in a way that wasn't surprising:

DIANNA: Probably here, just because it's close [to where they live].
STEVE: It's where we started going.
DIANNA: And we know everybody here and we like their wine.
STEVE: I think they have really good people that work here. You feel like you know all of them after a while. It's not because we come so much, but from the very beginning you start learning people and you get accustomed to a place that you like really well. And I think even though it makes it tough to get in because it makes it so busy, the entertainment . . . they are starting to get some really good entertainment here. They have some really good groups. We won't name any [laughing].

DIANNA: I liked Huber [Huber's Orchard, Winery and Vineyards in Starlight, Indiana] real well when we were there. It is so large and, you know, it's not something you buzz out to on an afternoon like this and have a glass of wine. But it was very nice.

Laura Richardson gave me her take on why customers such as Steve and Dianna enjoy the winery experience at Mallow Run, echoing Oldenburg's (1989, 1999) account of third places:

I think seeing how people respond to a casual, positive, generous environment is remarkable. And maybe that's just my perspective. I can't prove anything, but I think people are seeking a place where they can relax, enjoy themselves, be with their friends, listen to music, enjoy wine, and just feel comfortable, and there aren't a lot of rules. And you know, I've never thought about that, but now I think about it, and it is hard to find those kinds of places. I mean, along with the product being good—we couldn't do it without the product being good—but I think that whole other side of what we offer is just as important as the product, and I think we just have responded to that and learned it and have been flexible. Sometimes it's hard to keep doing that, but I think that's what we've done—to be flexible and respond to the feedback that we get. I think it's just really nice to see good things happen and people enjoying themselves. That's the best part about the winery.

This idea that wineries are a shared place, not just a business providing a product or service, was echoed by numerous winery owners across the four states I studied. As Joel Kopsa put it, "We like the people to think it's their winery. That's what we love to hear, when people come and say, 'This is ours'; when they bring friends and they say, 'Yeah, this is our winery.'"

Other winery owners talked about this laid-back but engaging and convivial third-place quality as a community benefit their wineries provide. Joe Henke, the owner of Henke Winery on the west side of Cincinnati, said, "We have that kind of a Cheers-type atmosphere where you get to know the people that come in; you know what's happening in their life." Jackie Trexel, owner and winemaker at Quail Crossing Cellars, an urban winery on the north side of Columbus, Ohio, described how community groups and nonprofits benefit from the use of her tasting room:

I think it's a gathering place. I think the fundraisers, and I've had a lot of them . . . I think it's a good place because people can decorate how they want. I allow them to bring food in, just not alcohol. They can order food from some of the places around here. I don't have too many rules that I make people stick to to be a gathering place. And it benefits me, too. We had a pop-up art gallery in the fall. That was fun. I would do that again.

Of course, wineries vary in terms of what they allow customers to do. Wineries with restaurants typically do not allow outside food to be brought in. State regulations restrict customers' use of alcohol other than what is purchased at the winery. Incivility and profanity are not appreciated, but it is other customers more often than owners who make this known to offending customers. Well-behaved children and pets are commonly welcome. Owners will occasionally make a rule clear when they have had enough of something, so Mallow Run has "no smoking" signs posted throughout its grounds, not just in enclosed spaces. They also have signs up about when the winery grounds close, since people have a tendency to hang out well past the tasting room's closing time, especially when the weather is nice. But compared to a workplace or other institutional settings, lists of rules are rare at wineries.

Customers are typically quite loyal to their local wineries, yet it is common for them to develop an interest in visiting others. The differences in terms of settings, local communities, and the interests, tastes, and capital investments of the owners give each winery its own unique characteristics. These differences encourage customers to visit a variety of wineries to experience those special qualities for themselves. I asked Steve and Dianna how many wineries they had visited, and they mentioned nine. I asked if they had been to any outside the state, and they said no, but they were thinking about trying some in Michigan during an upcoming visit to a relative there.

During a meeting with someone at my university one day, I mentioned that my band plays at Mallow Run. She told me that she and her husband, who was a student in our university's MBA program at the time, weren't really wine drinkers, but he had been assisting Chateau Thomas with some aspect of the winery's business, and they had started going there. Then they started traveling to other wineries in the state. Now when friends or family come to town, they often suggest visiting a winery as a possible thing to do together.

Butch's favorite Indiana winery is not near his home. Thomas Family Winery, about two hours from Indianapolis, is often a weekend destination for him and his girlfriend. As he explained it:

> It's not that they make the best wines. They make very good wines and I like them. But again, to me wine is part of an experience. I could sit on the back porch and drink an outrageously good wine by myself, but it's much more fun if friends are there . . . Just having gone to [Chef] Joseph's wine dinners and the capacity of wine to enhance flavors . . . I've known him for about twelve years, and that's where my understanding [pause]—let me rephrase that—the *enhancement* of my drinking perspective, maybe, I don't know what to call it, developed [his emphasis]. It's matching wine and it's the food and it's the people. And that's why Thomas Family is my favorite, the food and the people.

Many of the Midwestern wineries are family operations. When I visited John Ernest Vineyard and Winery for the first time on an unusually warm March day in 2015, the Kopsa brothers and their brother-in-law were working out in the vineyard. Five members of the Ferrante family were working at their winery and restaurant in Geneva, Ohio, when I visited in April 2015. Generations of Hubers continue to work at their winery and farm. The list of Midwestern wineries with two or three generations working together or that have been passed down in families is a long one. I will examine the importance of family to winery owners in the next chapter. The point here is that wineries often extend that sense of family to customers who volunteer to help out with big events and pick grapes at harvest time. In addition to the extended family who help out at Mallow Run, including Laura Richardson's parents, some of the customers helped out in ways that one might associate with family. Steve assisted with parking cars at events. The fiancé of an employee spent many hours assisting with picking, crushing, and other tasks. Many regular customers would show up to pick grapes just to enjoy the experience and help out. Butch talked about exactly this kind of experience as an important quality of the small Indiana wineries:

> I'm going down to Mallow Run, and, you know, you can go work that day, and it takes a lot of people to get the work done. Okay, this is too big for us. Well, we'll let people volunteer, and they can come in and we'll be nice to them and they'll be part of the family.

Wineries often serve as community cultural centers. In a small town or a rural community, a winery can be the primary attraction. Many wineries offer music, food, and informal (and sometimes formal) instruction about drinking wine. Some feature local artists' and craftspersons' work and provide them with a retail outlet. Some have yoga, knitting, or art groups who meet there for activities. Wineries commonly collaborate with other businesses in an area. For example, the owners of Tonne Winery near Muncie, Indiana, hold what they call their WINOS (Women in Need of Shopping) event every couple of months, where local vendors can come in and set up booths. Wilson Winery in Modoc, Indiana, is an added attraction for those staying at a privately owned campground in the area. Conversely, those who visit the winery may discover the campground, and together they become a weekend or vacation destination. A number of wineries mentioned bringing food trucks in. Wineries participate in local festivals, adding to the fun while educating and attracting new customers. Christine Lawlor-White, owner of Galena Cellars, was instrumental in starting a Nouveau Wine Weekend in Galena, Illinois, which has been held on the Friday and Saturday before Thanksgiving weekend since 1985. Her winery releases a Gamay-based nouveau wine (blended with a little Marechal

Figure 3.3. Blue Sky Vineyard in Makanda, Illinois, as viewed from the patio area outside the tasting room, May 21, 2015. Photo by Greta Pennell.

Foch) in the French Beaujolais tradition for the event, which is delivered to businesses in a pickup truck accompanied by a horse-drawn wagon carrying some revelers. Some shops and restaurants in the historic river town hold wine and cheese parties and serve French-inspired cuisine or food prepared or served with the nouveau wine. Thus they have turned what used to be a dead weekend for businesses into a regional attraction.

Many Midwestern wineries reflect qualities commonly found in other communal gathering places such as parks, country clubs, and even religious settings, but in contrast to city, county, and state parks in most Midwestern states as well as most churches, possessing and drinking wine is permitted on winery property. Midwestern wineries have begun to capitalize on customers' desire to use these special places for social events such as weddings, receptions, family reunions, anniversaries, and birthday parties. Vinoklet Winery in Ohio, Whyte Horse Winery in Indiana, Blue Sky Vineyard in Illinois, and Cedar Valley Winery in Iowa are among the wineries in these states that prominently advertise themselves as a site for weddings or receptions. Jim Ewers, co-owner and general manager of Blue Sky Vineyard, told me that he was flooded with inquiries about holding weddings there in the first month after they opened.

It is not surprising that couples would want to share their vows and celebrate in the scenic setting, which looks like a postcard of Tuscany brought to life. Some wineries have limited space and can offer only outdoor venues that require tents in case of inclement weather. Others have dedicated event spaces. I observed many very nice facilities specifically built for events, including the Winery at Wolf Creek outside Akron, Ohio, and Cedar Ridge Winery in Iowa, and was informed of a number of others. The demand for event space pushed Mallow Run to build a separate venue, the Sycamore, on the farm property so that winery events and private events could take place simultaneously. The event structure at Rocky Waters Vineyard and Winery in Hanover, Illinois, is awe-inspiring. A construction marvel styled much like a Western mountain lodge, it features a soaring ceiling supported by whole bald cypress tree trunks. Unlike private clubs or churches, wineries do not expect or demand continual financial or time commitments. They are there when patrons want them.

Wineries also give back to the community through collaborative and philanthropic activities. Many host benefit events, such as Mallow Run's "Wine at the Line" 5K run/walk for breast cancer or their Labapalooza benefit for a Labrador retriever rescue group. (Cooper, the Mallow Run Winery dog, is a rescue Lab.) Blue Sky Vineyard frequently donates the overnight suites located on its southern Illinois winery property for charitable groups to auction off. Many wineries allow their event spaces to be used during the week for meetings. As a result of their generosity and visibility, some winery owners I interviewed reported being overwhelmed by the number of requests they receive from organizations wanting them to take part in benefits. Some had to start limiting their participation or had become more selective about their charitable work due to the associated costs. A number of wineries moved to offering free wine tastings at nonprofit events instead of donating wine since this is mutually beneficial, providing a service to the nonprofit and an opportunity for the winery to gain some exposure, educate visitors about wine, and attract new customers.

Winery owners also serve on the boards and event committees of community organizations. Joe Henke mentioned serving as a board member for a number of community organizations and thought that his winery served as a community anchor. John Richardson serves on the board of directors of the Johnson County Historical Society. His daughter-in-law Laura Richardson has served on the board of directors of the Greater Greenwood Arts Council, and Mallow Run dedicates a portion of the proceeds to the council each year from wines with labels featuring local artists' work.

One difference between wineries near high-traffic or high-population areas and smaller wineries in more isolated, rural areas is that the latter are more dependent on both regular and occasional customers from their immediate

Figure 3.4. Rocky Waters Winery in Hanover, Illinois, May 4, 2015. The building houses the tasting room, event space, production facility, and owners' quarters on a hill overlooking the vineyard. Photo by Greta Pennell.

communities to stay in business. Those regulars and occasionals also create much of the social life and conviviality of the place. Ferrante, Oliver, and Huber's are regional destinations. Ferrante Winery and Ristorante is immediately off I-90 just outside the Lake Erie summer resort town of Geneva, Ohio. In addition to being one of the most highly regarded wineries in the state, it also has a highly rated restaurant. Ferrante is part of the Grand River Valley American Viticultural Area (AVA), which includes a cluster of other wineries nearby such as Debonne, making the wineries a tourist destination in their own right. In Indiana, Huber's depends heavily on tourists and successfully attracts them due to its variety of goods, things to do, and proximity to Louisv and surrounding towns. Oliver has benefited greatly from its ideal location on State Road 37 at the north end Bloomington, home of Indiana University. The winery is a common stop for travelers to sporting and cultural events, or parents dropping off or picking up their children attending the university. On a weekend, the parking lot is peppered with license plates from Ohio, Illinois, and Michigan, as well as Indiana plates from around the state. The tasting bar can have customers packed in three and four deep.

When I asked Bill Oliver how important the winery's location was to its success, he replied, "Huge, huge, huge, huge. There is no question we have a good situation." He noted that it isn't just the high traffic count at the location, "but it's also who is driving those cars." A high percentage of the parents of Indiana University students are middle-class professionals, and there are a lot of professionals who work at the university as well. Thus the winery is easily accessible to the primary demographic group that purchases and enjoys fine wines (Scarborough Research 2003). It will be interesting to see if the winery is affected by the conversion of State Road 37 to I-69. Cedar Ridge Winery and Distillery also benefits from a high-traffic location just off I-380 between Cedar Rapids and Iowa City, home of the University of Iowa.

Other wineries benefit from their share of tourist traffic as stops along well-traveled routes or in combination with other attractions in their areas. While traveling through Illinois, my wife and I stopped at Cameo Vineyards just off I-70 in Greenup, and were pleasantly surprised to find some nicely made red and white wines served in a tasting room in a family barn that had been relocated to the winery property. On a different trip we stopped at Sleepy Creek Vineyards, a few miles off I-74 in Fairmount, Illinois. We discovered a rather large selection of well-made wines served in a spacious and attractive tasting room, as well as a quirky tomato and jalapeno wine that is probably best used to make Bloody Mary drinks. A "novelty wine," part humor, part marketing ploy, can be quite popular and gives customers something to talk about and share. I confess that we bought a bottle to share with friends at some future brunch.

The winery owners I interviewed who were near population centers typically reported faster growth than those in more remote areas. Andy Troutman, owner with his wife, Deanna, of both Troutman Vineyards and the Winery at Wolf Creek, told me that because of Wolf Creek's proximity to Akron, Ohio, people stop in after work on weekdays and show up in large numbers on weekends in the spring, summer, and fall months. When I visited Wolf Creek in late April 2015, friends, couples, and coworkers started coming in around four o'clock in the afternoon. In contrast, Troutman said that his other winery, near the much smaller town of Wooster, attracted much less customer traffic.

Wineries are increasingly destinations for a day or weekend trip, or they are part of a broader itinerary that includes outdoor activities such as hiking and

Figure 3.5. Buck Creek Winery benefits from its location along I-70 at the southeast edge of Indianapolis. Photo by Greta Pennell.

boating, historical and cultural attractions, and shopping and dining. Butch often visits the Thomas Family Winery in Madison, Indiana, when he is in town to attend the River Roots Music and Folk Arts Festival (formerly the Ohio River Valley Folk Festival) or the Hot Luck and Fiery Foods Festival. My band used to play at the Chateau Thomas tasting room in Nashville, Indiana, a favorite weekend and vacation spot near Brown County State Park. We were gratified to develop a regional following of people from Illinois, Ohio, and Kentucky who would time their return visits to hear us when we played there. Southern Indiana and southern Illinois are covered with wineries near parks and other tourist destinations. Wineries line Lake Erie; not only does the lake provide some moderation in climate that is amenable to growing grapes, but it is a tourist destination. County visitors' bureaus and state tourism offices often produce pamphlets and sponsor websites that promote their areas' variety of leisure amenities.

Many Midwestern wineries have formed wine trails, groups of wineries that are clustered in an area or along common travel routes, to collectively promote their businesses. Mallow Run, for example, is part of the Indy Wine Trail, which includes six other wineries. As of summer 2015, Indiana had six wine trails. Ohio had six promoted by the Ohio Wine Producers Association, plus the Three

Rivers Wine Trail, which is promoted by the Coshocton [County] Visitors Bureau. The Iowa Wine Growers Association listed seven. Illinois has only four: the Shawnee Hills Wine Trail in the southern part of the state; the Northern Illinois Wine Trail, which is divided into three loops across the northern end of the state; the five-winery Mississippi Valley Wine Trail in western Illinois; and the five-winery Wabash Valley Wine Trail in the southeastern part of the state, which includes one Indiana winery. Wine trails encourage customers to visit multiple wineries and offer the opportunity to sample different wines as well as different styles and qualities of the same grape. Wine trails are especially important in helping wineries become destinations in areas that are distant from population centers. Paul Renzaglia, the owner of Alto Vineyards, told me that the wineries on the Shawnee Hills Wine Trail in southern Illinois depend on tourists from Chicago to make ends meet. Chris Lawlor-White, the owner of Galena Cellars, which is part of the Northwest Loop of the Northern Illinois Wine Trail, said the same thing. Making a wine trail work requires collaboration and coordination among wineries, often giving owners a sense of a shared identity and purpose, or at least creates a shared identity in the minds of customers.

Midwestern wineries make their customers feel as if they are part of something and that they matter. Walmart and other big retail stores cannot create this kind of experience no matter how often they give out hot dogs or school supplies to community groups. When those who weren't wine drinkers discover a place with people and products they like—some sweet wine, perhaps—they can enjoy sharing what seems to be a hidden treasure in their own back yards with friends and neighbors as well as the occasional visitor from out of town. Even those with more cosmopolitan tastes and experiences, who may have visited many other wineries in the world, appreciate the way a local winery can come to feel like home after repeated visits—and it will often have some very good wine to suit their tastes.

Wineries can run into the dilemma of becoming so popular that at times the crowds are a bit overwhelming. People want to be at a place that is happening, one that others want to be at as well. But they also want a personal rather than an impersonal experience. They want to talk with the winery owner or the server. They want to be able to find a seat or sit in their favorite spot on the lawn. Most of the Midwestern wineries are small enough that they would love to face this dilemma. But as they grow, they risk losing that intimate feeling. Good wine and an enjoyable place are always works in progress, requiring constant refinement and adaptation to circumstances to maintain their attraction. They also require much work, as the next two chapters examine.

4

Becoming a
Midwestern Vintner

Midwestern winery owners have become involved in the business in a number of different ways. As the industry has begun to mature, some are second- or even third generation owners who have taken over the businesses from their parents. Most others are wine lovers who started making wine in their homes as a hobby. Some were looking for something challenging and rewarding to do after successful careers in other lines of work. Some, although not many, were farmers, and had farms they were hoping to keep in the family. Wineries offer a way to diversify or shift over farm production to a more profitable finished product. Many owners I interviewed saw owning a winery as a way to bring together their different interests and talents. All had developed a desire to create quality wine and an enjoyable experience for others, and found satisfaction in the interesting, meaningful work that owning a winery affords—work that is often done with one's family and friends.

The Second Generation of the
Midwest Wine Industry

Winery ownership in the Midwest is now in its second and even third wave of ownership as the industry has matured. Owners of newer wineries have benefited greatly from those who came before them in terms of making the industry possible and developing the knowledge and skills necessary for success. Some of these newer owners have taken over wineries started by their parents or grandparents. As might be expected, most of these descendants of founders grew up in the industry and find much meaning in the close connection between their lives, families, places, and work.

The Second (and Sixth) Generation in Indiana

Ted Huber, Bill Oliver, and Mark Easley are second-generation Indiana winery owners. Although I did not interview him, Steve Thomas is also a second-generation winemaker, having worked for his father, Dr. Charles Thomas, at Chateau Thomas Winery before starting the Thomas Family Winery. Bill's father and Mark's parents were instrumental in restarting the industry in Indiana, and it was Bill's father who helped author the legislation for the 1971 Small Winery Act. Ted's father, Gerald Huber, and his uncle, Carl Huber, started Huber's Winery in 1978, with Gerald as the head winemaker. Ted described his start in the winemaking business to me in the large restaurant area of the winery on a cold day in December 2011.

> I actually made wine back when I was thirteen, fourteen years old as a hobby, and not in the commercial setting. I helped my father in the commercial setting up here, but in one of the out garages, I actually had my own glass carboys, made my own wine, and then made my own spirits as a youngster. Dad was making wines in a particular way, and then I was reading my books and I thought maybe this way is good and it's working. So I started my own experiments. I had all these glass carboys down in the old garage making my own products. So I did it both as a hobby and in a commercial setting.
>
> JP: So you just knew you were going to do this?
>
> TED: It's an interesting thing. Since I was in high school, I would help. I would come home as a freshman or sophomore in high school and actually help my father blend the wines for bottling. And so my dad picked me out of all the family members, the eight of us family members growing up on the farm, as the one who had a great palate for blending and tasting and that. So I helped. I got the very . . . this is a great privilege when you are a teenager, to be working with wines as young as that. And then one thing we have always done here at our winery is always compare our wine to its counterparts both as far as domestic wines as well as imports. So growing up, I always had the opportunity to taste our wines versus the Italian counterparts, French counterparts, the California counterparts, and in a lot of cases the counterparts here in our state and the surrounding states, too. And so you can say that I got the wine bug young.

Even though the most recent incarnation of Huber's Winery was officially founded in 1978, it may well be the oldest property in Indiana where wine was made before Prohibition. When Ted referred to himself as a sixth-generation winemaker, I asked him if the first settler, Simon Huber, grew grapes and made wine.

> The very first year, in 1843, when the property was bought and they clear-cut and planted apples and grapes, those were the two original crops on the property and they are still our two top crops today. And we've been in continuous production. And the farm, as you can tell, we do diversify a little bit, and right now we are looking at Christmas trees, pumpkins, and we do tourist fruits, and the farm itself is a fruit farm first. And if you look at our website, we start with strawberries, black raspberries, blackberries, and then the red raspberries and then blueberries,

then peaches. Then our grape season starts, and then our apple season starts. When we wake up here we aren't winemakers, we aren't this, we aren't that, we are farmers at heart. And we've been brought up that way, and my children are being brought up that way—that this farm, and this company, is an agricultural company, not a production company. So we are totally different than any other Indiana winery that you'll come across, [in] that we pride ourselves on being estate bottled. And that goes back to the fact that we were farmers and still are.

Huber's Orchard, Winery and Vineyards is a sprawling operation compared to most Indiana wineries, with a number of buildings on more than six hundred acres surrounded by fields of fruit trees, bushes, and vegetable plots. The main building houses a large restaurant, a banquet room, and tasting rooms upstairs and in the cellar. There are also a market building, an ice cream and cheese shop, and a number of production, storage, and implement buildings, as well as a small amusement park. The large tasting room on the second floor has a long bar at one side of the room. Wines are displayed with medals alongside various wine-related gift items and knickknacks. Ted Huber told me that for many years he resisted displaying the medals, but his marketing department finally convinced him that he should do it. He thinks it drives customers to particular wines and interferes with their ability to form judgments based on their own preferences and a given wine's merits. They may miss an opportunity to expand their knowledge and refine their palates or even pass up wines they might otherwise enjoy.

Huber's Winery is part of the Indiana Uplands American Viticultural Area, formed in 2013, and a member of the Indiana Uplands Wine Trail. The Uplands are highlands north of the Ohio River Valley that stretch a little over one hundred miles, from just north of the Ohio River to just north of Bloomington, Indiana. The region shares a common type of terrain and soils, but the low temperatures can range substantially in the winter from Butler Winery at the far northern end to Huber's, Turtle Run Winery, or Best Vineyards near the Ohio River. Like many of the wineries in or near the Ohio River Valley, Huber's can grow *vinifera* grapes such as Cabernet Sauvignon and Cabernet Franc. This allows them to produce wines that rival many California reds. Their Heritage wine, a blend of Cabernet Sauvignon, Cabernet Franc, and Petit Verdot, would have many wine aficionados thinking they are drinking a $30 or $40 bottle of California red wine in a blind test. At the annual Indy International Wine Competition, Huber's Winery has won more awards than any other winery in the state by far. They have won so many Governor's Cups, awarded to the Indiana winery with the most medals, that Ted noted: "I think my wife calculated that the next winery would have to win the Governor's Cup for sixteen straight years to just tie us." The winery is still an extended-family operation; Ted shares ownership with his cousin Greg, Carl's son. Greg focuses on the farming side of the operation.

Figure 4.1. Two generations at Huber's Orchard, Winery and Vineyards in Starlight, Indiana. *Left to right*: Gerald Huber; his son, Ted; Greg Huber; and Greg's father, Carl, at the "still house" on the anniversary of Repeal Day, December 5, 2014. Photo courtesy of Huber's Orchard, Winery and Vineyards, used by permission.

Unlike the sprawling Huber property, Oliver Winery, at the northern end of the Indiana Uplands Wine Trail, is tucked behind a hillside off State Road 37 on the outskirts of Bloomington. Bill Oliver took over the operation of the winery from his father, William Oliver, in 1984. Bill talked with me on a crisp, clear December morning in 2011 between phone calls, and described his entry into the business as follows:

> You know, the real heyday, the early heyday of the wineries in the mid- to late seventies, when Camelot Mead sales were just booming and we were largely about that, I think our late-seventies production was about eighty-plus percent Camelot Mead sold through distribution, and we didn't manage that terribly well. That kind of collapsed and left us in a pretty bad way in the early eighties when I got my undergraduate business degree, and I just saw it as an opportunity, a challenge, and a way to help out my dad's struggling business. So that's why I joined in 1983, and, you know, a real period of refocusing the winery on the retail end. The early

model was to just make us a really well-run retailing operation with good wines, nicely packaged, a pretty place—I think everybody has those expectations—and about service. And as we've grown, we know that—sort of have this understanding that—wine is an aesthetic experience. Wine is not a beverage [pounding his desk and laughing]. It's an aesthetic experience that involves so many nuances of that experience. And we're gonna be thoughtful of a broad range of that stuff, about how you serve it, with what you serve it, the glass we'll use. I mean, it's so much you have to think about. And I think because we have a deep understanding of that, we've been successful.

Bill worked to broaden the wine portfolio and transform the image and physical features of the winery. He told me that he is an "operations guy," and while he has a hand in the winemaking, the business employs a winemaker with assistants. The setting has come a long way from the cozy, rather subterranean tasting room and Quonset hut production facility my wife and I first visited in February 1982. Oliver has some of the appearance of a midsized California winery. A few grapevines decorate the front of the property. A walkway winds from the parking lot through attractive rock and flower gardens with a small waterfall and pool to the front door of a two-story wood structure featuring a wraparound covered porch and wood decks. The building would be right at home in Sonoma. When you step in the door, a large, four-sided tasting bar dominates the left side of the room, which is open to the roof rafters. To the right are checkout counters, wine displays, and coolers with white wine, cheeses, and other goods requiring refrigeration. Cases of wine are stacked, with varieties scattered around the room. A deck on the north end of the building drops off to a small pond. Chairs and tables provide a great place to view the pond and share a bottle of wine. The original tasting room building on the property serves as an overflow tasting room on busy days as well as an event space. The winery schedules occasional music performances and events, but the focus is on the wine experience. A large production facility is located to the south and back of the building that houses the tasting room. Additional tanks and production equipment are outside, including a tall ninety-thousand-gallon tank that looks quite a bit like a silo.

In 1994, the Olivers planted fifty-three acres of grapes on their Creekbend property, located a few miles west of the winery, and their estate wines are made from those grapes. I think their estate-produced Chambourcin is consistently one of the better ones produced in the state. Oliver has a big portfolio of dry and semi-dry red and white wines, both estate-grown wines under its Creekbend label, and wines made from other states' grapes under its Oliver label. Even so, the number one seller is its Oliver Red, a Concord-based sweet wine made from purchased juice. According to Bill Oliver, the grapes they grow account for only about 5 percent of the wine they produce. Like many Indiana wine-

Figure 4.2. Front and entrance to the main tasting room of Oliver Winery, Bloomington, Indiana, November 19, 2011. Photo by Greta Pennell.

makers, they procure grapes and juice from California, New York, and other states. Unlike most wineries in Indiana, Oliver makes most of its income—95 percent, by Bill's estimation—from retail sales through wholesale distribution.

I was surprised to learn that in 2006 Bill and his family made the winery an employee-owned business through an Employee Stock Ownership Plan. This information is now noted on their website, but was not yet there when I interviewed him. Interestingly, it also wasn't noted in an article in the *Journal of Values Based Leadership* (Baughman, Schroeder, and Schroeder 2011) that highlighted the winery's "value orientation." As Bill explained, he continued as company president, concentrating on the winemaking operation and the Creekbend vineyard, although the vineyard also has a manager and assistant manager. His wife, Kathleen, took over many of the management duties as general manager in 1993. Considering the extent to which a winery is shaped by its geographical and cultural location, it is reasonable that it would have an influence on the owners' interests and values as well. So it shouldn't have surprised me that a progressive form of ownership would exist in the most progressive city in Indiana. But Indiana hasn't been known for many progressive things in its past beyond being the birthplace of Eugene Debs and Kurt

Vonnegut and home to a rather high percentage of unionized manufacturing workers in the 1950s and 1960s.

Another son of an Indiana winery-pioneering family, Mark Easley, literally grew up above the winery in downtown Indianapolis. His parents, Jack and Joan Easley, were active in making commercial wineries legal in the early 1970s. As Mark told me:

> I was born into it . . . I was introduced to it by a family association and said, "Hey, this is a pretty good gig. I like this!" There are times when you are on 110 percent, and then there are times when it's a little slower and you can enjoy it . . . We as children grew up in this building. My family moved here in 1976 to the building. We sold our home. We were spending our time between the farm and here and we said, "Something's got to give," so we got rid of the house . . . lived upstairs, worked downstairs. It worked very well. You know, at six, the front doors locked. Everybody leaves, from customers to staff, and the place becomes yours. Obviously it was a slower time then. I mean, we've had quite a bit of growth, you know. But I like having my children here now. They're here on a daily basis. They get off of school, come here. I'm working with my wife daily. You know, that aspect, we spend more time at work than we do at home, and it makes the conversations interesting. They can cross back and forth between family and work. When my mother, who just passed away, was here, it was kind of interesting. Folks used to say, "Mark, why do you call her Joan? She's your mother, isn't she?" And I would say, "Yes, she is, but in the business it's a little funny to say, 'Hey, Mom, come here!'" So you know, we had an understanding early on: Mom is Joan at work. And at six o'clock when the doors lock, I'll say, "Hey, Mom, what's for dinner?"

Easley Winery was the first urban winery in the state, and it is still the largest, located in a two-story brick factory building about seven blocks from Monument Circle, which marks the center of Indianapolis. The tasting room, offices, and a dining room for events are located on the first floor toward the front of the building and are accessed from a parking lot. The back of the building houses the production facility.

Growing a winery to the level at which the owner can afford to give up a full-time job with medical insurance and perhaps hire some part-time help can be a tremendous challenge. This is one reason why Midwestern wineries are often a family affair.

MARK EASLEY: Traditionally, up until the 1980s, the wine industry was multifamily generational, the reason being the capital investment of the operation, in conjunction with the longevity required to establish the vineyards, required multigenerational approaches. You know, something on that subject that sticks to mind is when Robert Mondavi, back when he was still in the wine business and was still alive, was interviewed by publications and . . . at the time he was going around the world and establishing partnerships, he said he would not talk to any partners in Europe or in South America that were not at least at the third generation. That is, the family was in the third generation, with the thought process being that you have to cultivate this industry into the fabric of the people, in that you can't approach it as a business, as a heating and air business or a contracting business or something of that nature, to the extent that the timelines are too long. I have to anticipate what our customers are going to be doing five to eight years from today. Because I have to go find that farm ground, match it to what I think the demand will be. Is it red grapes, white grapes, dry wine, sweet wine? And then put those grapes on the right soil with the right climate, give them three to four years to begin growing, and then bring it into the winery and spend another year to three years perfecting the flavor and taste. So when you start looking at ten-year timelines, you can't approach this as "Oh, I'll get into the wine for a couple years and then get out." Now don't get me wrong here, there are people that do that, but they buy existing operations and hire trained folks and . . .

JP: Which is what is going on in California.

MARK: Right, at the end of the day, when they look at the finances, it's just a big hole, you know. They took a big pile of money and made it a small pile of money. But they are in the wine business.

The Second (and Third) Generation in Ohio

Despite stretching back to the repeal of Prohibition, Ohio's wine industry floundered until the 1970s. By then, the second generation of the Ferrante family was already into winemaking. Peter and Anthony Ferrante, the sons of Nicholas and Anna Ferrante, moved the winery operation from Cleveland to the family's farm and vineyards outside Geneva. Peter's son Nick started working at the winery along with Nick's brother and cousin.

I interviewed Nick Ferrante on a cold late April morning in 2015 with snow and sleet blowing—not the kind of weather that makes vineyard owners happy. After the loss of their grape crop and substantial vineyard damage caused by the record cold temperatures in January 2014, weather problems were on his mind. Sixty-five acres of grapes, including fifty acres of *vinifera* varieties such as Chardonnay, Riesling, Pinot Grigio, and Cabernet Franc, were budding. Vineyards can still get a secondary growth that produces grapes if the first is lost to freezing temperatures, although the yield is often less, and for *vinifera* it can be substantially less or none depending on the variety.

The winery is still a family operation, with five relatives currently working there. Nick, the head winemaker and general manager, didn't have any formal training; he just started making wine, and his brother focused more on the operation's business side. Nick took me on a tour through what seemed to be a maze of steel tanks and oak barrels in multiple rooms. He explained that the

Figure 4.3. Ferrante Winery and Ristorante as viewed from the northeast.
Photo by and used with the permission of Nick Plus Danée (www.nickplusdanee.com).

different oak barrels—various kinds of American oak, French oak, Russian oak (the latter in larger barrels), and hybrid barrels of Minnesota and French oak—imparted different flavors. He also had some acacia barrels. The stainless steel and sealed glass bottling line looked like something that might be found in a pediatric ward to protect premature babies. Nick said it could turn out seventy bottles per minute. With a production capacity of two hundred thousand gallons or sixty thousand cases of wine, Ferrante is the largest single brand in Ohio. Although Meier's produces more wine and other beverages, it does so under various labels. Ferrante's popularity is well earned. The wines are of high quality but reasonably priced. When my wife and I attended a charitable art event and wine tasting in southern Ohio, in November 2014, the attendees wiped out the Ferrante wines first among the many Ohio wines available. The 2012 Vidal Blanc Ice Wine, Grand River Valley, won the Sweepstake Award for best dessert wine at the 2014 San Francisco Chronicle Wine Competition.

In addition to the fine wines he produces, Nick also spoke proudly of the beautiful restaurant and tasting room, which was built in 1995 to replace one built in the 1980s that was destroyed by a fire in 1994. The high ceilings, different levels, and numerous windows that allow diners to look out over the vineyard offer a relaxed, casual setting for fine dining and wine drinking. But wine is clearly the focal point, with racks of wine for sale in the tasting

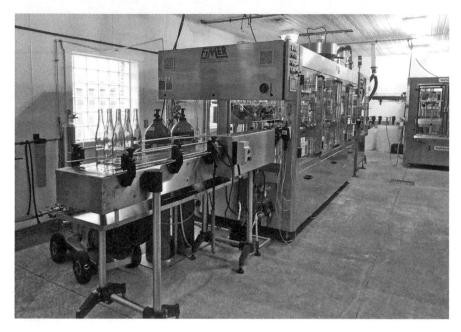

Figure 4.4. Ferrante Winery's automated bottler, April 23, 2015. Photo by Jim Pennell.

room near the entry door. Unlike some wineries in the Midwest that I would describe as restaurants with wineries attached, producing middling and in some instances terrible wine, Ferrante is a high-quality winery with a fine restaurant attached.

Ferrante is in the Grand River Valley AVA. The area lacks the density of Napa or Sonoma, but its concentration of wineries exceeds what is commonly found in the Midwest. Driving west on State Road 307 from Ferrante on the north side of the Grand River, one passes Harpersfield Vineyard, Hundley Cellars, and St. Joseph Vineyard in short order. St. Joseph has large wind machines, basically vineyard fans on tall stands, that help with frost problems. One of the wineries I visited on the south side of the river, Debonne Vineyards in Madison, had a beautiful restaurant, event spaces, and a tasting room surrounded by 175 acres of grapes. In the family since 1916, Debonne is the largest producer of wine grapes in Ohio. Tony Debevc Jr. opened the winery with his father, the late Tony Debevc Sr., in 1972. Similar to Ferrante, the winery produces high-quality wines at reasonable prices. Although I did not get an opportunity to talk with Debevc, I tasted some wine, ate some food, and ended up purchasing a mixed case of wine. (Winery research is not a cheap endeavor.) Other winery owners I interviewed in Ohio told me they purchase *vinifera* grapes from Debonne, especially Cabernet Franc.

Sometimes the winery bug skips a generation. Just outside the small town of Waldo, in north-central Ohio, Van and Emily Creasap took over the ownership and operation of Shamrock Vineyard in 2011. The winery was started by Van's grandparents Dr. Thomas and Mary Quilter. The Quilters had raised and sold grapes to wineries and home winemakers before opening the winery in 1984, when "Dr. Tom" was sixty-four. Van said that his grandfather, a physician by trade and a pioneer in cold-climate grape production, loved to educate people about grapes and wine. Van seemed to have picked up some of his grandfather's storytelling skills as he explained how he got into the business:

> I got involved when I was sixteen. You know, you get a car and you want to go somewhere. I grew up in Marion, which is fifteen minutes from here. I'd say, "Hey, Mom, Dad, I'm going to go for a ride." And they'd say, "Why don't you go help your grandfather today?" So I'd get in the car and cruise out, and then I'd sit on the mower, or I'd carry cases of wine from the cellar upstairs to the bond room, or do this, do that grunt work—and I kind of enjoyed doing it. Then I went to college, to Ohio State, got a degree in business administration with a focus in economics. And as I was going through school, I was working at BP Oil. I was the guy behind the register . . . and I worked out here [at the winery] basically one day a week on my day off from school and work. By the time I was a sophomore, my grandfather's health started to go downhill, and at that time he was just slowing down to where he couldn't keep up out here. So I volunteered to leave my other job with BP because I had enough saved to get through school for the next few years and was ready to come out here and help him more because I love being out here. I love being outside, having the freedom to just get the work done . . . By then, he pretty much needed me full time doing grunt work. Then it turned into doing more of the winemaking side of things; he just couldn't do it. And there was a heck of a learning curve for me, not partaking much in those seasons except for learning little bits here and there, and then actually being the one to do it. It was a lot of culture shock on my end. It's not as simple as one, two, three and you've got good wine. That was a very, very difficult time. And of course, being nineteen years old, I can't even go to the store and buy wine, and here I am making it. By the time I graduated in 2004, Gramps had pretty much been forced into retirement due to health issues, and I began running the winery full time and basically just never left.

Tucked between corn and soybean farms, Shamrock is at the end of a driveway that extends a few hundred yards down a narrow strip of land with a few rows of grapes to the left, then opens up to the old farmhouse, a new tasting and event room, and a gravel parking lot surrounded by the vineyard. Unlike the gently sloping river valley vineyards in northeast Ohio or the hillier vineyards in the southern part of the state, Shamrock is located in some rather flat farmland. Van said that through the oddities of topography and climate, his plot of land is in a part of Ohio that typically suffers the coldest winter weather in the state. As a result, the vineyard is planted with native and hybrid grapes such as Niagara, Concord, Delaware, and Seyval to battle the potentially killing freezes. Van is trying to get the number of varieties down to about ten from the twenty-five his grandfather started with as a "hobby grower." The winery also purchases other grapes from Ohio growers. Van thinks a commitment to Ohio grapes is important to the long-term health and identity of the state wine industry.

Another second-generation owner, Kenny Joe Schuchter, runs Valley Vineyards in Morrow with his wife, Dodie. The winery was started by his father, Ken, in 1969, with Kenny Joe and Dodie becoming partners in 1988. Their son Joe also works in marketing and sales at the winery. The Schuchters are also strongly committed to producing wines from Ohio grapes, with eighty-six acres of grapes on a hill above the Little Miami River.

The Second Generation in Illinois and Iowa

The rather late development of the wine industry in Illinois and Iowa in comparison to Ohio and Indiana means there are fewer second-generation owners. When Kelly and Brenda Logan took over the operation of Baxter's Vineyards and Winery in 1987, they bought it from the family trust, making Kelly the fifth generation to operate the winery since it was founded, and the fourth generation since the repeal of Prohibition. Paul Renzaglia joined his father, Guy, in 1985 to assist with the operation of Alto Vineyards. So he was already involved when they started selling wine in 1988. Jared and Phyllis Spahn share the ownership and operation of Rocky Waters Vineyard and Winery, which includes a twenty-five-acre vineyard, with their son.

An owner who did not take over her family's winery, but instead developed her skills working for another owner before setting out on her own, is Peggy Harmston, owner with her husband, Greg, of Massbach Ridge Winery just outside Elizabeth, Illinois. Peggy began developing her winemaking and business skills under the tutelage of Chris Lawlor-White at Galena Cellars. Located high in the Jo Daviess County hills, on the elevation for which it is named, Massbach Ridge is surrounded by a vineyard that was started in 2000. The tasting room opened in 2003. Following in Lawlor-White's footsteps, the Harmstons opened a tasting room in downtown Galena in 2011. They have also begun releasing a nouveau wine before Thanksgiving, although Harmston doesn't use Gamay grapes.

Most of the wineries in Iowa are relatively new. One of the exceptions, Ackerman Winery in Amana, which specializes primarily in fruit wines, was taken over by Harry and Louisa Ackerman's son Les and his wife, Linda, in 1974. They sold it in 2015 to the owners of Fireside Winery in Marengo, Iowa. Many of the Iowa wineries have two or more generations working together. For example, ten members of the Kopsa family collectively own John Ernest Vineyard and Winery, and all contribute to its operation as they can. John Ernest Kopsa and his wife, DeDe, are the patriarch and matriarch. Their children, Vicky, Karen, Joel, and Jeff, are co-owners along with their spouses. Joel cares for the vineyard with the assistance of family members; he and his brother Jeff make the wine; John and DeDe help with bottling; and Joel's daughter markets and distributes the family's wine to retail stores in Iowa.

Second-generation family owners spurred the Midwest winery boom, along with some long-time original owners who continue to run their wineries today, such as Chris Lawlor-White in Illinois, Jim Butler in Indiana, and Ron Mark of Summerset Winery in Iowa. These owners inspired others who visited their wineries, helped develop the knowledge and skills instrumental to making good wine in the Midwest, and have given substantial time and financial support to further the development of the industry in their states. They have served on state wine and grape councils and committees and on the boards of their industry associations, and generously provided advice and assistance to new winery owners. Second-generation owners grew up in the business and are in a different place in their development and operations. So what motivates others to start from scratch?

Motives for Getting into the Winery Business

Wineries require a lot of time, energy, and capital to start and successfully operate. They are like any small business in these respects. A common joke I heard from winery owners was that it takes a large fortune to make a smaller fortune from a winery. A number of owners also joked that their wineries were their retirements. For some, that meant they had invested money put aside for retirement into their wineries. For others, it meant they were working during the typical retirement years. And for some, it meant both. Starting a winery is not a leisurely retirement job. So what attracts people to the demanding work it requires?

Many winery owners started as home winemakers, echoing Fred Koehler's often-quoted statement that his winery was the result of "a home winemaking hobby that got out of hand" (Daley 2011). They were making wine that their friends and acquaintances enjoyed, and some were making it in quantities that called for another outlet. Joe Henke started out in this manner, as did Larry Satek. As Satek explained:

It actually starts back in 1975. I was a college professor. I was an assistant professor at Washington College in Chestertown, Maryland. And I liked wine, and of course I was on a poor assistant professor's salary and had rented a house that had some grapevines in the back yard. And I was sufficiently arrogant to say that I have a Ph.D. in chemistry and should be able to figure out how to make wine [laughing]. And so that is how it was started. So I had these grapevines, and I made wine and started making other kinds of wine, and at least, oh, other people at the college and other people around us seemed to think it was drinkable. So I made wine as an amateur on and off for, oh my, until about 1992.

Andy Troutman, who with his wife, Deanna, owns both Troutman Vineyards and the Winery at Wolf Creek, became interested in winemaking somewhat by chance:

When I was about ten years old, I took grape growing as a 4-H project. My dad was the county extension agent in Wayne County, where my other winery is, and he'd bring home a book, and I'd go through it and I'd quiz him on what projects had people taken and had they not taken. And grape growing was a project that no one to his knowledge had ever taken. So I'm like, I'll take that. So being the extension agent, he took me out to the OARDC, and I met Dr. Garth Cahoon, who was essentially what Imed [Dami, viticulturist at the OARDC] is doing today. Dr. Cahoon was a wise gentleman, and he gave me about a half-dozen potted table grapevines, kind of patted me on the head, and said good luck. It was a project that took three or four years. There was a different book every year about planting and training and harvesting and marketing your crop. Of all the projects I took, that was kind of the one that stuck with me as sort of a hobby even after I had finished the project, just something different and kind of fun. So, as a result, I remember in ninth grade trying to make wine out of those grapes in a jar down in the basement. My mom couldn't figure out what the smell was. I think I used baker's yeast that I took out of the cupboard, and it ended up being a complete disaster. But my friends thought it was cool.

After spending a year at Ohio State trying to figure out what he wanted to do, Troutman took a summer job that led him back to his interest in grapes and wine:

The following summer I worked at the 4-H camp on Kelly's Island, and got to know a lot of people that lived there year round. And they were nice enough to show me where all the old cellars were. You'd have these tiny little farmhouses with these massive wine cellars under them that were ten times the size of the farmhouse. And it really got me interested in the history of the Ohio wine industry and just grape growing in general. I kind of put the two together, and I think I went back to school that second fall and said, "You know, I think I want to be in the wine business." My parents had been in agriculture, my aunts and uncles. I think my mom cried when I said I was going to go into agribusiness. So I studied horticulture and food microbiology, and was about to head off to grad school in California, and I met the owner of Wolf Creek at one of the conferences. I think it was the grape wine conference in the spring. And he said, "Why don't you come work for us for the summer?" I said, "Sure." And life kind of happens. I was dating this girl and I didn't really want to go to California yet, and ended up staying here quite a few years, and have been here nineteen years now.

Dr. Charles Thomas owns Chateau Thomas Winery, located in Plainfield, Indiana, just west of Indianapolis. Thomas gravitated to winemaking out of a more general interest in wine:

Well, actually, when I was young, I was never a really big wine fan. I drank wine, but I wasn't really into it until I got married . . . 1970, 1971, along in there. And my wife and I both sort of got into wine together. Obviously it became more of a passion for me than it was for her. But anyway, characteristic of me, you know, when I get into something I get into it full bore. So I started reading everything I could read about wine, and believe me, you'll never read everything about wine, but I read as much as I could. Then I started drinking wine. And I started out actually by getting a kit from Wine Art. And that was the first thing that I did. But I quickly decided that I didn't particularly care for the wine that I made from the kit . . . I experimented with a few concentrates and so on, but I started to look around. So then I called Sam Rose, who's a local fruit merchant, and he would haul different fruits in from California. I got him to haul me some grapes, and we did that for a little while, and I continued to make wine. Then I joined a club that had their club meetings at Easley Winery. And there were several different people that were home winemakers, and it was called the Society of Cellar Masters.

Larry Elsner, owner with his wife, Donell, of Cedar Creek Winery near Martinsville, Indiana, learned how to make beer and wine with a friend:

Me and a friend of mine started doing beer kits and got me interested in it because it tasted really good, and I was interested in doing that stuff on the weekends. The beer kits just got bigger, and instead of bottling, I went directly to kegging, and then ended up buying a refrigerator and doing the Kegerator refrigerator, and the CO_2 tank, all that type of stuff. After a while we started doing wine, and he had an interest in wine. He's very outgoing, and so he showed me pretty much what to do and everything. The steps were the same; you still have to clean, rinse, and sanitize everything you do. The only difference between wine and beer, you don't have to boil your hops and do all that with the wine. Pretty much all the other steps are similar. Same equipment. Starting out small like that, we were able to do both of those. So in 2009, I had a building at our property. I bought some fermenters, me and Bryce [his son], and we started fermenting larger quantities of juice. At that time I was pulling our permits from the federal and state, and it would have been . . . December of 2009, when we got incorporated and became an LLC.

Winery owners often found their inspiration by visiting wineries in their states or other states. Jeff Durm, owner of Buck Creek Winery in Indianapolis, talked about his experiences visiting Shamrock Winery and its influence on his decision:

> Basically my wife and I visited some wineries in Ohio over twenty years ago and fell in love with one in particular called Shamrock. And it was a doctor that had bought an old farmhouse, had three acres of vines. Tasted the wines out of the old farmhouse with mismatched chairs and an oak table, and the vineyard was really neat. The wines were really good. And I said, you know, if they can grow grapes and make good wine in the middle of Ohio, we can do it in the middle of Indiana. That was twenty-two, twenty-three years ago. So we started looking, came back, got the bug, and said I want to pursue this. I started looking for land. I was on the Marion County Sheriff's [department]; I had to stay in Marion County because at the time you had to be within the county. So I started looking for land, which was being built up pretty quickly. I grew up on the northeast side in the Geist [area], and I knew that wasn't going to be possible. [JP: It's pricey.] Yeah, a little pricey to start a vineyard and a winery. So, you know, I just started looking for land and found this land. My mother-in-law and father-in-law and wife and I, my mother-in-law bought a lot, my wife and I bought two lots, and it ended up being, I don't know, nine or ten acres. And then later on we bought another acre and a half on the corner down here. So we have about twelve acres total, and purchased it contingent on getting a use variance for the winery. We were granted that and went ahead with the purchase, and then we waited almost fifteen years to actually start the winery. We planted the vineyard right away.

John and Lindsay Fouts, owners of the now closed Grateful Goat Vineyard and Winery, which was located in Harrison County, Indiana, in the far southern part of the state, started their winery at a much younger age than many winery owners. John found inspiration from a visit to some wineries in Illinois while he was attending Purdue University:

> I don't know what year it was, but near the end of my college experience at Purdue, I traveled to southern Illinois. I went to the Shawnee Hills Wine Trail down there. And there were probably nine wineries there at the time. We only hit up a few of them, but before that, I had only known about wines like Chardonnay, Merlot, Cabernet Sauvignon. I didn't realize that there were other wines out there, and I really got exposure to a lot of small winery-made wines, and learned how different they are than, you know, just your regular Chardonnay, for instance. I think peach and blueberry wine are what my first wine purchases were from a small winery [laughing].

The pleasure of combining the science and art of winemaking with running a business was a common theme in my interviews with winery owners. Fouts said:

I've always wanted to own and operate my own business, and this really gave me an opportunity to do that. And I always had a love for art and a love of science. And before the winery, there was no way that I could see that I could meet the goal of owning my own business and consolidating art and science into one direction. And the winery's allowed me to do that . . . I mean, I love chemistry. I always have since I was a little kid. There's a lot of chemistry behind wine, a lot of chemistry.

Jeff Quint is a certified public accountant and chief financial officer for a corporation in Cedar Rapids, Iowa, a job in which he continues to work full time. He and his wife, Laurie, started Cedar Ridge Winery with an interest in wine, but also with the benefit of his business experience to guide their decisions. As he explained:

My wife and I started this business because of, if I was to say it in one word, I'd say lifestyle. We both kept our day jobs. We were wine enthusiasts, and we started doing research and learned about these new varieties, these new French-American hybrids that had been developed. We concluded that this wasn't a fad; this was a permanent change. And we now have the ability to make wine in the Upper Midwest. So we thought through that if we're going to do this, we needed a good location. We weren't going to be leaving the area, so let's find a plot of land that's conveniently located, somewhere between Cedar Rapids and Iowa City, so we could support what we refer to here as the corridor. So we bought this property. It's twenty-seven acres, and we added another nineteen and a half. So it's forty-seven acres now, at exit 10 right off the freeway, and we started planting vines. Before we started planting vines, we kind of laid out where the buildings would be. So we put the vines around the hill.

Jeff described planting vines in 2003, 2004, and 2005 while planning the winery, opening a winery in some rented space in downtown Cedar Rapids until they could afford the building they wanted to build, and hitting on the idea of opening a distillery to differentiate their business from others in the state. He added, "We got into the food and event business because we were trying to run a business and make a living."

Many winery owners had business careers and interests that mixed with their interest in wine. Perhaps not so surprising given its chemistry, microbiology, and laboratory elements, a number of owners I interviewed had science backgrounds. Larry Satek, who has a Ph.D. in chemistry, talked about how creating a winery satisfied his desire to put together a successful business plan in ways he never achieved while working for a major oil company. Jim Butler's lab training in biology and lack of funding support while doing his Ph.D. at Indiana University led him to a job at Oliver Winery and ultimately to opening his own winery. A limnologist, or freshwater biologist, he told me his "standard line" with people is "that winemaking is just limnology with ten

Figure 4.5. Cedar Ridge Winery and Distillery, Swisher, Iowa, May 6, 2015.
Photo by Jim Pennell.

percent alcohol." Andy Troutman studied horticulture and food microbiology. Bill Richardson had a degree in agricultural science from Purdue. Kevin Tonne of Tonne Winery had a background in food science. Jared Spahn of Rocky Waters majored in biology and minored in chemistry. The only owner I interviewed who was a college-educated enologist was Chris Lawlor-White, who studied at Fresno State. Others had taken courses. Mary Hofmann at White Oak Vineyards had a certificate from the University of Missouri. In whatever manner the seed of inspiration was planted—growing up with a winery, making wine at home that others liked, visiting wineries in other states, enjoying the blend of science and art that winemaking offers, or enjoying the business of putting together appealing beverages with appealing places—winery owners took a variety of paths to ownership.

Getting into Winery Ownership

I observed five general paths to winery ownership: (1) second-generation ownership, as described at the beginning of this chapter; (2) winery ownership as a second career; (3) winery ownership as a repurposing of resources to make it possible to retain them and/or make them more profitable; (4) winery ownership as a career trajectory within the industry; and (5) winery ownership that starts as a small-scale, part-time endeavor and evolves into a full-time one. There is some overlap between the categories in some of the cases I studied, and this typology doesn't capture a few unique circumstances. But these paths offer a general outline for understanding the different trails and travails faced by those starting a winery.

A number of winery owners had successful careers prior to opening their wineries and were able to retire or change professions at a fairly young age. Thus they had financial resources that many younger people would not have. Charles Thomas was an obstetrician and gynecologist for over thirty years. Jared Spahn was a successful computer consultant. Larry Satek was a chemist for a major oil company. Jeff Durm was a deputy sheriff who was able to retire at an early age.

Others changed their professional trajectories to pursue what seemed to be a more interesting opportunity. Kevin Tonne was looking for a business opportunity in Arizona when he was asked by his brother-in-law Larry Simmons to start a winery with him. Jim Ewers, co-owner and general manager of Blue Sky Vineyard, had a degree in forestry and had a job he enjoyed at a mill when he partnered with his father-in-law and started planting grapes. Bill Richardson left a job as a stockbroker and moved to his grandparents' farm to work with his father, John. All three Richardsons found second careers at the winery, including Laura, although until recently she continued to work part time as a speech therapist.

Wineries and vineyards can serve as an alternative or a supplement to large-scale industrial farming, helping to maintain the agricultural character of a property while adding value to it. Mallow Run enabled the Richardsons to keep their farm in the family and operating. As John Richardson told me,

> I retired in '96. There was an article in the *Louisville Courier Journal* saying that Indiana winemakers were wanting farmers to grow grapes as an alternative crop. So I had the idea of moving back home—I grew up on this farm—and grow grapes to sell. And so after I moved back here in '98, in 2000 I planted an acre of grapes, half-acre of Chardonel, and half-acre of Leon Millot, and actually had talked to Bruce Bordelon, at Purdue, who is the grape-growing guru of Indiana. And Bruce came down, looked at some of our possible sites on the farm, and suggested varieties. So that's how I got started.

Larry Elsner was also looking for an opportunity to expand his interest in making wine that would both fit with and take advantage of his job as a construction contractor. He was able to get the property he purchased for his winery because the owner wanted to retain its agricultural character. As he told me in 2011,

> I went to about every farmer in the county, and nobody wanted to sell land. We looked at downtown Martinsville about buying a building, you know, we weren't happy with that. So then we talked to the lady right down the road who owned the

property here, she owns Red Horse Farms, Kris Thomas. You are welcome to use her name because I know she wouldn't mind. Her husband was Doc Thomas, who was a well-known veterinarian in the county and through Purdue. Everybody thought a lot of him. He passed away ten, eleven years ago of cancer. Anyway, I talked to her and just did not know her, and I stopped by one day and knocked on the door and said, "I'm looking for land." You know, when I told her exactly what I wanted to do—it would be a small farm winery, I needed ten to twenty-five acres, you know, set up back here, it would be all family oriented, told her that I wanted to build some buildings and all this—and she pretty much said, "Honey, you are the guy I'm looking for." She did not want houses going back here, and since her business is farm oriented, she wanted to keep it farm oriented, which, you know, that's what a farm winery is. And I assured her that I would be planting vines every year, plant more, and keep it like a park. And her main concern was, "I just don't want fifty houses going back here," because she was always getting people wanting to buy the property for that reason, and she wanted to keep it farm oriented.

Simmons Winery, located near Columbus, Indiana, and owned by David Simmons and his wife, Brenda, transitioned to wine production as an outgrowth of its farming operation and fruit production, and features wines made from its own fruit (Butler and Butler 2001, 191). Aware of his cousin David's success, Larry Simmons decided to put some property he owned near Muncie to a different use. He and his wife partnered with her brother, Kevin Tonne, to start Tonne Winery. Larry explained:

My wife, Kathy, and I—my wife is Kevin's sister—we own garden centers here in town. This one here [next door to the winery] used to be Waldo's Greenhouse years ago. There is one in town and I've owned it since 1977. It is a long-time business. It's been in Muncie since 1935, so you know . . . since I graduated from Ball State. I went to work there. Going to college, I wanted to earn money for essentials and stayed. Well, anyway, up to the present, then, this property, um, the greenhouse never really grew into the property. There is a little over eight acres out here, and the greenhouse never really grew into the potential we expected either. You can call it the economy, or you know, because Delaware County lost ten, twelve thousand people during that decade.

Perhaps the most colorful Indiana winery owners were John and Jim Wilson. The brothers moved back to the farm in rural eastern Indiana where they grew up and started Wilson Wines in 2000 (Butler and Butler 2001, 203). The winery is near a large private campground with a small lake that is quite busy in the summertime. I did not formally interview either brother, but Greta and I had the pleasure of enjoying some Wilson wines served by Jim, the winemaker, along with some humorous banter on a cold, sunny Saturday afternoon in November 2011. Their Marechal Foch was quite good, as was a dry, hard apple cider. Their sweet and semi-sweet wines were well made and would appeal to many Midwesterners' taste preferences. The Wilsons pretty well pummel the notion of a highbrow wine experience with some of their events, such as "John on the John" (John sitting on a toilet telling humorous stories) and BYOM (Bring Your Own Meat), a common Friday evening event during the warmer months, when a grill is fired up and customers bring their own food to grill. Wine tastings are served in plastic cups. If you are looking for social class pretensions with your wine, this is not the place, but Jim knew how to make wine from a variety of fruit in a range of styles. Unfortunately, he died in October 2015. The brothers were extremely close. I wish John well and hope he will find a way to carry on his and his brother's traditions.

As the industry has grown, so have the career opportunities. Many wineries employ winemakers, assistant winemakers, tasting room managers, event specialists, vineyard managers, and other positions. These positions offer an opportunity to develop interests and skills and may serve as a springboard to winery ownership. Andy Troutman was vineyard manager at the Winery at Wolf Creek before starting Troutman Vineyards, later purchasing the place where he started. Both Jim Butler and Peggy Harmston worked for other winery owners prior to starting their own wineries. As the wine industries in Midwestern states grow, this is likely to be more common. I talked to a number of young people, including assistant winemakers and tasting room managers or servers, who worked at the wineries I visited. Some talked about starting their own wineries at some point. This is a logical development as the Midwest industry matures. Those now working in the industry will have much of the knowledge and skills needed to be successful owners.

One reason startups have proliferated throughout the Midwest and will likely continue to do so for some time is that in contrast to the wine regions of the West Coast or even New York, it is still possible to start a winery in this part of the country without a small fortune. One can rent, lease, purchase, or build a building, and purchase suitable vineyard land at a fraction of the cost of property in those other places. Many winery owners have done this and transitioned slowly into the business. Jeff Durm of Buck Creek had been growing grapes on his own land for fifteen years before opening his winery. Joe Henke worked twenty-seven years as a programmer/machinist and spent the last five of those years starting up and running his winery in Cincinnati. Jeff and Donna Clark, owners of Old Mason Winery in eastern Ohio, are both basically working full-time jobs that have some flexibility as their vineyard matures and their winery business grows. He is a masonry contractor, and she is a realtor. Jackie Trexel, the owner of Quail Crossing Cellars in Columbus, Ohio, puts in eighty-hour weeks at the winery in the evenings and on her days off while also working full-time as a project manager. Jeff Quint continues to work full time in his job as a chief financial officer while running Cedar Ridge with the assistance of his wife, Laurie, and a sizable staff compared to most Midwestern wineries.

It is not unusual for winery owners to live in a house on the property, since it is considered an agricultural endeavor. John Richardson lives in one of the farmhouses on the family's historic property where Mallow Run Winery is located; Bill and Laura Richardson and their family make their home in the other. Van and Emily Creasap live in the old farmhouse at Shamrock that used to be the tasting room. The farmhouse basement continues to serve as the production facility. Jared and Phyllis Spahn live in the winery and event building at Rocky Waters and use the well-appointed kitchen built for catering to cook their own meals. The Kopsa brothers, Joel and Jeff, both live with their families on the vineyard property.

Winery Ownership as Meaningful Work

Study after study has found that we are stressed and dissatisfied at work, even if we are successful and well paid. Wineries hold the promise of being one's own boss in a meaningful endeavor. The successful independent entrepreneur is the archetype of the American dream. Winery ownership satisfies that entrepreneurial desire, although to a person, the owners I interviewed would add that wineries are a tremendous amount of work and should not be undertaken without a serious commitment.

Rudi and Mary Hofmann of White Oak Vineyards helped me understand how winery ownership has a kind of pioneering quality that harkens back to earlier European immigration and westward expansion. Rudi is a German immigrant, and Mary lived in Germany for many years before moving back to Illinois to be near family. Rudi grows the grapes, and Mary makes the wine. As they told me,

> RUDI: I put the first couple acres of plants in there by myself. We cleared the land and we did everything here, so I'm really tied to this part of land. It means a lot to me. And I'm actually not satisfied until we see some success. That's my nature anyway. If there is something that has to be done, it has to be done right. I have to do it perfect. Otherwise, I won't be satisfied. Maybe it's just me, but it's how I feel.
>
> MARY: It's personal. It means a lot. It means a lot because we came to the States with—yes, I had a job, and yes, we had this and all that—but we came with virtually nothing else. We came with that typical European attitude [of] this is where your dream can come true because we could not do this in Europe. This is something that you have to be born into in Europe.
>
> RUDI: Especially a farm over there, it goes from a generation to the next one. And for ninety-nine percent, if there is a son, the oldest one, he gets it, and the other one, he has to do something else.

MARY: For me, it's a vision. We set a goal and we made it happen. And that is, it's a sense of pride knowing that we came with nothing and with such adversity, people telling us "You cannot do this." Especially in this particular area. We had a lot of people who were against what we were doing, and some still are. I don't know how to express it in English, honestly. It's satisfaction, knowing that we started with nothing and we came with nothing, we came with money, now we have nothing [laughing].

When I asked Jim Ewers what Blue Sky meant to him personally, he also spoke of the rewards along with the challenges:

I will say over time, and I don't want to use the term "burnout" or anything like that, it is everything I hoped it would be and it's everything I dreaded it would be . . . After doing anything you've been doing for a while, you will tend to gravitate towards the negative. And it's just the occasional kick in the butt to say there's a lot worse things to be doing. It's very life consuming, but at the same time, it's extremely rewarding.

Starting up and running a winery requires attending to a whole host of tasks that must get done for the business to be successful. The individual's identity and the ownership role merge as a result of the all-encompassing nature of the work. As Jim Butler put it:

It's what I do [laughing]. I suppose you could say a lot of people work in jobs where they are just working a small piece of something. When you have a winery, it's the total thing, you are responsible from beginning to end, and some would say it's a very creative type of thing. We have essentially created an industry from nothing over the years. And it's the same thing for a winery, you're starting from nothing and you're creating something or producing something that you hope will carry on. I tell people it's too late for me to change now to something else [laughing]. That's the other thing.

One theme that came out of my interviews with winery owners is how closely their work is tied to their identities. When I asked them what their wineries meant to them personally, the response was fairly consistent. Bill Oliver said, "Oh, wow. I mean, to a fault I probably define myself by what we've done here . . . it means everything to me. I'm incredibly proud of it. I mean, every day I show up here, and I'm like, wow, nice!"

Mark Easley shared similar feelings about his family's winery:

Personally, it becomes a personal extension to the extent that a local grocer once said that my name is on the front of the building. You know, to that extent you do tend to take it personally. I would say that of many small businesspeople that I talk to, it becomes your baby, as they say. And you know, what motivates someone to put in seventy, eighty hours a week, week in and week out? And suddenly it becomes your identity. The winery to me is a pride thing. How can you do it and carry it on for the next generation? Because I mean, I certainly do, and my wife as well thinks of it as multigenerational. Will we force our children to do it? No, you can't force people to do things. But you can certainly build it and show them that, hey, this was good for us, it was good for your grandparents, and it may be good for you.

Owning a winery that carries on a family legacy can be very meaningful. This was especially the case with those whose families had tended the same land. As Bill Richardson observed:

> I'm glad that I am still on the farm, sort of working the same land that my grand-father, great-grandfather, and great-great-great-grandfather did. Certainly walking in the same footsteps, so that's meaningful. I hope we can preserve it for future generations. I don't know if that's always the case because of property taxes and other taxes that come into play. But certainly the history of the family does mean a lot, but it's more being on the farm than the winery itself.
> JP: So you actually like the farm work better than the winery work, you think?
> BILL: I don't think I like it any better. It's just more the history. I mean, if my grandfather had grown grapes, I might feel differently about it. It's certainly my kind of thing, where obviously they didn't do that. You know, I think I would know more about grapes than maybe my grandfather, great-grandfather did. So that's something that I feel like I can contribute, I guess, to the history.

Some winery owners viewed running a winery as a way to connect and work with family members, and in some cases, as Mark Easley noted above, as a way to build a legacy for their children. Some children—or grandchildren in the case of Van Creasap—were already working at their parents' wineries and seeing it as a career opportunity. Paul Renzaglia shared the operation of Alto Vineyards with his father for well over two decades. Tony Debevc ran Debonne with his father for four decades. Bill and Laura Richardson work with Bill's dad, John. Among the wineries at which parents work together with their sons and daughters are John Ernest in Iowa, Rocky Waters in Illinois, Buck Creek and Cedar Creek in Indiana, and Valley Vineyards and Old Mason Winery in Ohio. When I asked Larry Elsner what his winery meant to him personally, he told me:

> Just something different than construction [chuckles]. It'll work out good in the future for my son and daughter, trying to get them a start. They both have an interest in it and hope to make a career of it. We still have a lot of work as far as construction, but like I say, getting all the assets and all the fermenters and filters and the vines in the ground and the shelter houses and the barns and all that, you just can't start and go get a loan to do that. So that's how I can help them out by doing it. And the advantage I have being a contractor, I can do all this, and if I had to pay somebody to do this, I wouldn't be able to do what we're doing.

Despite the general enjoyment of working with family members and a commitment to creating or continuing a family legacy, a few winery owners I interviewed were quick to note that it would be up to their children whether or not to work in the family business. Parents' hopes and desires are not necessarily their children's. One owner noted that it was not "a big family dream," and he didn't "really wish it" on his children, mostly due to the heavy work demands. In addition to wanting to empower employees when he made Oliver Winery employee owned in 2006, Bill Oliver said, "We did that because we were not interested in our kids taking it over, because I've got a very strong feeling that generational transfers of businesses aren't always the best things for your kids and limit their opportunities rather than expand them."

Wineries are commonly husband-and-wife partnerships. Wives run the tasting rooms, handle business records, work in the vineyard, assist with production, do marketing and sales, and in some cases make the wine. When I asked Laura Richardson, who oversees food and events at Mallow Run and assists with many of the day-to-day and seasonal tasks, what the winery meant to her, she replied:

> Much more than it ever used to. Um, now I feel I am fully committed, and it's in my heart. When you work that hard and you see the positive effect it's had on so many people, and also feeling the responsibility for having employees and knowing that's a livelihood for other people, I mean, it's important.

Phyllis Spahn manages the twenty-five-acre vineyard at Rocky Waters with her son. Bill Oliver's wife, Kathleen, is the general manager at Oliver Winery. Ted Huber's wife, Dana, oversees marketing at their winery and farm. Brenda Logan makes the wine and manages the tasting room at Baxter's, while her husband, Kelly, assists when he can while working as a trucker full time. Although it is common for a spouse to be heavily involved in the winery business, it is not universal. Some continue to pursue their own careers and interests. Some, such as Donell Elsner of Cedar Creek, Emily Creasap of Shamrock, and Laura Kopsa of John Ernest, have full-time jobs in part so their families can have another income and medical benefits, or because they have their own professional pursuits. Even in those cases, spouses often help out in the evenings and on their days off. Donell has donned a costume that resembles grape clusters for some occasions. Laura Richardson continued to work part time for a number of years while committing a substantial amount of time, including many weekends, to the winery. She had to give up the other job as the winery and event demands increased.

At a few of the wineries I studied, the wife or husband was not directly involved. For example, Chris Lawlor-White's husband raises cattle. But that was clearly the rare exception. I noted a few cases where wineries were a source tension between husbands and wives beyond the usual frustrations of any nily business. Winery ownership is not simply an occupation; it can be a occupation that prevails over other interests and activities and can interfere h relationships if everyone isn't on board.

Most of the winery owners mentioned the pleasure of meeting interesting ole who frequent their wineries as a positive aspect of their work. Jackie el of Quail Crossing Cellars said that she had "met so many great peo- and that operating a winery had expanded her horizons. Brenda Logan ter's said, "It's fun coming to work every day. I get to meet interesting people. People ask questions and I like to answer them. After twenty years, I still enjoy coming to work." Van Creasap said, "I get to meet people from all over the globe; people make the job so interesting." Almost every one of the winery owners I interviewed mentioned at some point that they got to meet interesting, well-educated, widely traveled people who enriched their lives, something not experienced in many lines of work. Mark Easley observed:

> I like the people aspect, in that wine attracts a very educated, very worldly-thinking group of folks. I mean, when I go to small business gatherings and talk to folks that own gas stations and convenience stores and listen to the horror stories of dealing with what I would refer to as the general public, the folks that all the systems in the world have to be set for, I go, "Wow, we really have it good." When I hear that someone gets out and starts smoking while they are pumping their gas and you have to get out and go, "Sir, can you put your cigarette out so you don't blow up the station today?"

Despite satisfying the entrepreneurial spirit and providing an opportunity to work with and benefit one's family and community, use a variety of skills, and meet interesting people, winery ownership is far from the leisurely dream job people often imagine when they visit a winery and enjoy a relaxing afternoon. Larry Elsner put it quite well:

> It's funny because everyone says, "You are building my dream!" Well, it's a lot of hard work and money. I doubt I'll retire now. My retirement's gone. It's just something my kids can take over someday, and I can come back and enjoy doing what we're doing.

Starting and building a winery business is demanding work that requires constant engagement and attention to many details if the operation is going to succeed. Winery owners are responsible for creating an experience combining product and place that is drenched in meaning not only for them and their families but, more importantly in terms of long-term survival, for their customers. As Ted Huber put it, "In the wine business, you better have wine as your passion to be successful in it, because it is a lifestyle choice." Karen

Hand, the winemaker at Blue Sky, agreed: "It's a lifestyle, it's not a job." As Joe Henke, owner, winemaker, and restaurant host, put it, "It's my blood and my life. You have to live and breathe it."

One thing that struck me on my many visits to wineries and in my interviews with winery owners is what a nice group of people they are. They are considerate of their customers, but they also tend to be generous with their employees and communities. They are very hard working, as I will describe in more detail in the next chapter, but enjoy having a good time and sharing their knowledge of wine with others. They take pleasure in creating quality wine and a positive experience for their customers and find satisfaction in the interesting, meaningful work that owning a winery affords, work that is often done with one's family and friends. They also get along and collaborate well with their peers, as I will discuss in chapter 6. In short, to paraphrase a hokey beer ad campaign, they are some of the most interesting people you might meet.

5

Wineries Are Work

Going "Backstage"

When I was a child, I loved the part in *The Wizard of Oz* where Toto pulls the curtain back to reveal "the great and powerful Oz" as a bumbling old man who realizes his cover is blown. Winemakers are real wizards, mixing science and craft. They occasionally provide a glimpse of a barrel and perhaps a little taste from it on a tour, but much of their work goes on behind the scenes. Anyone can make wine, but making good wine involves a kind of artistry mixed with some science that takes time and effort to master.

Customers at wineries are often fooled into thinking there is a kind of effortlessness to the endeavor. When you walk in the front door of a tasting room, you are commonly greeted by a server and asked if you would like to do a tasting. At the smaller wineries, you will likely be served by the owners or their relatives. You are likely to be asked if you have been there before while being given a list of the wines available for tasting. In the Midwest and South, you will likely be asked if you prefer dry, semi-sweet, or sweet wines. The comfortable setting, laid-back atmosphere, range of available wines, and friendly, service-oriented owners and employees make wineries rather magical, idyllic places. These qualities mask much of the activity behind the scenes, or what sociologist Erving Goffman (1959) referred to as the "backstage" work that goes on in a winery.

Wineries are work in two ways. First, they require a great deal of time, energy, and capital to start and successfully operate. Second, they provide employment, careers, and meaningful work for some people, and transitional employment or part-time income for others. They are like any small or growing business in these respects, but due to the nature of the business, they have unique qualities and demands that can easily be underestimated even by those who have tried to do their homework. Jim Butler observed:

> It's like any other business, but it has these long lag times. They are very capital intensive. And you've got to plant grapes, build up inventory. And you just don't stamp out widgets and turn your inventory over every month. Any mistake now is going to be hanging around you for a good while.

He also noted:

> We typically work in the wintertime. Right now, we are probably just working sixty hours a week [laughing]. You know, come season, you're putting in eighty hours and more. So I say this is the slow time.

Most Midwestern wineries experience seasonal fluctuations in their income streams. This is less a problem for wineries near population centers, but even they suffer during bad winters. Joel Kopsa at John Ernest put the seasonal fluctuation and money flow problem bluntly when I asked him about the drawbacks of the business:

> Money. Money is always there. From May, June, July, August, September, October, November, it's pretty good. But boy, winter is tough. It's hard. If it wasn't for those three months, it would be a lot better, and I hear that even from the big wineries.

Starting a winery takes a lot of both time and money. Jim Butler shared a couple of his and Bill Richardson's exchanges about the required time and financial commitments:

> I knew [Bill] before they started the winery because people usually start hanging around the wine industry going to wineries, making wines. So he was coming in getting some winemaking supplies at the shop in town. I got to know him a little bit. I said, you know, if they wanted to start a winery . . . it will take twice as long and cost twice as much. And then he left, and they started the winery and he came back, and I think at one point he said, "You were wrong about that, it's three times [laughing]." So you know, one concern of the industry is that the people coming in know enough, and I would say a number of them are probably undercapitalized starting up, not realizing what it's going to take. But on the other hand, we have wineries coming in that are very well capitalized. So this is really, in the last six to seven years I would say, we are drawing people into the industry from other businesses . . . so it's drawing in new money, new experience, and new talent.

In order to thrive, any business must cover its costs and provide a return that both allows it to remain in operation and is sufficiently remunerative (and, I would also argue, experientially rewarding) to keep the owner committed. Otherwise he or she will likely pursue different investment or career alternatives. To support the owners and, in most cases, provide work for others, wineries must be economically successful, and much work goes into making and keeping them that way.

Recent startups commonly suffer from shortages of their more popular wines and often struggle to find ways to deal with products for which there is less demand. Not everything a winery produces is going to be good or appeal to customers, and a talented winemaker must make decisions about what to do with marginal creations. A small tasting room and/or unskilled or too few servers can frustrate a crowd that shows up anticipating a great experience. Well-managed growth and a tidy profit can help address these problems and elevate a winery quickly to destination status for locals and tourists. But it requires a lot of work; it doesn't just happen.

Wineries provide employment, careers, and meaningful work for some people, and transitional employment or part-time income for others. As might be expected, the smaller wineries are simpler operations where the owners are "jacks of all trades," raising or procuring the grapes or juice, crushing the grapes, fermenting and bottling the wine, selling the wine, and marketing the wine and the winery. Family members often pitch in to help out, as do friends and even customers. This is especially the case with picking grapes and bottling wine, jobs that involve hand labor and require intensive work in a short amount of time. As they grow, small wineries typically add a full-time employee or two and some part-time or occasional employees to assist. At the larger wineries, full-time employees and technology take over much of the work, and it becomes more specialized.

From Vine to Bottle: Growing Grapes and Making Wine

My first experience picking grapes was on a beautiful Monday morning in early September 2010. I had no classes on Monday mornings that semester and decided to play hooky from the university "administrivia" that dominated part of my life. Mallow Run Winery had eight and a half acres of grapes at the time. Different varieties attain their ultimate ripeness at different times, so picking can be spread out over a month to six weeks in late August, September, and early October, depending on the weather in a given year. As a smaller winery, Mallow Run sought volunteers to help with picking, since once grapes are ready to come off the vine, they need to be picked within a few days. The winery also had most of the full-time employees and some of the part-time employees assisting, depending on the number of volunteers who showed up and the amount of grapes to be picked. Picking grapes is usually an "all hands on deck" task at small wineries.

That Monday morning, volunteers and employees gathered as the sun peeked over the trees east of the winery property. A heavy dew covered the ground, as well as the leaves and bunches of Chardonel grapes we were going to pick that day. Coffee, juice, donuts, and fruit were laid out on a table under a tent, and John Richardson greeted each volunteer and directed everyone to the food and beverages. After twenty minutes or so, Bill Richardson showed up and demonstrated how to use the pruning shears to cut the clusters of grapes, which

Figure 5.1. Picking grapes at Mallow Run Winery, September 4, 2011.

clusters to pick, how to clean them up if they contained rotten grapes, and how to put them in the plastic lugs used to haul the grapes out of the vineyard.

After receiving instructions, shears, and gloves for those who wanted them, twenty people spread out along the rows of Chardonel vines. Some people had come with spouses, children, neighbors, and friends; others, like me, came solo. Some were retired, others had the day off, and still others were unemployed. One person was hoping to start a vineyard and winery. It is difficult to capture the sense of calm and serenity I experienced in the shirtsleeve weather that morning. Periods of quiet concentration on the task at hand were broken by small talk among the volunteers and employees. I was having a lovely conversation with a woman I couldn't see on the other side of the row, and at one point it dawned on me that I was talking with Laura Richardson. I peeked through the vines, and we both laughed. Picking grapes with others, and perhaps any task that blends moderate effort with a group on a beautiful day, fosters a kind of friendly banter and camaraderie that bridges social, political, and economic differences. Working with cultivated nature under such pleasant conditions makes one feel very close to the land. I picked a grape off a cluster and tasted it. I was somewhat surprised at how much the grape tasted like Bill

Richardson's bottled Chardonel. I knew this crop was going to be good, and about a year later, the vineyard-sourced Chardonel proved me right.

Growing grapes entails a tremendous amount of work that goes on nearly all year round. One of the most demanding jobs is tending the vines. It's common in the Midwest to start pruning in early April. Bill Richardson starts pruning vines in late January or early February. The idea is to force the vines to produce fewer clusters of grapes, which will allow those clusters to use the vines' nutrients to grow mature, sweet grapes with just the right acidity. Immature clusters are tart, even sour, and make poor wine. It is necessary to tend and prune vines and grape clusters throughout the growing season. Grape leaves can provide shade from the sun for those varieties that need it. Conversely, removing vines and leaves can expose grapes that need more sun to ripen and achieve maximum flavor and sugar content. Removing leaves and vines can also help control mildew, a big problem in the Midwestern, Eastern, and Southern regions of the United States, since sun and airflow are mildew's enemies. There are also different methods of trellising and pruning grapes, and these often vary by region. Joel Kopsa said that it was common for him to handle every plant in their six acres four or five times in a season.

How vines and grapes are handled might be considered part of the terroir of a region, since it affects how the plants grow and use nutrients. Terroir has commonly been thought of as the combination of terrain, soil, and climate (or microclimate) that gives a wine its character, or as Veseth puts it, the "special taste of a place" (Veseth 2011, 4). Increasingly, the traditions of how vines are cared for are also recognized as expressions of place, in part because the practices are a response to the different physical conditions and because these treatments affect the grapes produced. Arnie Esterer, the owner of Markko Vineyard in far northeastern Ohio and an inspiration for many Ohio winery owners, developed his own trellising system, the Markko Trellis. The vines, or "cordons," which are trained to grow horizontally along wires, are raised to promote greater airflow and leaf exposure. This also eliminates the need to tie the "canes" from which the grape clusters grow (Esterer, n.d.). Even the taste preferences of a wine region and its winemakers, which affect how the wines are made, are included by some (e.g., Trubek 2008) as an element of terroir.

During the spring, new trellises may be installed and vines planted. Selecting and appropriately planting varieties that will grow well in the terroir of a particular vineyard is an important task. Pick the wrong grape variety, and much expense and work may lead to low or no harvests and/or poor quality. Spring in the Midwest can also bring killing frosts, which freeze buds. Vines put out a secondary growth when this happens, but the quality of the grapes and the volume produced are usually lower, and some varieties produce

Figure 5.2. Joel Kopsa (*left*) and brother-in-law Duke Upah prune vines at
John Ernest Vineyard and Winery in Tama, Iowa, on a beautiful late
winter day, March 13, 2015. Photo by Greta Pennell.

no secondary growth at all. Some large wineries use giant fans to keep frost
from settling or spray water to protect the buds. I noted earlier the enormous
wind machines at St. Joseph Vineyard in northeastern Ohio, one of the larger
vineyards in the state. But most wineries in the Midwest cannot afford this
technology, or it doesn't make economic sense due to the small scale of their
operations. Selecting varieties that are hardy and bud a bit later can help, but
warm February and early March days, or an extremely cold April or early May,
can thwart the best-laid plans. Farming is a risky business.

Late spring and summer work involves spraying insecticide and fungicide,
pruning vines and grape clusters, and putting nets over the vines as the grapes
ripen to keep out the birds. Grapes must be the equivalent of filet mignon to
some bird species. They can wipe out a vineyard when it is about ready to harvest. I heard a lot of stories from winery owners about their bird encounters,
none of which ended well. I also saw the birds lined up on power lines just
waiting for the nets to be removed during a harvest at Mallow Run. Joel Kopsa
talked about his challenges dealing with Mother Nature:

Figure 5.3. Trellised vines at Rocky Waters Vineyard and Winery, May 4, 2015. Photo by Greta Pennell.

At harvest it's the bees. They poke the grapes, or wasps poke them. They drip out and the birds smell them, and then its game on.

JP: Do you put nets on yours?

JOEL: We do not. We use distress calls and we just are real vigilant. We test our stuff all the time so we know when the Brix [sugar levels] are getting to where the birds are going to be hitting them. And you know, sometimes if the Brix aren't all that right and everything isn't lining up but the birds are starting to hit them, we'll just go get them. We figure it's better to have something than not. I don't know if that's right or not, but that's how we've been doing it. It'd sure be nice to get all the TAs [total acidities] right and this just right and that just right, but it's just real hard because you're working with Mother Nature.

Some grape varieties have clusters that are easier to cut from the vine than others. Catawba grapes grow in large clusters that can leave little room to get to the stem to cut. Some clusters are so big that they wrap around the wire trellis. It can be difficult to even find a piece of stem to clip, and a cluster may have to be cut in multiple places to get it loose. It's easy to clip a finger with the garden shears if one isn't careful. The bigger hazard in the Midwest is yellow jackets. They are always a nuisance at picnics in August and September right up to the first hard freeze, and an occupational hazard in the vineyard. They really like rotten grapes, burrowing deep into hollowed-out spots. A handful of yellow jackets in a grape cluster can be a nasty surprise. I saw John Richardson break out the first aid kit a few times the day we picked Traminette. The grapes appeared to have been attacked by grape berry moths, a common nuisance whose larvae make holes in the skins, giving the yellow jackets easy access to a sweet treat.

In some areas, deer wreak havoc on young vines, and raccoons, turkeys, and other critters feast on the grapes. Karen Hand said they lost 50 percent of their crop at Blue Sky in 2014 to wildlife, and that wildlife management is a major task in managing a vineyard. Even domestic animals can be a problem. Rocky Waters lost thirty-six hundred new plantings in 1996 when the electric fence that normally protected them was being repaired and cattle got into the vineyard and destroyed the plants.

Fall is an intensive time at a winery. Those with vineyards must harvest, crush, and press the grapes. Even wineries that purchase grapes must live by harvest and delivery schedules. Grapes start to lose their quality as soon as they are picked. Some hold up better than others to short periods of storage or shipping. But the quicker the grapes are crushed and put in a vat or tank, the better. I heard quite a few stories from winery owners about receiving shipments of unusable grapes, but most said that improvements in handling and shipping, including freezing grapes, have reduced that problem. White grape varieties are often crushed at the vineyard, and the juice is shipped in refrigerated tanker trucks.

At Mallow Run, stacks of lugs full of grape clusters were hauled to a concrete area outside the production facility right after they were picked and emptied into the crusher and destemmer. Fourteen-hour days are not unusual at this time of year. If the picking crew is short-handed or bad weather blows in, grapes will occasionally be covered and crushed the next day. Crushed white grapes go to the grape press immediately. Crushed red grapes are put in vats

Figure 5.4. Tom Morton (*left*) shovels grapes into the crusher-destemmer at Mallow Run Winery, August 28, 2015, while J. P. Pitcock retrieves a bucket of crushed grapes that will go into the bladder press (*far right*). The juice flowing into the barrel is pumped through the hose (*foreground*) to a tank in the production building.

or tanks and left for a period of time from days to weeks to benefit from the color, tannins, and other flavors and qualities provided by the skins.

Greta and I talked with Jim Pfeiffer, the owner of Turtle Run Winery, in his tasting room one Sunday in June 2011. He said there are more than fifteen hundred natural chemical compounds that affect the flavor of wine. Seeds can present the most problems for a wine's flavor. Stems can also affect the flavor. They can provide some tannin structure, but too much stem flavor and the wine can taste green. The skins are where most of red wine's desirable flavors come from, which is why juice is commonly left on the skins for part of the fermentation process. White grapes are typically pressed immediately, separating the juice from the skins, since skins can pose flavor problems for white wines. In some places such as the Douro Valley of Portugal, one reason winemakers still prefer the use of feet for pressing grapes rather than equipment is to avoid crushing the seeds. Perhaps the attention to detail is one reason for Turtle Run's wide variety of very good wines.

Figure 5.5. A canopy is raised at Mallow Run Winery to help protect a shipment of Illinois Chambourcin grapes from the sun to prevent spoilage, August 28, 2015. Photo by Greta Pennell.

Wines are bottled when the winemaker decides they are ready. The time this takes can vary widely, depending on a lot of factors, including the grape variety and desired style. They may not be fully fermented to retain some sweetness, or, more commonly, some sugar or unfermented juice will be added. Wine-makers make choices about the desired level of dryness or sweetness, the kind of fermentation process, and the amount of aging or contact with oak, if any. A Beaujolais-style nouveau wine can take as little as six weeks; white wines can ferment for months; and big, full-bodied red wines might spend a year or two in oak barrels. Again, I am not a winemaker, so there are a host of factors I am leaving out. The point is that making wine involves multiple decisions and year-round monitoring to determine when the various wines being produced are ready. When a batch is ready, it can be kept cool in a tank for a short amount of time, but it is usually bottled within two weeks. Making a variety of wines means that bottling can occur year round.

While I was assisting at Mallow Run, Bill Richardson had an assistant winemaker, a young man who had taken some wine courses at Purdue as an undergraduate. I observed him checking the Brix (sugar content), pH (acid strength), and total acidity (percent of acid by weight) a couple of times, and gladly assisted with taste testing from the tank as wines neared their finish. After a wine has been checked, the tank may be topped off with wine from another batch (or bottles from previous years), or in the case of Mallow Run, a movable lid is lowered onto the tank. Air is an enemy of wine, so tanks and barrels need to be kept as full as possible. Tank temperatures may be lowered to slow the fermentation process or raised to speed it up.

In addition to picking grapes and observing some of the winemaking process, I spent much time bottling wine. Wineries vary in the automation of their bottling process. Small wineries, especially startups tight on money, often fill one bottle at a time and use a corking machine that requires someone to place a cork in the appropriate position and then use a hand lever to push it in. Mallow Run uses a five-bottle filler that supplies wine through a hose from a wine tank raised in the air on a forklift. One person unpacks the bottles from the cases they come in and sets them on a table near the filler. The person operating the filler places the bottles under the spigots until they are full, then pulls them out and puts them on a table to the other side of the filler. Mallow Run's corking machine automatically inserts the cork when the operator places the bottle in the appropriate position, which is recognized by a spring trigger. Occasionally, the operator also has to stop and manually dump corks from a bag into the cork hopper. When I was helping with the process in 2011, I got pretty good at working the corking machine and keeping up with the filled bottles. If they sit too long, those pesky little fruit flies can invade and the bottle must be discarded.

After the wine is corked, capsules are put on the tops of the bottles by hand, and heat is applied with a wine capsule heat shrinker to shrink them. Mallow Run's looks like a blow-dryer. The labels are then applied on the front and back of each bottle. In 2011, Mallow Run was still using a hand-cranked labeling machine; they have since replaced it with an electric machine that is operated by foot. Any mistakes, and the bottle is relegated to the tasting room. Then the finished bottles are placed, corks down, into boxes, which are sealed with tape, labeled, and stacked on a pallet. The process is labor intensive and works best with five people. In 2015, Mallow Run handled over 115,000 bottles of wine this way.

I found bottling to be repetitive, back-breaking work, and the sessions could last between three and six hours, depending on how much wine needed to be bottled that day. Still, the atmosphere when I was there was quite pleasant. As customers Steve and Dianna noted in chapter 2, the Mallow Run owners and employees are some of the nicest people you will ever meet. Since the work was rather repetitive, there was much opportunity for small talk and friendly banter. But as the hours dragged on, it was difficult to maintain the enthusiasm.

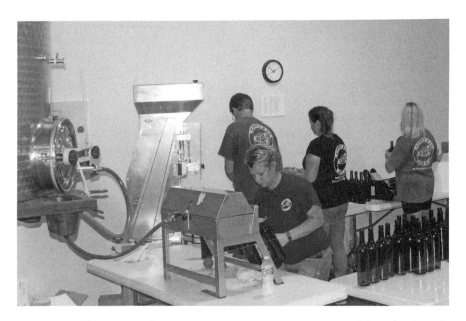

Figure 5.6. *Left to right*: Becky Kirby, Jeremy Racke, Lindsey Jacob, and Dana Stockwisch bottle Mallow Run's Vino Rosso, August 17, 2015. Photo by Greta Pennell.

This is one of the important tasks that must get done in a winery. Not surprisingly, wineries automate the process as much as possible as soon as possible. I saw an old automated system at Chateau Thomas that could be effectively operated by two people. The system at Oliver Winery was world class. It was completely automated, with empty bottles taken out of boxes, sterilized, filled, capped, and labeled, then inserted back into boxes and stacked. The equipment needed only a caretaker and occasional maintenance, but it pretty much monitored itself. Ferrante Winery also had the latest in bottling technology. High-end bottling systems not only reduce the labor needed for the process, but they keep out contaminants such as fruit flies and inject nitrogen to remove oxygen, which can damage the wine. This extends the shelf life of the wine. Nick Ferrante said they can bottle seventy bottles of wine in a minute. I'm guessing we were lucky if we finished fifteen bottles in a minute at Mallow Run.

At the other end, Brenda Logan of Baxter's Vineyards and Winery, and John Fouts of the now defunct Grateful Goat filled and then corked the bottles one at a time with a manual corking machine. Fouts described pulling all-nighters bottling wine by himself while working a forty-hour-a-week day job. I interviewed Fouts the month he had transitioned from part-time to full-time operation at his winery in 2011. Except for a little part-time help in the tasting room and some temporary help during picking, it was a one-man operation. He described the range of things he did on "slow" days in addition to manning the tasting room when customers arrived:

> Well, in the summertime, I'm out there in the vineyard a lot, and I'm weeding around vines, or I'm tying up shoots, or I'm inspecting wires, or I'm inspecting for disease, or I'm spraying fungicides, or I'm spraying insecticides, or I'm fixing issues with poles or wires. So I do a lot of that, or I'm mowing. I spend a lot of time mowing in the vineyard. In here in the winery I'm usually either labeling or I'm bottling or I'm measuring free SO_2 [sulfur dioxide] levels, doing some chemistry, or I'm titrating, or I'm cutting out the scarves that go on my bottles—these things [shows a little bottle neckerchief to me]. Or I'm designing my labels, or I'm talking to the state about getting road signs. I don't know. It's very varied as far as duties go. I try to stay up on Facebook and post something at least every few days. We try to make sure all of our events are posted on our website, on Facebook, on Twitter, on Metromix, the *LEO* Weekly [the *Louisville Eccentric Observer*—an arts, entertainment, and issues newspaper].

Unfortunately, Fouts had to close in 2013 for reasons that I won't go into here. It was due to circumstances beyond his control, not to a lack of love for the work or of knowledge or planning on his part.

The point here is that viticulture is labor intensive. Winery owners may be most interested in making and selling wine, but there are challenges involved, and additional knowledge and investment are required to establish a vineyard. Consequently, many wineries in the Midwest do not grow their own grapes, or they tend only a modest number of vines to add some ambience to their settings and serve as a backdrop for events. This reduces their startup time—it takes from three to five years for grapevines to begin to produce suitable grapes for making wine—and reduces the costs of land and associated labor.

Some wineries buy only juice instead of grapes, so they can dispense with the task of crushing and pressing. Urban boutique wineries often do this because they have limited space. It also saves the expense of crusher destemmers and presses. Some purchase concentrate, since it is cheaper than juice. I will discuss these practices and the issues that surround them in the final chapter. Most wineries have found it necessary to purchase at least some grapes or juice so they can produce enough wine to keep up with demand. Even wineries that have fairly large tracts of vines may still need to purchase grapes to meet demand or to provide varietals that do not grow or are in limited supply. Wineries are left with little choice but to purchase grapes after a bad winter or spring that damages buds or if diseases and pests devastate their crops.

Whether a winery grows grapes or purchases grapes and/or juice, it must produce a sufficient supply of wine of acceptable quality and with the right product mix to meet demand. A number of small, relatively new wineries found it difficult to keep up with demand, especially for their most popular wines. As Larry Satek noted,

> We opened in 2001—in the summer of 2001—with what we thought was enough wine to last for a year or more, and by early November, we were sold out of wine [laughing] . . . I was still doing it on a weekend, part-time basis, but it was so successful, I knew I had to retire or hire somebody to do it.

Paul Renzaglia said that Alto Vineyards opened in December 1988 with twelve hundred gallons of wine and sold out in two days. That was probably the most extreme example I heard, but many of the smaller wineries reported challenges with maintaining sufficient inventory.

Even for the larger wineries, ensuring a sufficient supply with the right mix and quality can be a challenge. Mark Easley's comments in the last chapter about ten-year planning timelines come to mind. I have been the beneficiary of his winery's $6-a-bottle clearances to get rid of inventory that may be getting past its prime or has not attracted strong demand. Sometimes it is a matter of quality, but typically it results from overestimating demand for a particular variety or just having a bumper crop. I suspect that some especially abundant Chambourcin harvests led to some innovation, with rosé being produced along with the typical red styles.

Winery owners spend much time engaged in or overseeing financial activities. One important job is to determine when and how much to invest in expanding and upgrading production capacity. Invest too much too soon without a corresponding increase in sales, and the winery becomes insolvent. Invest too little, and customers can become frustrated with a lack of availability or poor quality. New wineries may start with procured juice or concentrate, plastic tanks, and some oak chips for flavor, but keeping up with industry standards ultimately requires the purchase of expensive stainless steel tanks, then larger tanks, then oak barrels, then a larger building or addition to hold the tanks and barrels. In the early years of the reestablished Midwest wine industry, procuring a loan to upgrade and expand was extremely difficult. That is why most wineries in the 1970s and 1980s developed out of farming operations or were funded by owners who had successful outside careers. Banks have caught on to the fact that wineries are a solid investment, but they are still judged by the standards of other businesses. Prospective owners must have reasonable business plans and demonstrate the likelihood of profitability in the not-too-distant future. They also must grow to meet demand, which requires more planning and purchases. Financial matters are much like grapevines: they must be tended constantly.

Getting over the capitalization hump can be a challenge for new wineries. Constructing new buildings or adapting old ones for production facilities and tasting rooms is expensive, typically requiring more money than most owners have on hand. Steel tanks cost thousands to tens of thousands of dollars depending upon the size and features. Cooling jackets, pumps, bottling equipment, a tractor or forklift—the list of necessities is long and expensive. So one must borrow.

John Fouts found himself in a dilemma: he would need to quit his full-time job to grow his winery, but he was not in a position to borrow any more money until sales increased. He had difficulty keeping up with the demand for his most popular wines and was often out of some of them. This is a common situation for many small wineries in their first few years.

Even as wineries get over the initial startup hump and begin to grow, owners often keep little or no income for themselves, choosing instead to invest and pay employees. Joel Kopsa told me that after they opened John Ernest Winery and Vineyard in 2005, their business growth was "just steady" and that he was "trying to pay stuff off." Kopsa worked full time at the winery but paid himself half time. The winery had a full-time tasting room manager and four or five part-time employees. His wife worked full time for the city of Tama. I found this sort of arrangement repeatedly at small wineries. In order to grow, wineries must hire employees.

Making Wine and Jobs

Midwestern wineries have expanded rapidly in number and size in the last twenty years. As wineries grow, owners must hire and oversee employees to accomplish the essential tasks. Getting grapes from the vine and turning them into bottled wine in sufficient quantity and variety is only part of the work entailed in operating a winery. Wineries also require financial planning, purchasing, accounting, marketing, and sales. Oliver Winery has over 90 full- and part-time employees. Huber's has 125 to handle its huge farming operation, winery, restaurant, ice cream and cheese shop, farm market, and events. Ferrante has 15 full-time employees working in the winery, vineyard, and restaurant, and up to another 25 or 30 part-time employees during the busy summer months. Ten years after opening, Cedar Ridge Winery in Iowa has 17 full-time and 14 part-time employees. Even the smallest wineries tend to have two or three people working full time and two or three working part time.

An analysis of the wine and grape industry's economic impact in Iowa in 2012 estimated that the industry was producing 2,678 full-time-equivalent jobs in the state (Frank, Rimerman and Co. 2014b). This number included jobs that were indirectly related, such as in the tourism industry. The same research firm estimated that in the same year, the Illinois industry produced 3,887 full-time-equivalent jobs (Frank, Rimerman and Co. 2013). A report commissioned by the Ohio Grape Industries Committee estimated that the Ohio industry generated 5,291 jobs in 2012 (Frank, Rimerman and Co. 2014a). There is no economic impact research available on Indiana, but it is reasonable to estimate, based on the figures for Iowa and Illinois, that the industry there generates substantially more than 2,000 full-time-equivalent jobs.

Thinking about the job prospects for his children and other families in the business, Mark Easley observed:

> Circumstances may change, but what's interesting between the farming of the grapes, the winemaking process, the wine marketing process, you can find a lot of talent areas within the business. You know, you need marketing people, you need mechanics, you need chemists, you need agronomists and ag specialists that do viticulture. So, you know, if they've got any interests at all, you can find your niche. And you know, there are large families that have done that. Obviously, Hubers have shown that you can find an area anywhere in the business for a family member having that big of an extended family.

In order to sell their product, wineries must find ways to reach customers. They get some help from their state industry associations. Donniella "Donnie" Winchell, executive director of the Ohio Wine Producers Association, assists wineries with marketing and oversees a website (www.ohiowines.org) that includes information on member wineries and wine trails in the state. Ohio, Indiana, and Iowa also have state-funded organizations that assist with marketing as well as educational support. I will focus more on these industry-related organizations in the next chapter. Even with assistance, a winery's own website, Facebook, and Twitter presence, or whatever web-based efforts are pursued, as well as print and radio advertising and other forms of outreach, come with a cost and require the time and attention of the owner and/or employees. The demands of this work are much different from those that result in a well-made wine.

In the Midwest, most wineries' sales depend on customers who visit the establishments and make purchases there. This allows them to earn the full retail price for their wines. Consequently, most Midwestern winery owners spend a lot of time and money on their tasting rooms. Tasting rooms must be open and sufficiently staffed to move product. Initially, the Richardsons shared the job of supervising the tasting room at Mallow Run. Part-time employees were hired to assist with pouring wine, and some friends and family members volunteered to help out on busy weekends. As the demands of the winery quickly escalated, a tasting room manager was hired to work with the owners in the supervision of part-time employees. This is a typical pattern of growth.

In Indiana, amendments to the original Small Winery Act of 1971 allowed for satellite tasting rooms and tastings and sales at events such as festivals and farmers' markets. These outlets provided opportunities for customers to learn about wineries and purchase their wines. All these activities require employees (and in a few cases trained volunteers) to pour wine for tastings and handle sales. In addition to its tasting room at the winery, Chateau Thomas opened three additional tasting rooms in Nashville, Fishers, and Bloomington. (The latter was short-lived, and the Fishers location closed in 2015.) Both Butler and Oliver opened downtown Bloomington tasting rooms in addition to the tasting rooms at their wineries north of town (Oliver closed its downtown location in 2015). Butler's is run by a daughter-in-law of Jim and Susan Butler. Butler also has a tasting room in northern Indiana, in Chesterton, run by a son and daughter-in-law. Cedar Creek opened a second tasting room in Nashville in September 2013. Chateau de Pique, in Seymour, has tasting rooms on the north side of Indianapolis and in Clarksville in far southern Indiana.

Illinois also allows tasting rooms offsite. Lynfred Winery was the first in the state to add an offsite tasting room and currently has three. Galena Cellars has two offsite tasting rooms, and Massbach Ridge Winery has one in Galena. Alto Vineyards has a second site in Champaign.

Most wineries have expanded their participation at local events to supplement sales and help raise awareness of their brand among people who live in the surrounding area. Larry Elsner at Cedar Creek and Jeff Durm at Buck Creek are among those who reported significant sales from participating in community events. These events commonly require at least one and often two employees. Since they are often held during winery business hours, additional personnel are commonly needed to cover them. Dave Smith, the owner of Smith Winery in Columbus, Indiana, sells his wine only at community events and farmers' markets, doing the pouring for tastings himself. All four states have statewide and regional wine events, which I will discuss in more detail in the next chapter.

As Butch noted in chapter 3, part of having a good experience at a winery or tasting event is a knowledgeable server. Most of the winery owners I interviewed agreed that it was not difficult to find people to work in their tasting rooms, but finding people who are somewhat knowledgeable about wine, especially Midwestern varieties, can be a challenge. Since much of the pleasure of wine comes from talking about it with others, tasting room and event servers need to be skilled at engaging customers, judging their knowledge and taste preferences, assisting them in exploring the available wines, and answering their questions in an informed manner.

Some of the wineries I studied focused heavily on distribution to retail outlets through wholesalers. In Indiana that was especially true of Oliver and

Easley, whose wines are distributed in a number of other states. Both wineries have sales representatives to promote their wines. Rettig Hill, in southern Indiana, distributed only by wholesale and at some events. Ferrante Winery in Ohio sold about 80 percent of its wines through wholesale distribution. At Alto Vineyards in southern Illinois, that proportion had recently increased to about 40 percent. Working with distributors and managing sales is time-consuming work, which again requires different knowledge and skills from those needed for making good wine. Many wineries in all four states self-distribute, but there are restrictions on that practice, which I will talk about more in the next chapter. Self-distribution also requires someone to do sales and maintain accounts.

Although most winery owners in the Midwest are also the winemakers, some are businesspeople who hire, or are in partnership with, winemakers. This is sometimes partly a function of scale. The larger wineries have professional staff who are responsible for certain tasks with input from the owner or owners. Oliver, Huber's, and Easley, the three biggest wineries in Indiana, have employees who specialize in different aspects of the business. Oliver has employed a winemaker since early in its operation. In contrast, Ted Huber and Mark Easley are the master winemakers, with assistants to help with the production process. At Mallow Run, the Richardsons have distributed many of the business and marketing tasks, but Bill has become the winemaker, despite his father's interest in it and years of home winemaking. They also employ an assistant winemaker. At Tonne Winery, Kevin Tonne does the "chemistry," but he and Larry Simmons, who also owns a garden center, collaborate on making taste decisions.

At Blue Sky Vineyard in Illinois, Karen Hand was brought on board by Jim Ewers to make the wine, and she has an assistant. Chris Lawlor-White at Galena Cellars is the master winemaker but also has an assistant. In Ohio and Iowa, one can find the same arrangement as wineries mature as business operations and owners delegate some if not all of the winemaking duties to employees.

Some wineries have focused on pairing their wine experience with food beyond the cheese plates or hummus commonly found at most wineries. In Ohio, Debonne, Ferrante, Henke, and Valley Vineyards have restaurants, and there are many others across the state. Some offer full menus and serve lunch and dinner. Blue Sky in Illinois serves both, as does Cedar Ridge in Iowa on weekdays, with a Sunday brunch on the weekend. Ertel Winery in Batesville, Indiana, has a full-service restaurant that serves lunch and dinner Wednesday through Sunday. When I visited there, it seemed more restaurant than winery, with a very small tasting counter at the entrance, but large stainless steel tanks could be viewed from windows at the back of the restaurant. Huber's is a foodie experience with a restaurant, ice cream and cheese shop, and farm market.

J & J Winery in Richmond, Indiana, serves food Thursday through Saturday, and features an outdoor pizza oven. Other wineries may serve sandwiches and small plates or offer food for special events. Mallow Run commonly serves food on weekends or brings in local restaurants or food trucks for some events.

Serving food requires additional employees, creating job opportunities not directly related to making and selling wine. Add in wedding receptions and the other kinds of events that many wineries host, and the range of employment opportunities expands. As Jeff Quint of Cedar Ridge noted, the restaurant and events were important revenue streams along with the winery and distillery. Joe Henke saw his restaurant as a "necessary evil" for selling his wine, adding, "If you wanted to curse somebody, curse them with a restaurant."

The Challenges of Getting the Work Done

As Midwestern wineries have boomed over the last twenty years, even during economic downturns, they have needed to find ways to address that growth by hiring more employees to handle the various work tasks. The large majority of the owners I interviewed reported no problem with attracting good employees. When I asked Laura Richardson how difficult it was to find good people to work at Mallow Run, she said:

> Well, most of the good people that work here have found us. And that's the key [laughing]. You know, and it's happened, it just happened. And very little have we had to try to find additional help, and those attempts have not been so successful . . . It's been a networking . . . And the full-time people aside, which, I mean, obviously they need—this is their job, but we have a good handful of people that don't need to be working here, and it's fulfilling something for them besides just a paycheck. I mean, that's remarkable for us to have that.

Markko Vineyards owner Arnie Esterer explained to me that one of the positives of owning his winery is being a vertically integrated business that raises the grapes, makes the wine, and sells it. He added:

> The other great thing is developing a workforce. We didn't have a workforce here. So we're working with people. The first lady came up to me and said, "I've worked in vineyards. I know how to tie grapes and I know how to do what needs to be done. I've done it for years." I said, "Okay, come and do it." And she did, and she brought all of her friends. So she's the crew leader and has been for twenty years. Nobody here had grown wine grapes before. They'd grown Concord. And so it was a small change, but it was easy and she knew how to manage it . . . We've always used local people that are out of jobs and looking for work. People come and say, "You need some help?" "Yep, sure, we got a job for you." Part time—kids, and they can bring their families. You know, the mothers that come, they'd have

kids running around the vineyard. We'd feed them. And, babies, one, two years old all the way up. Then by the time they got to high school or something, they were working in the vineyard. We can find a job for about anybody.

Bill Oliver viewed this matter quite differently, perhaps due to the size of his operation and the large number of positions it requires, but also as a result of its employee stock ownership model:

> Hiring people, for us, is just a hand-wringing experience fraught with all sorts of uncertainty. And we are really deliberate about it. Our expectations are really high. Our culture is very tight. New people have to be absolutely certain they are going to fit in—just from a personality, cultural, skill level, energy, vision, all that stuff. It's really been tough. But, you know, you keep at it. And ultimately you've got a crew. And some people, it doesn't work out. It's not often, but occasionally. I've been willing to recognize when someone is not a good fit.

He also noted that Oliver has very little turnover except for the tasting room staff, about half of whom he estimated are college students, who tend to be temporary.

As wineries grow, they must adopt many of the practices of larger firms, which means they need people to handle the scheduling and management of personnel, the human resource dimension of hiring, firing, procuring benefits, and negotiating disputes, and the exacting work of addressing federal and state employment requirements. Mark Easley talked about the shifts in his life from his first love of farming and making wine to turning those tasks over to others and becoming the business manager of a successful, growing business.

> I'd say the most stressful part is the growth we have experienced. It has caused us to go from us doing it to hiring folks, and then you have a lot of assumptions. You have to put in systems and operations and trainings. That part's been difficult to handle. Cash flow is always a hard part. As an agriculturally based business, you receive all of your year's inventory in a sixty-day window. So you've gotta be good financial managers, in that everything you're gonna work on for three hundred and sixty-five days shows up here in sixty.

Some have worked at or run other businesses and are used to these kinds of responsibilities. Others are not. Laura Richardson shared her struggles as one of the Mallow Run bosses:

> Well, it's hard. There are natural things that happen human resource–wise when you have employees and people and conflicts, and there have been—that is what just rips my heart out—when bad stuff happens with people, and then it's just hard for me to say it's okay, I'm the boss. I'm still trying to be okay with not being liked sometimes. And I think when I go to the hospital and I'm just a speech therapist two afternoons a week, it's just so affirming and I'm just responsible

for myself and the job that I do, and people like me and it's nice and it's a good feeling. I mean, I'm not trying to make too much of that because we have amazing, good people here and great relationships, and lifelong friendships that have been formed all the way around. But I think that's just a part of having a business and having employees that can't be avoided.

One area where employment patterns and weather work against industry growth in each state is in the production of grapes. I will focus more on this problem in later chapters, but I will reiterate here that tending vines and picking grapes involves a tremendous amount of work. Few laborers are available in agriculture today in the Midwest due to the decline in the diversity of crops grown (now mostly corn and soybeans) and the mechanization of production. So there are limits to how many acres a winery owner can tend and harvest without investing in a harvester or paying at a level sufficient to attract and retain additional employees. Rocky Waters Vineyard and Winery in Illinois uses a mechanical picker for its twenty-five acres. Tassel Ridge Winery in Leighton, Iowa, uses a harvester for sixty-seven acres. Michael White, viticulture specialist at Iowa State University, reported that in 2012 there were six wineries using pickers in the state (White 2012). Some larger Ohio wineries, such as Klingshirn Winery and Firelands Winery, use mechanical harvesters. Debonne Vineyards shares its harvester with South River Winery. But using a mechanical picker on eight or ten acres of grapes makes no sense due to the cost of the picker. Consequently, some wineries recruit friends, relatives, and customers to volunteer some time for the task. When I mentioned this to Bill Oliver, he said:

> I hear wineries have people that volunteer to pick grapes. I was like, wow! I don't think that's even legal, and not necessarily moral. That's wrong [laughing]. Once a winery gets [on] their feet financially, they ought to be paying for their help. That's just the way I feel about it. You know, if you're starting up and your friends are helping you, then of course, of course!

As the owner of the largest winery in the Midwest, Oliver is in a very different position than most. At the other end of the spectrum, John Fouts, who in 2011 was one of the newest winery owners running probably the smallest winery in Indiana, said he preferred to pay pickers because he thought he could count on them more than volunteers to show up. Chris Lawlor-White at Galena Cellars said that she prefers not to use volunteers because, "frankly, they are lousy pickers." She and other owners also mentioned the 2014 case in which the Westover Winery in California was heavily fined for violating the state's labor law, which does not allow for-profit companies to use volunteer labor.

I should note that as Mallow Run has prospered, it has paid temporary workers to pick while continuing to use volunteers. One retiree reported being paid $11 an hour, well above the minimum wage, which in fact does not apply to farm workers. Mallow Run also provides volunteers with vouchers for two bottles of wine in exchange for a morning's effort. People do it both for fun and to help out, as I did well before I started this book project, and a few do it because they are thinking about starting a winery and want to learn. A number of owners told me they have community groups who assist with picking in exchange for donations to their organizations. As Greta suggested to me, the use of volunteers has some similarities to the rural tradition of a barn raising. People pitch in when things need to be done, which is part of being a community member.

Although employment prospects in the wine industry look fairly good in the Midwest, I don't want my account of Mallow Run or any of the wineries I discuss here to be interpreted as a claim that workers at Midwestern wineries are all happy employees working for enlightened employers. I do think that as a group, the winery owners are a pretty progressive bunch, and the social conditions of the work are generally pleasant. But most of the jobs available at the smaller wineries are part time. As small businesses, the wineries find it hard to provide for more than a few full-time workers in most cases. It is difficult for owners to afford retirement and health benefits for employees as well as for themselves (remember, some are investing their retirement money from previous careers). This is a problem for most small businesses in the United States. Profits are often reinvested to meet the demands of growth. Stainless steel tanks and equipment, oak barrels, attractive tasting rooms, and buildings to house it all are expensive. My focus in writing this book was not on the conditions of employment in the winery industry, but on the attraction of wineries, the owners' experiences, and the kinds of work that go into a successful operation. Consequently, I did not formally interview employees. More research into the growing opportunities and possible drawbacks of wine industry employment in the Midwest is needed.

Success also breeds problems. I have already described the phenomenal success of Mallow Run Winery. When I asked Bill Richardson in 2012 about the drawbacks to the job, he noted:

Certainly the hours and the commitment. It's much more work than any of us thought it would be. And part of that is that it's grown much faster than we ever thought it would. We went from thirty-five hundred [gallons] the first year, double the first couple of years, up to—we bottle twenty-five thousand [gallons] . . . We are finally getting into the situation of now we made this wine, we have to sell it. Every other year it has been we have to make more wine to keep up. This is the first year you can look at it as prepared, or look at it as a situation that now you're more into the marketing and less into the production.

Owners of smaller wineries talked about the challenge of getting away for more than a few days. Donna Clark at Old Mason said that one of the drawbacks of ownership is that "You're married to it. You don't realize how much you traveled before." When I asked the Hofmanns at White Oak Vineyards how big they would like their business to be, Rudi responded, "Big enough so that we can have what we need to go somewhere on vacation like a regular person."

In short, wineries are time-consuming, capital-intensive efforts. They might be started on weekends with a modest investment, but they are not leisurely endeavors. Owners of small wineries have to rely on their own labor to meet most of the work demands, and they often feel overwhelmed in the early stages. Wineries require a substantial commitment of time and money to reach the point at which they can become financially stable and the primary source of income for a family. Due to their popularity, that time has tended to be sooner rather than later in the last two decades. Then the winery owner has to deal with the new demands of growth. Success is satisfying, but it can also be a mixed blessing.

Growth can also color customers' experiences. Big is not necessarily bad. Recall Steve and Dianna talking about enjoying both Mallow Run and Huber's—Huber's for the range and quality of its products and its ability to attract and manage large numbers of people, but Mallow Run for its intimacy and as a regular place in their lives where the owners are usually present and interact with customers directly. Growth presents a challenge for owners in terms of how to maintain the kind of ambience and experience they want to provide their customers. When Mallow Run holds events with many hundreds and even thousands of people attending, it has a different feel and can put a strain on employees and service. Regular customers tend to adjust their expectations and adapt to the situation. Some even volunteer for the day during big charitable events, assisting with parking cars or other tasks. But those who are drawn to the featured event and lack regulars' familiarity with the place take away a different experience. This has led some winery owners to avoid or pull back from big events to focus on a more laid-back wine experience. When I asked Laura Richardson how big she would like Mallow Run to be, she put it in terms of the talents and energies of the employees they have or might attract:

> It's all about the people. If we have the people that love being here and are capable and excited and have things that they're excited about, I mean, that to a huge degree will absolutely, literally direct where we go. If we don't have the resources and the people to do new things, I mean big new things, then we won't do them. I think the people have to come first. If we have the right people, I don't think there has to be a limit.

Gender and Ethnicity in Winery Work

As a sociologist, I commonly examine the ethnic and gender divisions found in work settings. When I started my research for this book in 2011, I was surprised to find that while women shared ownership with husbands and assumed a range of work responsibilities in Indiana wineries, they did not make the wine. Some owners I interviewed mentioned the short-lived Gaia Winery in Indianapolis, which had a woman winemaker. I found a number of instances where sons were interested in the winemaking side of the business, but I noted no daughters demonstrating that interest, although a number were involved in other aspects of the business. I asked Laura Richardson of Mallow Run about what some have referred to as the "wineglass ceiling" (Epstein 2015; Teague 2015), and she said:

> I just feel like, I mean, all I can think of is the skills that it takes to do those jobs are maybe typical gender strengths. And you know, like being able to fix things and work on a car and fix a tractor and fix a bottling line tends to be more of a guy thing, and then, you know, on the flip side being organized, having good verbal communication skills, being social, being flexible . . . I mean, it's kind of like why are there more female nurses? It's kind of that, I think. I mean, because I love being in the dirt and in the garden. I love that kind of stuff. But I feel like somebody had to do this [the jobs she does at the winery], too, and I mean for us, Bill had—I mean, he did go get an education. [JP: He has a degree in Ag.] Right. So that sort of made sense that he would be, he didn't come here by accident like I did. Not really an accident, but you know what I mean!

Although no wives of those I interviewed were deeply engaged in the winemaking process in Indiana, like Laura, many were actively engaged in various roles at their wineries supervising the tasting room, overseeing events, and purchasing or marketing products.

Fortunately, I had the opportunity to visit wineries and interview winemakers in other states, and I did discover women winemakers. I identified six in Illinois: Chris Lawlor-White, Brenda Logan, Peggy Harmston, Mary Hofmann, Susan Sullivan Danenberger, and Karen Hand. All but Hand were also owners. When I asked Hand what some of the drawbacks of her job were as head winemaker at Blue Sky, she said:

> I'm going to sound a little bit sexist, but being a female is a little bit hard, especially in southern Illinois. And I definitely understand that a lot of winemakers first were cellar rats, so they did do the equipment and all that, and that's how they developed. So it tends to be more of a male industry. But I think people are a little, like, if I were standing here with another male, people tend to give the male winemaker more respect.

I also found six women winemakers in Ohio. Three were at wineries I visited: Hundley Cellars (Traci Hundley-Pringle), the Winery at Wolf Creek (Carrie Bonvallet), and Quail Crossing Cellars (Jackie Trexel). Todd Steiner, enologist at the OARDC, told me of two more, at Laurello Vineyards (Kim Laurello) and Caesar Creek Vineyards (Patricia Chalfont), and I discovered Kelly Harvey of Signature Wines through an internet search. Nan Smith at Stone Cliff Winery in Dubuque was the only woman winemaker I could identify in Iowa. However you look at it, women are extremely underrepresented as winemakers even in comparison with California's industry, where in 2013 they made up about 10 percent of all winemakers (Gilbert and Gilbert 2015). In Illinois the proportion is a little less than 6 percent, and in Ohio it is less than half that.

Beyond winemaking, the division of labor varied among men and women. Some married couples were full partners and shared in decision making and management. They made business decisions as a team, although certain tasks were commonly divided. For example, Jared Spahn is the winemaker at Rocky Waters, and Phyllis cares for the vineyard with their son. At White Oak, Mary Hofmann makes the wine and Rudi tends the vines. Whatever the division of labor, of course, there are times that require "all hands on deck" for tasks such as picking grapes, bottling, or serving customers at big events.

In other cases, the husband took the lead in business decisions and ran the winery. Often the wives had full-time jobs elsewhere but assisted with certain tasks in the evenings, on weekends, or on days off. In a few cases, the wife played no role in the winery. A number of wineries were business partnerships among men. In those cases, they often split their areas of decision making. Ted Huber oversees the winery operation at Huber's, and his cousin Greg oversees the farm. Kevin Tonne and Larry Simmons, the owners of Tonne Winery, work together on business decisions, although Kevin is the winemaker. In these cases, wives played an advisory role or took on the responsibility for certain tasks. At Huber's, Ted's wife, Dana, is in charge of marketing and public relations, and Greg's wife, Jan, is the chief financial officer. These are extremely important positions for the success of their winery and farm.

In most cases, the division of labor reflects the interests and talents of those involved. The larger wineries seem to have more gender diversity in employment, probably in part because they have more positions to fill in management, marketing, and customer service. But gender differences in winemaking and vineyard work are quite evident.

Times change, and education combined with expanding opportunities seems to be playing a role in women's assumption of more winemaking roles, although the progress has been slow. When Greta and I were visiting some northern Indiana wineries in November 2013, we met a young woman named Nyssa

Boyd at Wildcat Creek Winery near Lafayette who said she had studied food science at Purdue. I checked with Dr. Christian Butzke, professor of enology at Purdue, and he told me that Boyd was Wildcat's assistant winemaker and had taken his Commercial Grape and Wine Production course. He also mentioned a number of other women involved in winemaking in the state. Purdue Food Science alumnus Jackie Kibler was assistant winemaker at Whyte Horse Winery. Although they weren't making wine, Jenna and Stephanie Cook started a vineyard in 2010 just northeast of Indianapolis and were selling grapes to wineries. And though she was not making wine in Indiana, Nancie Corum-Oxley, who graduated from Purdue in 2002, was the head winemaker at Michigan's largest winery, St. Julian.

There is an even more noticeable ethnic divide in the Midwestern wine industry. Dave Smith, the owner of Smith Winery in Columbus, Indiana, is the only African American winery owner in the state. He retired from Cummins Inc. after a career as an engineer and now makes wine and sells it at farmers' markets and events. In Ohio, Mansfield Frazier opened Chateau Hough in one of the most downtrodden neighborhoods in Cleveland. I had an opportunity to learn about his winery at a conference I attended in 2014 in Cleveland where he gave a presentation on his work. The winery is an ex-offender re-entry and training program as well as an urban-renewal project. Frazier planted three-fourths of an acre of Frontenac and Traminette in 2010 on a lot where a former crack house was torn down. The first wine was produced in 2014. The only other Ohio winery I could identify owned by African Americans is Markell-Bani Fine Wines and Sparkling Beverages, founded in 2007 by Gregory Markell Lawrence and Sean Bani Yisrael. The two wines it sells have been produced in Sonoma, California, since 2009 (Markell-Bani 2016).

Research evidence suggests that African Americans historically have generally been more conservative in their orientation to alcohol, especially women (Caetano, Clark, and Tam 1998). But that does not mean they do not enjoy wine. According to recent marketing research, as African Americans become more affluent, they are more likely to develop an interest in fine wines (Scarborough Research 2003; Forman 2011). Ethnic minorities certainly frequent Midwestern wineries. Easley Winery's "Groovin' in the Garden" music event drew a diverse crowd on Tuesday evenings and Saturday afternoons when my band played there during the summer from 2006 to 2011. Most likely, the capital investment that opening a winery requires and the tendency for Midwestern wineries to be located in rural, predominantly white areas contribute to the lack of black ownership and employment in the industry. Economic inequality and ethnic residential patterns, residuals of the U.S. history of discrimination, continue to shape opportunities to learn about winemaking and accrue or attract the capital to start a winery.

Be Careful What You Wish For

Owning or working at a winery may look like a dream job on the front stage—hanging out in the tasting room with a group of happy customers and celebrating one's efforts with them—but backstage it is a different story. A tremendous amount of work goes into producing wine and creating settings that customers enjoy. As Joe Henke put it, "Grapes don't just jump into the bottle." The work offers its moments of pleasure, and the pleasure is typically enhanced by having a pleasant group of people to work with. The Midwestern winery business seems to attract interesting, convivial people. I suspect it is that sort of person—smart, creative, and sociable—who gravitates to the industry, whether owner or employee. Managing a vineyard, making wine, and sharing it with customers is meaningful, satisfying work. Wineries take on a lot of the characteristics of their owners. As they grow, however, they become more complex organizations and require more personnel. It can be more difficult to retain those unique qualities and the personal relationships that customers enjoy with owners and winemakers.

Fortunately for newcomers to the industry in each state I studied, a tradition of winemaking and winery ownership is developing. An infrastructure of organizations and relationships has developed that means new owners are not starting from scratch, but have an extended professional family to draw upon. I turn now to an examination of these relationships and the ongoing challenges of maintaining them while adapting to or pushing back against the changing political, economic, and social landscape.

6

Organizing the
Midwest Wine Industry
to Address Challenges

Wine is a heavily regulated product. The purveyors of our Puritan heritage made sure that if they couldn't successfully ban alcoholic beverages through legal means, as they tried with Prohibition, then they were going to make sure that the producers of those beverages were subjected to more than market forces in their economic pursuits. The result was the Twenty-First Amendment, which gave states tremendous power to regulate alcoholic beverages. Mark Easley told me, "You know, we have an eternal family joke: it's the Twenty-First Amendment is our biggest problem in life." The state laws that resulted from that amendment put tremendous constraints on the production and sale of alcoholic beverages, effectively blocking the development of the wine industry in Indiana until 1971, in Illinois until 1979, and in Iowa outside the Amana Colonies until 1997. Only Ohio maintained the semblance of an industry prior to the 1970s, although it was in a state of serious decline.

By the turn of the twenty-first century, the political maneuverings and laws involving alcohol had settled down for the most part, but there were still rumblings of discontent. The use of the internet was growing, wine was becoming more popular, the winery business was booming, and some wineries were starting to achieve high enough production levels that they were seeking new outlets for their products. Wine tourism was big in California, and that state's wineries wanted to ship directly to customers throughout the country. On visits there, Greta and I would ask at wineries if they could ship to us, but they always said no, Indiana didn't allow it. Sometimes they suggested that we contact our state legislators and register our disappointment. We didn't really understand why our state didn't allow it except that Indiana tended to be quite restrictive about alcohol. We'd schlep a case or two back as luggage and hope the bottles didn't vanish or break in transit.

At the same time, Midwestern wineries, with the assistance of their industry associations and state agriculture and tourism agencies, were promoting themselves as tourist destinations. Some were forming wine trails so that tourists could make multiple stops at participating wineries. People started taking vacations or weekend trips that included visits to wineries. Trips to other states were also common. For someone who lives in Kalamazoo, Michigan, large parts of Ohio, Indiana, Illinois, and Wisconsin are closer than Traverse City, the area where many Michigan wineries are located. Back in 2000, if you liked the wine from a winery you visited in any of those four states and wanted to have some shipped to you in Michigan when the supply you had purchased was gone, you couldn't do that, for different reasons depending on the state. Illinois, Iowa, and Wisconsin were "reciprocity" states: they were part of a group of ten states that had signed an agreement saying that wine could be freely shipped or received between wineries and customers only in those states. If your state wasn't a reciprocity state, and Michigan wasn't, you couldn't get wine shipped to you from the reciprocity states. Indiana, Ohio, and Michigan had laws that permitted shipping within the state, but did not allow shipping to residents from out of state. So you couldn't get wine shipped to Michigan from Indiana or Ohio, either (Greenhouse 2005).

Granholm v. Heald and the Battle over Direct Shipping of Wine

In 2000, wine writers Ray and Eleanor Heald wanted to have some wine shipped to their home in Michigan from Domaine Alfred Winery in California, a reciprocity state, but couldn't. So they and the winery owner filed a lawsuit against the State of Michigan. Another lawsuit was filed that same year by a winery owner in Virginia who wanted to ship to customers in New York. The plaintiffs in each case thought the Commerce Clause of the U.S. Constitution was being violated. The clause places the power to regulate commerce among states in the hands of the federal government to prevent states from restricting interstate commerce in a discriminatory manner. In these cases, Michigan and New York were treating out-of-state wineries differently than in-state wineries by allowing only in-state wineries to ship to customers who lived in those states.

The cases made their way to the United States Supreme Court, where they were combined into a single case, *Granholm v. Heald*. The decision was rendered in 2005. The court agreed that states cannot create wine-shipping laws that treat people in other states differently than they treat the residents of their own states. Therefore, both reciprocity agreements and allowing only in-state shipments were in violation (Greenhouse 2005; Martinez 2005; Gary 2010). This meant that those states would need to change their laws, or their residents would be able to have wine shipped directly to them from any state that allowed it. It was the result those who had brought the suits were hoping to achieve. But a Supreme Court decision is often like eating sausage: you can't be sure how it will affect you until it has been fully digested. So the states in violation could go a different direction.

The decision did not change the right of individual states to regulate wine and other alcoholic beverages as specified in the Twenty-First Amendment so long as they did not violate the Commerce Clause. Fifteen states at the time of the decision completely prohibited direct shipping within, to, or from their states. Thus their laws were not in violation of the Commerce Clause, since they treated their residents and those in other states the same way (Greenhouse 2005). Everyone in those states had to go through the three-tier system, which strictly separates the roles of producer, wholesale distributor, and retail outlet (including bars and restaurants). No business in one of those roles can assume responsibility for another role at the same time, and no steps can be skipped. This means that no direct shipping is allowed from producers to customers or retailers. In some of these states, the retail outlet is the state itself, at least for some beverages such as spirits. Even in states such as Ohio and Indiana, where in-state wineries could ship to residents prior to *Granholm*, or Illinois and Iowa, where wineries could ship to other reciprocity states, the three-tier system was in effect for all other alcohol sales, including wine that could not be shipped directly.

The three-tier arrangement basically means that wholesale distributors get a cut of the retail price of every bottle of wine sold in a particular state. In Ohio, the size of the cut is even mandated by law with a formula. The distributors did not want state legislatures to develop direct-shipment laws that would eliminate their cut. As Gary writes (2010):

> The three-tier system is not required by federal law and is a product not of the marketplace but of state legislative preference. Regulators have generally favored the three-tier system, and wholesalers have strongly promoted it. Arguments in favor of the three-tier system are that it facilitates efficient tax collection, aids in enforcement of alcohol beverage laws such as underage drinking prohibitions, and promotes orderly market conditions.

The Indiana legislature took up the issue in its next session after the *Granholm* decision. Wineries were in support of allowing direct shipping to in-state customers as well as across state lines without restriction, including allowing wineries in other states to ship to customers in Indiana. The wholesalers wanted to protect their incomes. Their lobbying group, the Indiana Beverage Alliance, donated heavily to legislators' election campaigns. The combination of distributor financial influence and complaints that their businesses would be seriously hurt, coupled with the specter that alcohol could more easily end up in the hands of minors, posed a daunting challenge for the state wine industry. Jim Purucker, the executive director of Wine and Spirits Wholesalers of Indiana, argued that "unlicensed" UPS delivery people would make it easy for kids to get wine delivered (Foulkes 2007). No evidence was presented that this had ever happened in Indiana.

It shouldn't be news to anyone that those under the legal drinking age already have ways to get alcoholic beverages through the three-tier system. It also doesn't require much horse sense to know that kids aren't going to spend money on expensive fine wine and pay extra to have it shipped to them when they can get alcoholic beverages more easily and cheaply from stores. But Indiana's legislators were worried that wine ordered online or by phone could be carelessly delivered and end up in the hands of people under twenty-one—or at least that was what they were claiming.

Larry Satek of Satek Winery, who was the president of the Indiana Winery and Vineyard Association at the time, told me that the IWVA became more politically active in 2006 when many of the wineries found that their very existence was threatened by the legislation being pushed by wine and liquor industry wholesalers:

> For the first couple of years, up until 2005, the association more or less did the annual meeting and maybe a summer meeting for grape sales if somebody had some grapes. Our entire budget was about five thousand dollars. We had no lobbyists, we had no lawyers, we had nothing other than just a very simple 501c6 . . . After 2005, as we went into the 2006 legislative session, we started to realize that things needed to be changed dramatically. Pam and I went down to Indianapolis for what we thought was a one-hour meeting and didn't come home for four days. Because they almost . . . the house actually passed legislation at one point which would have required every Indiana winery to sell every bottle of wine to a wholesaler, and then we would have had to have bought it back in order to sell it out of the tasting room. That actually passed the house and was held up in committee by somebody who felt sorry for the industry in the senate in 2006.

Satek explained that since most Indiana wineries were small, the only way for them to turn a profit was by selling directly to customers at the wineries. If they had to give wholesalers a cut, only wineries that produced at least twenty-five thousand gallons would be able to survive. He estimated that would have only been a handful of wineries at most. He explained how the crisis was averted:

> When we got into real trouble, when Bill Oliver realized we were in trouble, he hired lobbyist Lisa Hays, who is still our current lobbyist. And I, on a whim and prayer, hired an attorney to represent us on the legal issues because we didn't know what the hell we were doing, and a publicist that would try to help get our story out. We charged assessing fees [to member wineries], and all of a sudden our budget went from, I don't know, five thousand to like a hundred thousand dollars in one year . . .

And it took forever—it seemed like forever—for it to finally get resolved. It got held up, and then the governor decided that we needed an alcohol bill. And he did what I think probably really should be obscene in the state, they call it a strip-and-insert piece of legislation, and in three days we drafted what is pretty much the current legislation. I was at a conference, the Eastern Wine Conference in Pennsylvania, and for three days I didn't go to a single meeting or a single anything. I just sat and faxed, emailed, and made telephone calls trying to hammer out the negotiations for getting at least some kind of deal, because we had three wineries that were totally dependent on wholesale, and that's why this particular obtuse way came together. They were not going to give wineries wholesale privileges, but we had three wineries that were going to go out of business immediately. One of them didn't even have their first tasting room. It was quite a mess. So eventually we ended up hammering out in the three days before the end of the session something for the strip-and-insert legislation which was not very well thought out and had lots of problems.

The compromise saved the Indiana wineries, but kept them hamstrung. They negotiated a law that allowed direct shipping to customers if they had (1) visited a given winery or purchased from its representatives at an event, (2) shown their driver's license or a state-issued identification card that indicated they were twenty-one, and (3) signed a card that the winery had to have on file before shipping telephone or online orders. In 2015, the legislature finally relented to complaints from winery owners and customers and changed the requirement to allow shipping with proof of age and a signature upon delivery.

Shipping directly from wineries to retailers such as grocery stores, liquor stores, and restaurants posed a second direct-sales issue, since it would also bypass wholesale distributors. States had been even more restrictive about this than about direct shipping to customers, probably because the latter are small change to the wholesale distributors. Grocery and liquor stores move volume. Compared with southern and eastern states, Midwestern states generally have made it a bit easier for wineries to sell directly to retailers. Ohio, Illinois, and Iowa allow direct sales to retailers with varying fees, requirements, and production or distribution limits that are fairly straightforward, with Iowa being the least restrictive. Indiana also has a "micro-wholesaler license" that permits distribution of up to twelve thousand gallons of wine and brandy a year to restaurants and retail stores. The oddity is that winery owners cannot hold the licenses. Someone else has to become the micro-wholesaler and help them out. The fee for the license is $100, but legal fees and insurance add thousands of dollars to the cost. So technically this arrangement maintains the three-tier structure while creating some legal and financial obstacles that can be discouraging to small wineries.

Mallow Run decided to go this route, assisted by a non-owner relative. While I was helping out with bottling one day, John Richardson showed me a small square painted on the production room floor, which every case of Mallow Run wine being distributed had to pass through to meet the letter of the three-tier law. This requirement captures the absurdity of the system pretty well. The wines distributed in this manner are still a very small percentage of total sales at most Indiana wineries, with the exception of Oliver, Easley, and Rettig Hill. But some direct distribution allows small wineries to generate name recognition and meet local demand at a nearby restaurant or liquor store on a limited basis outside the winery setting.

I will say more about the three-tier system in the final chapter. Suffice it to say here that many states were impacted by the *Granholm* decision, especially Illinois and Iowa, where the previous reciprocity arrangement was much less restrictive. Most states now issue permits to in-state and out-of-state wineries that allow them to ship directly to customers. There is substantial variation in the laws in these "permit states," including the fees and how many cases can be shipped. Wineries are required to file reports and pay excise and sales taxes. Some states require this monthly, others quarterly, and others annually. Consequently, a winery from a distant state, especially a smaller winery, is not likely to go to the trouble of doing all this for a handful of customers. In my visits to wineries across the four states, I noted that few ship out of state. So while technically in-state and out-of-state wineries have equal access to customers across state lines, in reality access to customers is still quite limited because of the reporting and fee requirements. If you are a customer, you still are not likely to be able to get that wine you liked from a winery in another state shipped to you.

We often assume in the United States that people can do pretty much what they want to as long as it doesn't violate the law. But we often lose sight of how laws can work in favor of one group and against the interests of others. When we don't like how we are treated and would like to see changes, we can join together with others who share our interests. This doesn't just happen; it takes a lot of effort. For many winery owners, as Larry Satek's account suggests, this is a whole other area of work that is required if their wineries are going to survive politically and be economically successful. They must spend time working together and with others to develop and maintain relationships and institutional arrangements that will assist them in their endeavors.

State-Level Wine Industry Organization

Winery owners have worked to organize their states' industries to further their interests in a number of ways. They have sought funding for educational institutions to advance research on grape and wine production and to provide assistance to winery and vineyard owners. They have created state-level industry associations to identify industry needs and serve as a collective voice when dealing with governments and the public. They have established state councils or committees to advise on government funding for research, marketing, and quality-improvement programs. And they have collaborated with state agriculture and tourism departments to attract customers and market their products and events. Each state is organized and operates a little differently, to a great extent due to differences in laws and how funding is channeled. Some wineries have also collaborated to establish wine trails and American Viticultural Areas. In contrast to most industries, winery owners often provide direct assistance and advice to each other. They see themselves as collaborators more than competitors. In the following sections, I provide an overview of the industry organization in Ohio, Indiana, Illinois, and Iowa, highlighting unique features and owners' perceptions of the strengths and weaknesses of their state-level systems.

Ohio: Strong State Support for Education and Marketing

Ohio began supporting the winery industry in the 1960s, when the Ohio Agricultural Research and Development Center (OARDC) in Wooster established viticulture and enology research and extension programs, as well as experimental vineyard plots along the Ohio River. The OARDC is one of many centers that are part of the very large Ohio State University system. Most people don't understand the labyrinthine structure of the contemporary state university. This isn't the place to go into that in detail, but I will try to put a few things in perspective for those less familiar. At state research universities such as Ohio State (and Purdue, Southern Illinois, and Iowa State, which I will be discussing below), tenure-track professors keep their positions and get promotions primarily through research and publication of their findings in peer-reviewed outlets. To a lay reader, this work is often perceived as rather narrow and esoteric, in part because that is precisely what much of it is. An academic researcher typically cannot move his or her area of study forward by rehashing what has been done, but must find questions to pursue that do not have clear answers. These are often little chinks in the generally accepted body of knowledge that typically makes up the introductory courses of disciplines and occasionally slips into the general public's awareness. Academic researchers are usually expected to procure funding for their research by writing grant proposals. Some research professors are expected to generate their own salaries, as well as the salaries of the extension specialists and graduate research assistants who work for them, through grant procurement. If there are no funded proposals, everyone involved may be looking for a new job. The pressure in terms of expectations and one's sense of responsibility for the livelihoods of others can be tremendous. Working conditions are commonly pleasant and even enjoyable, but this is demanding, stressful work.

Universities where agricultural research is an important part of the mission also typically have extension programs that make use of the existing body of knowledge in an area to help people working in agriculture and related industries. These programs are also increasingly involved in collecting data of various kinds, sometimes setting up experimental plots in different areas of a state and partnering with farmers or those working in an industry connected to agriculture to collect research data.

The OARDC does both research and extension work. As one of the largest state schools in the country, Ohio State has a dizzying array of campuses, centers, extension offices, and research stations throughout the state. In the area of wine and grape production, its program dwarfs those in the other three states in terms of the number of personnel involved. In addition to researchers, who may have appointments with centers and extension offices, these programs have other types of positions, which are often referred to as "staff" appointments in contrast to faculty appointments. Staff positions can range from directors of programs to specialists who may work in offices, in labs, or in the field assisting some industry or in some cases the general public. There are also faculty with staff appointments, but this is probably too much information, and you are probably thinking of reaching for your cell phone to check your text messages, so I will stop the general description here and get more specific.

Today, the OARDC has a number of specialists with various appointments across university and extension programs who assist with wine and especially grape production. David Scurlock, the extension outreach specialist, spends most of his time consulting with vineyard owners and managers in the northern part of the state. He also edits the *Ohio Grape-Wine Electronic Newsletter*. Todd Steiner manages the enology program. He conducts research on improving wine quality and also does much extension work assisting wineries with production problems. Dr. Imed Dami is both a professor at Ohio State and a viticulture extension specialist, focusing primarily on research. Other faculty members at the OARDC specialize in grape diseases, pests, and weeds that pose problems for vineyards. Most are located at the OARDC campus in Wooster, but one is at the South Centers campus in Piketon, and there is a research station in Ashtabula County in the northeastern part of the state that specializes in *vinifera* grape research. Research plots are located at each of these sites.

The OARDC has no dedicated enology or viticulture programs for students, but courses in these areas are offered as part of more general food science or horticulture and crop science programs. Kent State University offers two-year associate degree programs in viticulture and enology at its Ashtabula campus. Kent State Ashtabula is also part of the Viticulture and Enology Science and Technology Alliance (VESTA), which is funded by the National Science Foundation and administered by the University of Missouri. The program offers online courses through a partnership of seventeen universities and community colleges.

The Ohio Grape Industries Committee (OGIC), a state entity that works closely with OARDC wine and grape specialists and winery and vineyard owners, was established in 1982 by legislative mandate. Administered by the Ohio Department of Agriculture, the OGIC is chaired by the Ohio director of agriculture or the director's designee. The chair appoints five members, of whom two must earn their income from growing grapes and two from making wine. Three other members are the state liquor control superintendent or designee, the chief of the Ohio Department of Agriculture's Marketing Division, and an OARDC viticulture extension specialist who serves as a nonvoting member (Ohio Revised Code-924.51 2006). There are also five subcommittees with much broader representation that advise the OGIC. OARDC/OSU grape and wine specialists are represented on the Production Subcommittee, the Quality Subcommittee, and the Research Subcommittee, and are heavily represented on the latter. The other two subcommittees are Public Relations and Administrative/Budget (www.tasteohiowines.com). Winery and vineyard owners, others connected with the industry, and government officials fill out the various committees.

Christy Eckstein is the executive director of the OGIC. Winery owners, regardless of the size or location of their wineries and whether or not they had served on the OGIC, were quite effusive in complimenting her work. One owner captured the general sentiment of all I interviewed: "Christy Eckstein is always accessible. She's just the best. She's very helpful at all times."

Funding for the OGIC is provided by a tax of five cents per gallon that is collected on all wine sold in the state: three of the five cents are a permanent allocation from the state excise tax, and the other two cents are a temporary allocation from the same tax that must be renewed in the state budget every two years. The total excise tax is thirty-two cents on wine with 14 percent alcohol content or less, one dollar for wine that is over 14 percent, and more for vermouth and sparkling wines. Ohio's excise tax on wine that is 14 percent alcohol or less is the lowest of the four states I studied, and one of the lower rates in the country (Federation of Tax Administrators 2015). As a tax, these rates of course can change, and the uses to which they are apportioned can change.

One of the OGIC's projects has been to expand the production of grapes in the state. A couple of strategies have been tried, so far without much success. A pilot Vine Grant program provided funding to enable selected Ohio wineries to add one to five acres per vineyard each year, but it was later dropped.

The committee's Ohio Quality Wine program, which Todd Steiner oversees, recognizes well-made wines produced from Ohio grapes. Steiner told me that the program was a work in progress, but he thought they were making headway with it as a marketing tool. The OGIC also promotes all of Ohio's wineries through tasteohiowines.com and brochures, and funds market research to gauge public awareness of various initiatives.

The OGIC jointly organizes the Ohio Grape and Wine Conference with OARDC professors and staff and the Ohio Wine Producers Association (OWPA). The OARDC provides much of the programming, with wine and grape experts from around the country and even Canada commonly participating. Statewide conferences are common across the country. Most owners I interviewed religiously attend them to learn how to address various problems in the vineyard or winery. The OGIC also sponsors the annual Ohio Wine Competition, which is held every May at Kent State University Ashtabula, and is organized by staff there. Todd Steiner supervises the judging.

The Ohio Wine Producers Association focuses primarily on marketing and creating a positive identity for wineries in the state. In addition to the website (ohiowines.org), it promotes the industry to the public through brochures and events such as the statewide Vintage Ohio Wine Festival. The association also partners with groups in putting on festivals and other events throughout the state, and it manages most of the Ohio wine trails. The OWPA's board of directors is made up of winery and vineyard owners and employees. Donniella "Donnie" Winchell is the full-time executive director, a position she began on a part-time basis in 1978. Winchell is well known in the state and beyond, serving on many local, regional, and national boards and committees. For example, she serves on the board of WineAmerica, the National Association of American Wineries, and its government affairs committee (wineamerica.org/about/board-of-directors). She also serves on the Public Relations Subcommittee of the OGIC. The OWPA board of directors makes the formal decisions about the direction and programs the association pursues, but Winchell, who monitors industry developments both inside and outside the state, provides significant direction in relation to program and marketing ideas. In addition to Winchell, the OWPA has a small staff of full-time and part-time employees based in Geneva, located on the northeastern edge of the state along Lake Erie.

I first heard about one marketing workshop Winchell runs, "License to Steal," from some winery owners in Indiana, Illinois, and Ohio who raved about it and thought it was a great place to pick up new ideas. Winchell told me that the workshop developed out of gatherings that originally involved a small group of people from different states who wanted more opportunity to share marketing ideas than industry conference formats typically allowed. They met for a few years at a hotel near the Cleveland Airport before adopting the current name. She typically has participants from Ohio, Indiana, Illinois, Missouri, and Michigan, and at times from New York, Maryland, and Virginia. Attendees share what is working for them that other wineries can borrow or adapt. For example, Indiana borrowed the idea for creating the Vintage Indiana Wine and Food Festival from the Vintage Ohio event. Winchell said she "stole" the Indiana wine trails' "passport weekend," when customers receive a wine glass, a small gift, or a benefit of some kind for visiting multiple wineries along a trail.

The OWPA's services don't come cheap. Membership fees in the Ohio association are substantially higher than in the other three states. Some small winery owners felt that the cost of membership outweighed the benefits. As one explained, "I think that group is so geared to northeastern Ohio so much, they don't look at us very closely." On the other hand, this owner had participated in Winchell's "License to Steal" marketing event and was very positive about that. Another owner told me, "I was a member for many years. Donnie is a great spokesperson for Ohio grapes. But I decided not to do it, more or less for cost reasons. With Ohio Grape [Industries Committee] doing almost the same thing, I can save the money and buy a new tank." Others, whose wineries didn't participate in Vintage Ohio, thought the OWPA put too much effort into that event.

I mentioned these concerns to Donnie Winchell herself, and she said she hears them regularly. She told me the fees probably did seem somewhat high to those in the middle range of production, but that owners often lose sight of the benefits that are available to them as a result. Since the OWPA manages most wine trails, there is no additional membership fee to be part of a trail, whereas wineries in other states often pay thousands of dollars to belong to and promote their wine trails. Wineries can also get legal assistance through the OWPA that could easily cost them their membership fees and more if they were hiring an attorney on their own. She mentioned a number of marketing and advertising campaigns that drive customers to wineries along with the Vintage Ohio Wine Festival, which brings the wineries to the customers, and where participating wineries take home "big checks." In addition, the OWPA partners with and provides assistance to many local and regional festivals across the state. Winchell said these events have multiplied over the years, contributing to declining attendance at Vintage Ohio. Still, the festival attracted about twenty thousand attendees over two days in 2015. The event continues to generate substantial income for the association, which benefits all the members. The OWPA has supported grape research and the use of locally grown grapes, which is not a concern of wineries that use grapes and juice from California, New York, and other states. Winchell admitted that the office location and work demands made it difficult for her to get out to other parts of the state as much as she would like.

The complaints of some owners could in part be a result of a change in the OWPA's approach to working with them. Instead of initiating projects, the board of directors has shifted the association's focus to supporting members' initiatives. In my view, this is a logical outcome of the tremendous growth in the number of wineries across the state. In response to the criticism that Geneva-area wineries and vineyards received too much attention, Winchell pointed out that those wineries have worked collaboratively to make themselves an attraction and move the industry forward, and they grow most of the wine grapes in the state. As she noted, Geneva "painted the fire hydrants purple and green." The city also holds a fall Grape Jamboree.

A much smaller professional organization, the Winegrowers of Ohio, was organized by some of the larger wineries in the state to lobby for industry support after the *Granholm* decision. This makes Ohio different from the other three states, where the larger and more inclusive state industry associations take this role. While the Ohio Grape Industries Committee and educational opportunities pull Ohio owners together, the professional associations have generated some divisions. However, there is no doubt that the glass is well more than half full for the Ohio industry as a result of these different efforts.

Indiana: Small but Strong Technical and Marketing Support

One of the collective organizational efforts that have helped move the Indiana wine industry forward was the formation of the Indiana Wine Grape Market Development Council (more commonly referred to as the Indiana Wine Grape Council) and the Purdue Wine Grape Team. In 1989, Jim Butler and some other winery owners joined together to push for legislation that would allocate five cents of the forty-seven-cent state excise tax to support research, development, and marketing for their industry (Butler and Butler 2001, 146, 210). Whereas the similar tax in Ohio goes to the Ohio Grape Industries Committee, which is a state government agency, Indiana Code 7.1-4-13 channels the funds to Purdue's College of Agriculture.

The Wine Grape Council is an advisory group to the dean of the College of Agriculture, who appoints the members. The council consists of an odd number of seven to fifteen members, with the majority representing those who grow grapes or produce wine commercially. According to the bylaws, the dean designates the director of Purdue's Office of Agricultural Research as the council director, or that director can appoint someone else. The current director, Dr. Marshall Martin, is also senior associate director of agricultural research, an assistant dean in the College of Agriculture, and professor of agricultural economics. Got all that? Again, state research universities are big places, jobs get passed down and around, and people can have many titles and responsibilities. The council director, the chairperson of the Department of Horticulture and Landscape Architecture, and the chairperson of the Department of Food Science (or the designees of all three) serve as *ex officio* members, meaning they have no vote on council recommendations. The voting council members elect officers—a president, vice-president, and secretary (Indiana Wine Grape Market Development Council 2014).

The Wine Grape Team is housed on the Purdue University campus. It is funded by the excise tax allocation and provides support to the Indiana wine industry in the areas of viticulture, winemaking, and marketing. Dr. Bruce Bordelon is professor of viticulture at Purdue, and Dr. Christian Butzke is professor of enology, assisted by Jill Blume, whose job title is enology specialist. Jeanette Merritt was the marketing director until January 2016, when she started a new job with Indiana Pork, the state hog industry association.

I had met Jeanette Merritt before I interviewed her in 2011. She and her husband own a hog farm in Peru, Indiana, and she was roasting pigs for Mallow Run's anniversary celebration over a Labor Day weekend when my band was playing. Jeanette was responsible for marketing the whole wine industry in Indiana, or as she put it, "to make sure that people know that we have an industry in the state . . . and to make sure that they understand we have a *successful* industry, that we're not doing this by the seat of our pants" (her emphasis). She also assisted individual wineries, especially new wineries, with their marketing plans—"how we're going to do news releases and launch them and get social media plans put together."

In addition to providing Indiana wineries with marketing advice, Merritt was responsible for marketing initiatives such as the Vintage Indiana Wine and Food Festival and the "Try on Traminette" promotional campaign. She also assisted winery owners who wanted to set up a wine trail. She oversaw the Wineries of Indiana website (www.indianawines.org), which provides information on all the wineries in the state and links to their individual websites. In addition to serving as a source of information for customers interested in visiting wineries in the state, the website provides information on winemaking and growing grapes for amateurs and professionals.

Started in 2001, Vintage Indiana is a state festival devoted to "wine, food, and fun" that attracts wine enthusiasts to Indianapolis each year on a Saturday in June to sample wines and listen to music. Almost ten thousand people attended the 2014 event, tasting and purchasing the wines of twenty-seven Indiana wineries (Ganchiff 2014; www.vintageindiana.com). Attendance dropped to eighty-four hundred for the 2015 event, with twenty-nine wineries participating, or about 35 percent of the wineries in the state (Indiana Wine Grape Market Development Program 2015; www.vintageindiana.com). The event has become so popular that lines for tastings can be long and slow. There is no minimum case requirement for wineries to participate, but some wineries are hesitant due to inadequate stock. Larry Simmons, co-owner of Tonne Winery, told me during our interview in 2011 that Vintage Indiana was "a little out of our league yet." His cousin David, the owner of Simmons Winery in Columbus, had told Larry and Kevin Tonne they would probably need a hundred cases of wine and six people working the booth. Another winery owner who quit participating said it wasn't worth it: "Simply because it's become a place where people come to get free wine and they could care less what it is." Of course, it isn't free. Tickets for the 2015 event were $25 in advance, $35 at the gate, with a $50 early admission option for those interested in getting a head start and avoiding some of the lines. I have also attended the event enough times to know that while there may be some who come just to drink, many people are interested in learning about the wines and wineries.

For the wineries that do take part, Vintage Indiana provides an opportunity to introduce their wines to attendees who are mostly from densely populated central Indiana. It was at Vintage Indiana events that I first sampled a number of wines from wineries far to the north and south of Indianapolis. At the 2012 event, I tasted wines from Rettig Hill Winery for the first time. Rettig Hill doesn't have a tasting room, selling most of its wines through a handful of retail stores. I would have been hesitant to purchase its wines off the store rack without trying them first, but now I seek them out.

"Try on Traminette" is a marketing campaign that was launched when the Indiana Wine Grape Council adopted Traminette as Indiana's "signature" wine grape in 2009, at the recommendation of the Purdue Wine Grape Team. The idea was "to help create a regional identity for the state's wines" (Bordelon 2010, 1). A hybrid of Gewurztraminer and the French-American hybrid Joannes Seyve 23-416, the Traminette grape was first commercially available in 1996. Created for cooler climates and relatively disease tolerant, it was adopted in part because it generally grows well in any part of Indiana. The wine made from Traminette grapes also seems appropriate to me as the official Hoosier wine because it splits the difference for those preferring drier wines and the many Midwesterners who have a sweeter tooth. Commonly described as fruity and floral, and sometimes having some of Gewurztraminer's spiciness, it is produced by some Indiana wineries in two styles, a dry (although not necessarily completely dry) and a semi-dry or semi-sweet style, with the sweetness ranging according to the winemakers' preferences. Easley Winery's Traminette was selected as the "best off dry white wine" at the 2015 Mid-American Wine Competition.

In addition to these marketing efforts, Bruce Bordelon conducts research on grape production and provides support to grape growers, and Christian Butzke and Jill Blume conduct research and provide support to winemakers.

Bordelon's appointment is in Purdue's Horticulture and Landscape Architecture Department, and his responsibilities are split between extension work, research, and a course or two a year. Butzke's appointment is in the Department of Food Science, where Blume serves as enology specialist. Much of their time is devoted to helping commercial and amateur winemakers address problems with their wines and improve quality. They analyze a few hundred samples each year. Purdue does not have viticulture or enology majors, but students can take courses as part of their food science work. Butzke, with the assistance of Blume, teaches a very popular wine appreciation course that attracts hundreds of students interested in developing an understanding of wine. He also recently cofounded the company VinSense, which uses an integrated technology developed at Purdue to measure and map the distribution of soil moisture and temperature in a vineyard (Purdue University Research Foundation News 2015).

The Purdue Wine Grape Team is also responsible for the Indy International Wine Competition, the largest "scientifically organized and independent wine competition in the United States," according to the competition's website (www.indyinternational.org). Butzke serves as chief wine judge for the event and recruits a panel of judges from around the world. Blume is the executive director of the competition, and she and the marketing director assist with the arrangements and promotion. I am not sure how it stacks up with other competitions, since there is no formal ranking of these things, but it is a big event for a state that is not usually associated with wine. Many of the winery owners I talked to in Ohio, Illinois, and Iowa as well as Indiana participate, and their medals were proudly displayed in their tasting rooms. The competition has attracted entries from Europe, South America, Australia, New Zealand, and Africa in various years; thus the "international" label. When my friend Butch was visiting Canada, he and a winemaker in Ontario discussed the possibility of having Butch personally deliver some wine to the competition, since the winemaker was concerned about the cost and getting it there in a timely manner.

Indy International began in 1973 as the Indiana State Fair Wine Competition for amateur and commercial Indiana winemakers. It was held on the Indiana State Fairgrounds until it was moved to Purdue in 2010. Dr. Richard Vine, the first Purdue enologist, expanded the entries in 1992 and began accepting submissions from anywhere. Not only does the wine competition put Indiana on the wine industry radar, it gives Midwestern wineries the opportunity to compete with others nationally and internationally. Two Indiana wineries, River City in New Albany and Huber's, took home "Wine of the Year" awards for their Vignoles in 2012 and 2013, respectively. A California winery won in 2014, but Easley Winery's Traminette won in 2015. There is also a division just for Indiana wines, with a special award for the Indiana winery with the most medals, the Governor's Cup for the Indiana Winery of the Year. Huber's Winery has won this award eleven times since 1999.

The Indiana Winegrowers Guild, now the Indiana Winery and Vineyard Association (IWVA), was originally formed in 1975 to bring winery and vineyard owners as well as amateur wine enthusiasts together to promote the industry and improve viticulture. It was a loosely structured group that developed brochures with the Indiana Department of Commerce, started the state wine competition that eventually became the Indy International Wine Competition, and provided some technical support for its members. Much of that support was in the form of informal collaboration and sharing. Although industry advocacy was always part of its mission, the IWVA became much more politically active in the wake of the *Granholm* decision, and continues to pay for a lobbyist to pursue the industry's interests in the state legislature. It has also begun recognizing a state legislator each year for work that supports the industry.

At one time the IWVA put on its own annual conference to help educate its members with the assistance of the Purdue Wine Grape Team and other outside experts, but it now participates in the annual Indiana Horticulture Congress and Trade Show. The three-day "Hort Congress" is held in January and organized by Purdue and various horticultural associations, including the IWVA. Sessions address a wide range of crops, not just grapes, but the IWVA holds its annual meeting at this event and carves out a number of sessions dedicated to grape growing, winemaking, marketing, and other areas of interest.

Besides the Purdue Wine Grape Team marketing assistance, Indiana wineries receive less marketing assistance from the state than is the case in the other three states I studied. The Indiana Office of Tourism Development sponsors a website (visitindiana.com) and publishes a state travel guide, but wineries must pay to be promoted in these. Only eighteen wineries were listed on the website in August 2015.

Illinois: Nudging the Industry Forward

Illinois is unique among the four states I am examining here in that owners and specialists have taken on much greater responsibility for the welfare of the industry with much less state assistance. State funding problems and decisions effectively forced them down this road. Illinois at one time had an industry council along the lines of Ohio's and Indiana's. The Illinois Grape and Wine Resources Council, started in 1997, brought new resources to the industry. Similar to Ohio's, the program was funded through the Illinois Department of Agriculture. It was initially allocated two cents from the $1.39 per gallon wine excise tax, but legislation passed in 1999 changed its funding to $500,000 per year for a five-year period supported by hotel and motel taxes. The funding made it possible for the University of Illinois at Urbana-Champaign and Southern Illinois University Carbondale to partner for research purposes and maintain a state enologist, viticulturist, and marketing specialist. Imed Dami, now at the OARDC, was hired in 1999 as viticulturist at SIU Carbondale. A number of owners mentioned that Dr. Dami, a specialist in cold-weather growing conditions, had moved their industry forward. Jim Ewers, general manager and partner at Blue Sky, said that Dami helped them lay out their vineyard and select grape varieties. Paul Renzaglia, the owner of Alto Vineyards, said, "Imed was the greatest thing. He was the only true viticulturist in the state." Renzaglia said the experimental station Dami established provided helpful information about the appropriateness of certain varieties for that region.

The council's funding was cut in 2003 by Governor Rod Blagojevich, whom some winery owners referred to as "the crook" for reasons that they must have felt required no elaboration even though the previous governor also served prison time. Blagojevich, noting that the council had failed to spend $370,000, decided to address part of the state's $5 billion budget deficit by ending the program's funding. As a result, Dami moved to the OARDC, and the Illinois state enologist, Dr. Stephen Menke, became Pennsylvania's state enologist (Gregory 2003; Smyth 2003, 2004). For fiscal year 2006, the legislature subsequently restored $400,000 in funding, which went directly to the two universities and the Illinois Grape Growers and Vintners Association (IGGVA) for research and technical assistance (Illinois Department of Agriculture 2005), but the damage had been done: the council was defunct.

As a result of the state government's chronic financial problems, the IGGVA stepped up to take over some of the functions formerly handled by the Illinois Grape and Wine Resources Council. The IGGVA and universities continued to seek state funding and were awarded some, but it was sporadic. A program of agricultural research and effective extension support requires continuous funding. When $142,500 was cut in 2012, grape research and the state enologist position were again threatened (Ganchiff 2012). The IGGVA took over the responsibility of maintaining the state enologist position with some state assistance. The association also maintains a website (www.illinoiswine .com) that lists the state's wineries with contact information and links to their individual websites.

As of 2015, no state excise funds were dedicated to the wine grape industry in Illinois, even though its $1.39 per gallon excise tax on wine is one of the highest in the nation. Some research and program grant funding assistance continued to be available through the Illinois Department of Agriculture, but no consistent state funding was available. This situation leaves the state industry at a disadvantage in relation to long-term research initiatives and extension assistance. The Illinois Office of Tourism does maintain a website (www .enjoyillinois.com), which provides a list of Illinois wineries, divided into four regions, with one stretching the length of the state along the Mississippi River. The website promotes some wine festivals along with other major events and tourist destinations in the state.

As the primary source for technical and marketing support to Illinois wineries and vineyards, enologist Bradley Beam is known throughout the state. He assists wineries with production startup and problems and is responsible for organizing educational programs, which include the annual conference and workshops. He also instituted regional roundtables, where winemakers can discuss quality issues and bring samples of their wines at different stages of production for others to taste. These workshops were quite popular with the winemakers I interviewed. Beam also organizes the Illinois State Fair Wine Competition. Unlike the enologists affiliated with universities in the other three states, he has no laboratory, so wineries must send problem wines to commercial labs for analysis. Instead, he spends a lot of time on the road visiting wineries and providing education and assistance onsite.

Illinois is similar to Ohio and Indiana in that no university in the state offers dedicated enology or viticulture programs, but students can take courses in those areas as part of food science and horticulture programs. For several years, Rend Lake College in Ina offered two-year VESTA programs in enology and viticulture similar to Kent State Ashtabula's, but they were dropped in 2015. Dr. Bradley Taylor, associate professor and viticulture specialist at the Horticulture Center at Southern Illinois University Carbondale, conducts research and provides assistance to winery and vineyard owners. He was at Blue Sky Vineyard with a graduate student checking on some vines the day I visited. Jim Ewers told me that Taylor had asked him to cancel half an order of Cabernet Franc vines and plant three or four other clones of that grape variety for research purposes, which Ewers gladly did. Elizabeth Wahle also provides assistance with grapes and other crops through the University of Illinois Extension program. Both Taylor and Wahle present at the IGGVA Annual Conference and Winter Wine Festival and do workshops with Bradley Beam. The Winter Wine Festival is a wine-tasting and food-pairing event open to the public that kicks off the annual conference weekend. SIU Carbondale has established a Fermentation Science Institute, which will be doing laboratory analysis for beer, wine, and distilled spirits producers in the state. A new undergraduate degree in fermentation science was approved to begin in the summer of 2016 despite statewide cuts in funding that were affecting programs at SIU and other universities throughout the state (Krause 2016).

As part of the Grape and Wine Resources Council collaboration between SIU Carbondale and the University of Illinois at Urbana-Champaign, Dr. Bill

Shoemaker, now retired, and several other University of Illinois professors conducted cold-weather grape research at the St. Charles Horticulture Research Center. Part of the University of Illinois Extension program, the center was located outside Chicago. IGGVA funding and university funding helped maintain the experimental plot and support some research as state support dried up. Dr. Shelby Henning, took over as director in 2013. When I spoke with him in August 2015, he was making progress with bringing the vineyard research program back to life but continued to be stymied by the lack of state funding. Sadly, the university announced the center was closing that December. Henning confirmed the closing when I spoke with him in May 2016, and was quite dejected about the situation, describing his work there as his dream job.

With many industry resources skewed to the southern and central parts of the state, the IGGVA contracted with Denise Cimmarrusti to assist wineries and vineyards in northern Illinois. Cimmarrusti previously assisted with research and outreach at the St. Charles Horticulture Research Center. Chris Lawlor-White, at Galena Cellars, said she felt this gave the northern area some credibility relative to the southern area, where much of the state's research continued to be conducted.

I asked the Illinois winery owners I interviewed about their use of viticulture and enology specialists in the state. Most were critical of the lack of dependable state support for education and research in their industry, frequently mentioning that no funds come back to the industry from the wine excise tax. However, they were very positive about the support they had received under the circumstances. Beam, Taylor, Wahle, and Cimmarrusti were all mentioned as invaluable resources.

Iowa: Pulling Together for Rapid Growth

The Iowa wine industry has developed a supportive infrastructure that has contributed to the rapid growth of wineries since the Iowa Wine Growers Association (IWGA) was formed in 1999. Iowa's state government has done much to create a favorable climate for small wineries in rather short order. Perhaps most notable is that the $1.75 wine excise tax does not apply to retail sales at wineries for consumption on or off premise. The tax applies only to wine sold through wholesalers (Iowa Legislature 2015). This is a tremendous benefit for small wineries that mostly sell wine from their tasting rooms.

The Iowa Department of Agriculture and Land Stewardship formed the Iowa Wine and Grape Advisory Council in January 2000. The council was composed of representatives from the department, the Iowa Economic Development Authority, development districts across the state, Iowa State University, and vineyard and winery owners, and its objective was to reestablish the wine industry in the state. The hope was "to encourage agricultural diversity, economic development, tourism, and enhance the quality of life in Iowa" (Ovrom, n.d.). On February 20, 2001, Ron Mark, owner of Summerset Winery in Indianola, and Paul Tabor, owner of Tabor Home Vineyards and Winery in Baldwin, made a request to the Iowa Senate's Agriculture and Natural Resources Appropriations Subcommittee for ten cents of the state's $1.75 per gallon wine excise tax to "be designated to the development of an Iowa Grape Growers Industry" (Iowa Legislative Fiscal Bureau 2001). As the subcommittee minutes note, "It is estimated the funds would be approximately $223,000 and would be used to provide technical assistance to Iowa vineyards" (ibid.). No funds were allocated, but the Iowa Grape and Wine Development Commission and the Iowa Grape and Wine Development Fund were established to assist the state agriculture department in developing programs for "establishing, improving, or expanding vineyards or winemaking operations, including wineries" (Iowa Code 2009). Modest funding ($75,000) was provided for the 2003, 2004, and 2005 fiscal years, and then 5 percent of the excise tax was appropriated thereafter. The Development Commission and Development Fund were rescinded in 2014, and funding was shifted to Iowa State University and its Midwest Grape and Wine Industry Institute (MGWII).

The Iowa Wine and Beer Promotion Board was created in 1986, well before the establishment of the IWGA and other state programs. It was originally placed under the control of the Iowa Department of Economic Development, which was renamed the Iowa Economic Development Authority (IEDA) in 2011. Made up of three members representing Iowa breweries, wineries, and the IEDA, the board advises the IEDA on programs to promote wine and beer produced in the state. For many years, the amount of funding it received was determined by the commissioner of the IEDA (and the Department of Economic Development before that). Later it was allotted a portion of the excise tax after other legislated appropriations were deducted. In 2011, $100,000 of its funds were legislatively allocated to the MGWII. The amount was increased to $120,000 in 2012. In 2013, the Promotion Board was put under the institute's control despite the protests of the Iowa Brewers Guild (Real Beer 2012).

By 2013, $250,000 was being appropriated for the Midwest Grape and Wine Industry Institute from the excise tax, with the remainder of the income (projected in meeting minutes to be $25,000) going to the state economic development authority to fund the Iowa Wine and Beer Promotion Board (Iowa Wine and Beer Promotion Board 2013). The MGWII is a relative newcomer to the list of university enology and viticulture programs. Approved by the Iowa Board of Regents in 2006, initially it was more like the OARDC program at Ohio State than the Purdue Wine Grape Team because it did not have marketing responsibilities. Now the funding for the Promotion Board goes through the MGWII.

Institute staff conduct wine and grape research, provide extension services to wineries and vineyards, and are responsible for coordinating and evaluating wines for the Iowa Quality Wine Consortium. MGWII and Iowa State grape and fruit specialists are involved with the Northern Grapes Project, which is a collaboration of researchers across a number of cold-climate states led by a Cornell University researcher. It was launched in 2011 with a two-year $2.5 million grant from the U.S. Department of Agriculture, of which the institute received $500,000. After a year without funding, the grant was renewed for two years in 2014 (Iowa State University News Service 2011).

Iowa State offers some courses and workshops related to viticulture and enology, but no degrees. However, three community colleges offer programs. Des Moines Area Community College has a viticulture and enology program but offers a certificate only in viticulture. The program uses blended courses that require some classroom attendance but are predominantly conducted online. Northeast Iowa Community College, with campuses in Peosta and Calmar, offers certificate and associate degree programs in conjunction with VESTA. Kirkwood Community College in Cedar Rapids offers certificates in both viticulture management and winemaking and winery facility management. It has a 1.5-acre vineyard and operates a teaching winery that sells its wine to the public.

When I asked Joel Kopsa of John Ernest about his use of the enology and viticulture programs in the state, he told me, "Iowa State is probably for the bigger guys. But they've been good. I had a problem with La Crosse wine, and they helped me out. I do get a lot of good information from them." Then he quipped, "I should take that back since I'm a Hawkeye fan," referring to the University of Iowa nickname. He said he prefers to consult with his friend Lucas McIntire, Kirkwood's winemaker and vineyard operations manager, because the Kirkwood vineyard grows a lot of the same grapes as his vineyard.

The prime mover of the Iowa winery industry has been the Iowa Wine Growers Association. Vineyard owners Ron Mark and Paul Tabor were instrumental in its founding. The IWGA continues to press the legislature for additional funding to expand the work of the Midwest Grape and Wine Industry Institute (Iowa Wine Growers Association, n.d.). The IWGA also organizes an annual conference with presentations by MGWII staff and experts from other states on wine and grape production.

In 2000, vineyard and winery owners in Iowa's Missouri River Valley area, where the Council Bluffs Grape Growers Association once operated, formed the Western Iowa Grape Growers Association. The association is working to "rebuild the grape and wine industry of Western Iowa" (westerniowagrapegrowers.org).

The Mid-American Wine Competition is held in Iowa, sponsored by Des Moines Area Community College. It is open to wineries in all the "Mid-

American" states, as well as Montana, but there are relatively few participants from the more distant areas. Dr. Murli Dharmadhikari, director of the Midwest Grape and Wine Industry Institute, serves as a judge and technical advisor. In addition to a typical blind competition, there is a competition in which wines are paired with food for judging. In 2015, Eagles Landing Winery in Marquette, Iowa, near the Mississippi River, won four gold medals in the pairings contest. From the other side of the river, Galena Cellars won the pairing with lamb for its Eric the Red. There is also a wine label competition, with prizes awarded in various categories (including best label, best series, and most humorous). Iowa wineries are heavily represented in the competition, in part because there is a special competition for Iowa wines similar to what the Indy International competition does for Indiana wines (Mid-American Wine Competition 2015).

Dealing with Government Agencies and Regulations

Once political squabbles calm down and organizational relationships stabilize a bit, winery owners are still faced with responding to the existing set of laws and regulations. The regulation of wine is divided between the state and federal governments, with the state overseeing sales, distribution, and consumption, and the federal government regulating how the product is defined or classified and labeled. Both levels of government tax wine as well as all alcohol products, with the federal and most state taxes varying depending on the percentage of alcohol in the product. As already noted, excise taxes can be wildly different from state to state, from a low of eleven cents per gallon in Louisiana to a high of $2.50 in Alaska. Wineries that fail to abide by federal or state laws can be fined or lose their licenses, and their owners can even be sent to prison.

Product labeling is one of the areas controlled by the federal government. The Alcohol and Tobacco Tax and Trade Bureau (TTB), which is part of the U.S. Department of Treasury, oversees the rather tight labeling requirements. We all love reading federal regulations, right? No. So I will spare you all but a few details. You can learn as much as you want to about what winery owners must know and do with their bottle labels at the TTB's well-laid-out website (www .ttb.gov/wine/wine-labeling.shtml). While you are on the site, you can read all the tax requirements, too, just as winery owners must do.

A number of things need to appear on a wine bottle label, although there are many exceptions and intricacies in the rules. For example, wine is required to have the percentage of alcohol on the label, but there is an exception. If the alcohol content is between 7 and 14 percent, the label can have "Table Wine" or "Light Wine" instead of the exact percentage. One benefit of using the designation "Table Wine" is that the label does not have to be changed if the alcohol content changes substantially. The percentage here is significant because the federal tax is $1.07 per gallon up to 14 percent, and $1.57 over that up to 21 percent, where it then jumps to $3.15. Artificially carbonated wines are taxed at $3.30 per gallon, and sparkling wines that are naturally fermented at $3.40. Small wineries that make less than 250,000 gallons per year, which would be most all wineries in the Midwest, are eligible for a credit of ninety cents per gallon for amounts produced up to 100,000 gallons, not including sparkling wines (Alcohol and Tobacco Tax and Trade Bureau 2014).

There are also label rules about varietal designations, appellations of origin, and dates. In order for a label to carry a varietal designation such as Chardonnay or Vignoles, at least 75 percent of the wine in the bottle must be from that particular grape variety, and all of that 75 percent must be sourced from an appellation of origin indicated on the label. Wine labeled as Concord or one of the other *labrusca* grapes must have at least 51 percent of that variety. An appellation of origin can be a country, state, or county, or a geographic region that countries recognize, such as the AVA designation in the United States or the *appellation d'origine contrôlée* (AOC) in France. However, if the wine is from an AVA and includes the grape variety, it must contain 85 percent of that grape by volume from that area. In addition, not only does it matter where the grapes are grown, but the winery producing the wine must be within the area designated by that appellation of origin to indicate the grape variety on the label. Recent rule changes also allow wineries to use varietal labels for grapes from adjacent states (Alcohol and Tobacco Tax and Trade Bureau 2015).

There is an exception to the varietal rule. A winemaker can indicate the variety without an appellation of origin by including the wording "For Sale Only in" followed by the name of the state in which the producer is located and restricting sales. That exempts the winemaker from interstate commerce rules, and the appellation rule then doesn't apply. Jim Butler told me this is a good way to know that the grapes used to make the wine in that bottle were probably shipped in from out of state. Many wineries come up with fanciful names for their wines instead of indicating the kind of grapes they contain. This allows them to use the same label from year to year even though the grapes used to make the wine might change.

No approval is required for label changes pertaining to vintage—the date when the grapes were harvested. Dates can also be left off entirely. By not including a date, wineries can blend juice from different vintages. At Buck Creek Winery, Jeff Durm dates his corks instead of putting dates on the label since corks aren't regulated. Other wineries provide date information on their wine lists but not on their labels.

The label regulations were established for the purpose of protecting consumers from those who might attempt to sell swill as something better. This

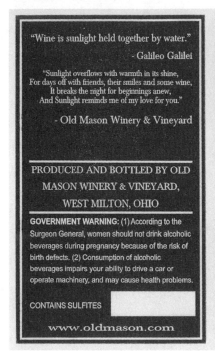

Figure 6.1. Old Mason Winery wine bottle label with fanciful name. The label reflects the masonry trade across three generations of the Clark family. Note the designation "Table Wine," which can be used for wines with an alcohol content ranging from 7 to 14 percent. Label courtesy of Old Mason Winery, used with permission.

was a real problem with alcoholic beverages prior to the establishment of regulations. Labels provide some useful information if you care to know more about your wine than the alcohol content. For example, according to the TTB's (2008) brochure on wine labels,

> "Estate Bottled" means that 100 percent of the wine came from grapes grown on land owned or controlled by the winery, which must be located in a viticultural area. The winery must crush and ferment the grapes, and finish, age, and bottle the wine in a continuous process on their premises. The winery and the vineyard must be in the same viticultural area. (Alcohol and Tobacco Tax and Trade Bureau 2008)

Mallow Run has often had an estate-sourced Chardonel made from the vineyard's own grapes. But the label cannot indicate it is estate sourced because the winery is not in an AVA. One year when they had a Chardonel made with their own grapes and another from Indiana grapes, they indicated their estate-grown version with a black capsule and also noted it on their wine list. For either version, they could only put "Indiana Grown Table Wine" on the label. If they bought the grapes from another state, they would likely put "American Table Wine." This designation is often used by a winery to avoid a label change when the source of its grapes is likely to change from year to year.

Another designation that can appear on a label is "Cellared and Bottled by." Most consumers probably aren't aware that this statement is used when a winery does not make the wine itself, but ships it in from another producer, puts it in "the cellar"—a tank or maybe an oak barrel if it is going to be further aged—then bottles it. This is not a deceptive practice because of the statement, even though the winery name on the label suggests to most customers that the winery made the wine.

In the days before the TTB approval process went online, wineries had to mail their labels in and wait as long as six months for a response. A rejection could really jam a winery up with finished wine in bottles that could not be sold without a label. Jim Butler said that at one time a service could be hired that would hand deliver labels and speed things up, but after the anthrax scares in 2001, submissions had to be quarantined until they could be analyzed. The new system has made the process faster, and most of the winery owners I interviewed said that continuing improvements had made it reasonably user friendly. Faster, however, does not mean fast. The TTB states that since the number of applications it receives has continued to increase, "you should allow adequate time for a 90-day application review process within your business plan and anticipate that we may require you to make revisions to your labels or formulas" (Alcohol and Tobacco Tax and Trade Bureau 2013).

Wineries must also keep extensive records and submit quarterly reports to the TTB on their wine on hand, both bottled and bulk, as well as on their sales. Larger wineries may report more frequently depending on the quantity produced. This is some of the time-consuming, routine drudgery that is absolutely necessary when making wine for public consumption. The TTB will occasionally send auditors to a winery to check its records and inventory and may do a chemical analysis. One owner told me that TTB investigators were at his winery for six days and were "very tough": they "put the fear of God in all of us in the state."

The TTB is also responsible for approving applications for the establishment of American Viticultural Areas. An AVA designation is a way for wineries and vineyards in a certain area to distinguish themselves from those in other areas in terms of certain unique characteristics, but it is primarily used for marketing purposes, in the hope of achieving some name recognition. The TTB requires "evidence" about the appropriateness of the name for an area, its boundaries, and distinguishing features such as climate, soils, and physical features and how these differentiate it from surrounding areas. They also ask for descriptions and locations of the vineyards in the area, and have certain requirements and restrictions about all these things.

At one time the Ohio River Valley AVA was geographically the largest in the country, with 16,640,000 acres stretching along the Ohio River through West Virginia, Ohio, Kentucky, and Indiana. It was unseated from the number one spot in 2009 by the Upper Mississippi Valley AVA, which includes parts of Illinois, Iowa, Minnesota, and Wisconsin, and covers 19,144,960 acres and 29,914 square miles. In 2013, the Indiana Uplands area became the first completely Indiana AVA, stretching from Bloomington to the Ohio River (www .indianauplands.com). According to Jim Butler, who did much of the work in establishing the area, one problem the effort ran into was that the proposed Indiana Uplands AVA overlapped with the existing Ohio Valley AVA. It is possible to have overlapping AVAs, but there are certain requirements and restrictions. The simplest solution was to remove the Uplands area from the Ohio River Valley AVA. Butler also told me that the Indiana Uplands wineries set themselves up as an agricultural cooperative along the lines of Sunkist and Blue Diamond to make themselves eligible for various federal grants.

Although AVAs are supposed to reflect some common elements of terroir, they also reflect political decisions in terms of which wineries get included and which get left out. The TTB offers a period for comment on proposals for those who have some concern. For example, in 2005, two proposals were submitted to the TTB for the Shawnee Hills region of southern Illinois, one for a smaller area that included only five wineries at the time (one of which made only apple wine—AVAs are for grapes), and another for a much larger area. Dr. James A. Osberg, a former employee of the Office of Economic and Regional Development at Southern Illinois University Carbondale, wrote a letter in support of designating the larger area. He indicated that he had assisted in the formation of the Illinois Grape and Wine Resources Council and other regional development efforts in the area. He argued that the larger area was not substantially different in degree days or heat and moisture, as claimed in the proposal for the smaller area, and noted that the larger area had "over 80 families of growers in the Greater Shawnee Grape Growers Association. These growers had been actively discussing the creation of a 'Greater Shawnee AVA' since 2000." Osberg suggested that the petitioners for the smaller area must be pursuing some competitive advantage by restricting the AVA footprint to "some gerrymandered version" of the region (Osberg 2005). Despite his protests and the competing proposal, the TTB went with the geographically smaller footprint.

In addition to shipping laws, states have a host of regulations governing the sale of alcoholic beverages, which can vary substantially from one state to the next. I remember going across state lines in the 1970s to purchase alcoholic beverages in a state where the legal drinking age was eighteen or nineteen. Ronald Reagan put an end to that, requiring states to make the minimum age twenty-one in order to receive federal highway funds. Other than this commonality pushed by the federal government, the variation in regulations from state to state can be substantial.

One area of difference across the states is offsite sales. In Indiana, Illinois, and Iowa, for example, wineries can offer tastings at farmers' markets. Ohio wineries were working to get that provision into the state law in 2015. I was told by a reliable source that the grocery stores were the obstacle because they feared that the growth of farmers' markets in the state would cut into their business (which is a national trend). Wineries also want to be able to offer tastings and sell wine at festivals or other events. In Indiana, wineries that want to sell at events have to apply to the state's Alcohol and Tobacco Commission (ATC) for a permit. This is the agency that also issues their license to do business. In 2014, wineries were limited to forty-five events. Many owners told me that sales at these events are extremely important to their bottom lines. Some complained about inconsistencies with how the law is interpreted by ATC permit processors. When I asked about his experience with these inconsistencies, one owner said:

> Well, you know, to their defense, the laws are so ambiguous and they leave a lot of stuff out. I really can't fault them for what happens. We just kind of hope that they're going to work with us and get it ironed out. We are trying to play by the rules, you know, as convoluted as the rules are.

Wineries also have to report the number of gallons of wine they produce, sell, and have on hand and pay the excise tax on any wine sold. Reporting and payment frequency varies by state and by the amount produced and sold, but typically the reports are submitted monthly. In Indiana, wineries have to file monthly reports with the Indiana Department of Revenue on the quantity of wine produced, purchased, and sold. There is a 10 percent penalty if the report is not submitted by the twentieth of the following month. The deadline is the fifteenth day of the following month in Illinois. Winery owners must pay close attention to tax requirements and any changes in those requirements. State industry associations are often helpful in tracking and reporting changes.

Wineries also face challenges at the state level in dealing with tourism offices and transportation departments. If your winery relies on customers coming to your door, then you want them to know where you are. Recall that I first discovered Mallow Run by seeing an informational sign on I-65 that was almost ten miles from the winery. In addition to regulating distribution, states also regulate highway signage. The sign regulation was a problem for Cedar

Creek Winery, since the road it is on intersects a less traveled highway, Indiana State Road 252. That was the only location where the state would allow Larry Elsner to post a sign. SR 252 intersects the heavily traveled SR 37 a couple of miles from the winery, as well as SR 135 in nearby Morgantown, a common route to the popular destinations of Nashville and Brown County State Park. The state wouldn't allow signs along either of the more heavily traveled state highways. Elsner finally had to pay for a billboard on SR 37 to inform drivers of the winery's location nearby. In contrast, Mallow Run benefits from state signage on SR 37, since Whiteland Road crosses it, as well as I-65 almost ten miles in the opposite direction, which I learned later is the state's distance limit for winery signage.

To be eligible for highway signs, some states set a mandatory minimum number of hours that a place of business must be open. John Fouts, owner of the now closed Grateful Goat Vineyard and Winery, had to quit his job in order to be open five days a week, six hours a day, since that was the Indiana require-ment to qualify for a highway sign. Although government regulations can be a heavy burden for new winery owners, over time the burden lightens as they become familiar with regulations, routinize related tasks, and add employees.

Costs versus Benefits of State Expenditures

States provide a tremendous amount of economic development money to all sorts of businesses through grants, subsidized loans, and tax abatements. Typi-cally those funds are targeted to businesses that show promise of economic growth and the potential to develop jobs. Clearly, the wine industries in the four states I studied are on an upward trajectory and have contributed sub-stantially to their states' tax bases and employment opportunities. Larry Satek put Indiana's investment in the state's Wine Grape Council and the Purdue Wine Grape Team this way:

> It was a tremendously wise investment by the people in 1990 when they chose to do that. The total expenditure since 1992, that's twenty years, probably six or seven million dollars. They have created a two-hundred-fifty- to three-hundred-million-dollar-a-year and growing tourism—agritourism—industry. I wish I had stocks that gave that kind of payback. And that's all the more reason to take some of the handcuffs off the marketing, because all we would do is grow and get bigger.

State support is not without controversy. A conservative policy group in Illinois objected to the use of state funds for the wine industry (Rasmussen 2014). This is somewhat ironic, since Illinois's allocation of funding has been the worst of the four states I studied in terms of providing the consistent long-term support necessary for further development of the industry. Some wineries in Iowa have also been criticized for receiving farm winery tax abatements even though they don't grow anything and because farm wineries' tasting rooms are taxed as farm buildings instead of commercial properties (Jordan 2014).

State funding of business is certainly a political issue and should be thoughtfully considered by elected officials, since their decisions determine the winners and losers in the contest over limited resources and shape their states' economic futures. The problem is that their decisions are often influenced by those who have the most resources to push the decision process in a certain direction. Political support commonly flows to big corporations, which have plenty of money to spend on lobbyists, managers, and political campaign donations to court politicians in a manner that local businesses and state industries cannot afford to do. Big businesses can make promises about creating a large number of jobs and bringing in a large amount of revenue for a state. The problem is that these businesses are often national or global and can expand and contract in unpredictable ways. The interests and decisions of major corporations are usually focused on factors much broader than their one manufacturing plant or office in a particular state. They may take a city's or state's money and start to get things rolling, then have a change of heart when circumstances change. Big corporations also have less of a sense of local responsibility to communities than local businesses do. This is part of the reasoning behind the "buy local" movement, which I will discuss in the final chapter.

States and the federal government also support educational institutions in part to prepare people for jobs. I work at a university, and a common discussion there is about the kinds of work we are, and should be, preparing our students for. Our students receive state scholarships, federal grants, and subsidized loans, which are commonly justified as necessary to prepare them for employment. The wine industries in each state, as well as nationally and globally, are creating jobs and need an educated workforce. Certainly states and the federal government must prioritize with the limited resources at their disposal. But consistent funding of research and educational programs pays dividends over piecemeal approaches. Wine industry knowledge and skills, though specific in some ways, are also quite transferable to other kinds of work.

Winery owners are not simply looking for handouts; they have put a great deal of work into their state industries themselves. Many vineyard owners assist university researchers by planting experimental varieties or sharing their expertise at state conferences and workshops. Winery and vineyard owners serve on committees and advisory councils, and they counsel and support those newer to the industry if and when they are interested in stepping up to leadership positions.

University experts have made the most of the limited funding they have been provided. Many work together across state lines, blending their different areas of expertise to conduct research on how different conditions and treatments affect grape and wine production. They serve as judges for each other at wine competitions, as speakers at each other's conferences and workshops, and as consultants when problems arise in a neighboring state.

Providing state support to grow good grapes and make good wine is certainly not as important as feeding the hungry and housing the homeless or researching and trying to understand the circumstances that contribute to those problems so they can be alleviated. But as Larry Satek argued, state support has provided a return on investment that suggests that it should at least be continued if not increased, and Illinois winery owners would like to see it become more stable. In the next chapter, I consider other problems and issues that cut across state lines and are on the minds of owners and industry experts.

7

The Challenges of
Identity and Quality

As a student of social and institutional change, I am interested in under-standing what brings changes about in the world as well as what keeps change from happening. One thing we can't change is where we are born or the circumstances we are born into. Winery owners certainly have some choice about where their wineries are brought into existence, but their decisions are often constrained by where they live, their relationships, and whatever resources they can bring to bear, such as existing property they wish to use, a comfortable retirement income or financial nest egg of some sort, and what they know about making wine and growing grapes. Their efforts can be aided by certain opportunities and resources, such as the opportunity to draw on the knowledge of industry specialists and the benefits provided by government assistance. At the same time, they are constrained by obstacles legal, practical, and, as I will explore more below, geographical.

One of the consequences of the division of the world into nation-states and the division of nation-states into states or provinces is that people or groups may find themselves having more in common in terms of geography and cul-ture with people who live nearby but just across state lines than with people in other parts of their own state. But each state has its own political system, which defines the legal circumstances for the people within its boundaries and requires them to share those circumstances whether they like it or not. That doesn't keep ideas from being generated or from flowing across state lines, with calls to be more like the state next door. Midwestern winery own-ers generally get along well with the other winery owners both within their own state and across state lines, and have worked together to create effective, collaborative state-level entities to advance their common interests, such as the councils, committees, industry associations, and educational resources discussed in the previous chapter. Nevertheless, winery owners often find it challenging to develop a common identity and sense of purpose with owners in other parts of their state. Differences in state laws also make collaborations across state lines difficult.

The four states I studied shared some general challenges, which many owners and industry specialists talked about as issues that needed to be resolved if their state wine industries were going to move forward. The biggest challenge they collectively face is that less than 10 percent of the wine purchased by residents in their states is produced within the state. In addition to the distribution issues discussed in the previous chapter, owners most frequently spoke of their challenges in relation to identity and quality. They were concerned about developing a definable identity in terms of what Midwestern wineries and their wines *are* collectively and what distinguishes their own state's wines from wines in other states or countries. Their concerns about quality were simply that Midwestern winemakers need to be producing the best wine they can possibly produce. Identity and quality are not mutually exclusive. If quality is poor, it can spoil the collective identity or reputation of wineries in the state or region.

The Identity Problem: What Is Midwestern Wine?

Midwest wineries have an identity problem. Unless wine drinkers have taken the time to do some exploring, they too often assume that the wines made in the Midwest are mostly sweet and generally inferior. And indeed, the best-selling wines at most Midwestern wineries do tend to be sweeter *labrusca* varieties such as Concord, Catawba, or Niagara, with some exceptions such as Mallow Run's popular rhubarb wine. A couple of owners did mention that a dry red was their most popular wine, and a few wineries focus their production on dry wines, but that was a rare exception. In terms of volume produced and sold, Midwest wines do tend toward the sweeter side.

The fact, however, is that most Midwestern wineries make an almost dizzying array of wines, to the point that it is hard to know what to expect when you visit a winery for the first time (unless you glance at its website, which I recommend). Midwestern winemakers want to make all their customers happy—they want them to have a positive experience—so they try to have something for everyone. But this means that collectively they aren't really known for anything in particular. Many wineries are likely to have more wines made from California or New York grapes than from their own vineyard or grapes sourced in-state. This is especially the case as they expand, because there aren't enough grapes being produced locally to meet their needs. Again, there are exceptions, but generally this is the case.

Another big part of the identity problem is the lack of geographical consistency across the region. The physical geography of the Midwest varies substantially. The wide-ranging terroir, the differences in the kinds of grapes that can be grown as a result, and the differences in settings, aesthetic tastes, and wine preferences of winery owners and their customers make it difficult to say exactly what Midwestern wineries are about or how much the wineries in each state have in common beyond the happenstance of past political decisions. Ted Huber saw this as a key issue:

> I think the biggest problem with Indiana is our geographic region, is the fact that what I can do down here on the Ohio River and the wineries down here do as flavors and as varieties don't work north of here and way north of here. And so there's this wild difference in flavors and styles of wines from southern to central to northern. There are very distinct regional differences that are *very* distinct [his emphasis]. When you talk about California, there are very distinct regional differences too, but California Cabs are California Cabs, and there are subtle differences. When you talk about Indiana, there are wild differences. That's a problem because it doesn't give Indiana a chance to really identify itself. And the whites are becoming better. Traminette is leading the cause of making Traminette a signature wine. But there are huge differences in the flavors that are being produced and the styles that are being produced from north to south.

The Indiana Wine Grape Council's adoption of the Traminette grape as the "signature grape" of Indiana was an effort to build a common identity because it theoretically could be grown across the state. It is certainly more stylish than Concord or Catawba, and it can be associated with a European grape and flavor profile while still reflecting Hoosiers' preference for sweeter wines, since it can be made in sweet, semi-dry, and dry styles. Still, the wide-ranging differences Huber speaks of remain.

The Wine Trail as a Collaborative Geographical Marketing Strategy

One way wineries can work together to promote themselves is by creating wine trails. These associations provide a collective geographical identity for their members based mostly on proximity. Once a wine trail has been established, its members decide as a group whether to add new wineries. Wine trails commonly have brochures, some have websites, many purchase advertising in print or online media, and most offer wineglasses with trail logos or a benefit of some kind to those who visit multiple wineries along a trail. The participating wineries are usually charged a membership fee to pay for these things, and they make collective decisions about any such expenditures. Participating in a trail also expands member wineries' opportunities to market themselves along with other tourist amenities in the area, such as hotels, inns, bed-and-breakfasts, restaurants, parks, and other businesses, to jointly promote their region as a tourist destination. Cross-advertising is common, through the use of shared ads and links on websites and collaboratively produced destination brochures, often with the assistance of the state or sometimes a county tourism office.

In 2015, Ohio had six wine trails affiliated with the Ohio Wine Producers Association. Coshocton County promotes a seventh trail on its website (www .visitcoshocton.com/things-to-do/wineries). Seven Ohio wineries are part of the sprawling Lake Erie Wine Trail, which also includes wineries in Pennsylvania and New York.

In Indiana there are currently six wine trails: three in the south, two central, and one in the northeastern part of the state. Over half of the wineries in the state are affiliated with a wine trail.

Illinois has the fewest wine trails, although the majority of wineries are on a trail. The Shawnee Hills Wine Trail is in the southern part of the state. The northern part of the state has the somewhat oddly organized Northern Illinois Wine Trail, which advertises three "loops": the Chicagoland Loop in the northwestern part of the state, the Fox Valley Loop a bit farther out of Chicago, and the Northwest Loop, which includes the Galena-area wineries and stretches across a massive tract of real estate. I say that it is somewhat oddly organized because while there are some clusters of wineries that lie along certain convenient routes, most notably in DeKalb County and Jo Daviess County, some of the wineries on the loops are not easily accessed from other wineries. Four wineries in the southwestern part of the state, plus one Indiana winery, make up the Wabash Valley Wine Trail. The Mississippi Valley Wine Trail consists of five wineries in the west-central part of the state. The trails in Illinois are autonomous and not directly associated with the Illinois Grape Growers and Vintners Association or any state entity, although they occasionally partner with the IGGVA and the Illinois Office of Tourism on events and advertising. The IGGVA's website makes no mention of the wine trails in the state. As of August 2015, the Illinois Office of Tourism website had a link that didn't work for the Mississippi Valley Wine Trail and what appeared to be a prominent paid advertisement and link for the Shawnee Hills Wine Trail. In May 2016, the Mississippi Valley link worked, but a link for a Southern Illinois Wine Trail went to a dead end, so if that trail ever existed, it appeared to be defunct. The Shawnee Hills Trail had a link that worked. The Illinois River Trail was indicated, but the link to its website went to the IGGVA website with no indication of the trail. With the exception of the Shawnee Hills Trail, Illinois wine trails seem to lack the attention to detail that would make them more effective as promotional tools.

Iowa has seven wine trails: one in each of the four corners of the state, one that stretches across the state along I-80, the Amana Colonies Wine Trail in

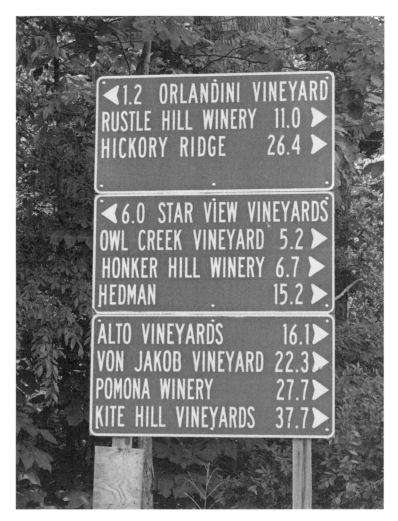

Figure 7.1. Directional sign for wineries on the Shawnee Hills
Wine Trail in southern Illinois. Photo by Greta Pennell.

the east-central part of the state, and one that covers the central part of the
state from north to south. Three wineries show up on both the I-80 and the
Heart of Iowa trails, and two on the I-80 and Western Iowa trails. The trails in
the northwest and central parts of the state and the I-80 Wine Trail are quite
spread out, with the latter clearly intended to attract those passing through
at some point along the way. A little over half of the wineries in the state are
affiliated with some trail.

Trails occasionally go beyond being marketing tools and develop other identities. At least two trails I studied became the foundation for American Viticultural Areas. The Shawnee Hills Trail formed the Shawnee Hills AVA, and the Indiana Uplands Trail formed the Indiana Uplands AVA. As mentioned earlier, Indiana Uplands also formed a cooperative association, a regional umbrella organization that can provide additional benefits to its members.

The most common complaint I heard from the owners of wineries that belonged to wine trails was that some members were not pulling their weight regarding the work of the trail such as attending meetings, developing marketing materials, and arranging events. My sense is that with so many demands on the owners' time, wine trail work can fall near the bottom of the priority list. Wine trails can be a time burden for newer winery owners who must wear multiple hats, and a bit of a nuisance to owners of more established wineries who already have a strong customer base. They seem to be especially helpful for smaller wineries that are a bit off the beaten path or that lack the resources to do much promotion on their own. But the fees for entering into that arrangement can seem rather steep for those in their early stages of development. Wineries may benefit from being on a wine trail initially, but trail events can be an added burden for successful operations that attract big crowds through their own efforts, have a prime location on a heavily traveled route, or are near a population center. I have seen the wine trail limos pull up at a winery. It's great that these customers are in limos and not driving, and they can be a blessing for a smaller winery if they purchase some bottles or cases. But if they are tasting and running, trying to hit as many wineries as possible, the winery owners can only hope they remember something positive about their short visit and come back later for the full experience.

I have visited wineries along a number of trails, and one thought that continually occurred to me was that quality can range widely among the members of a trail. Much as visitors may damn an entire state's wineries based on visits to only one or two of them, wine trails can cause themselves harm in the same manner. On a trail that included wineries that produce high-quality wines from their own or local grapes, my wife and I visited a member winery that offered only "cellared and bottled" wine, meaning that it had not actually been produced there. It was also poor to middling in quality. Greta and I decided to drink the bottled beer that was served at the establishment instead. The wines I tasted on other trails were of radically different quality and had little consistency in the sourcing of grapes. The only thing these wineries had in common was proximity and a nice setting, although in some cases even the latter was lacking. The reputations of the many fabulous Midwestern wineries that make excellent wines are tarnished by association with the underperformers. How can Midwestern wineries get to consistent quality across the board?

The Problems with Achieving
Consistent Quality

High-quality wine comes from two things: using high-quality grapes and then realizing the best expression of those grapes through the winemaking process. Bruce Bordelon, the viticulturist on the Purdue Wine Grape Team, has produced numerous guides and technical reports on growing grapes in the Midwest, drawing on his research and the work of others in his field. He is part of a consortium of wine grape researchers from different states doing long-term research, and he has experimental sites at Purdue and in Vincennes to study different grape varieties and how they respond to differences in terroir and treatment. He had been studying the Traminette grape prior to its release, so he had almost two decades of research to draw upon in recommending it as the state wine grape. As he told me in November 2011,

> It's not that difficult to grow grapes. It's more difficult to grow really good-quality grapes, and that's the real trick. It's not just the disease management, but can it be managed and all that—recognizing, you know, do I have the right amount of crop on these vines? Do I have my canopy management handled well? Have I pulled enough leaves? Is that fruit exposed enough, or too exposed? Those are the little nuances that growers learn to recognize. That's where you start moving your industry forward and your wine quality up.

I asked Bordelon to walk me through the kinds of things he would do for me if I were thinking about growing grapes. He recommended the *Midwest Grape Production Guide* (Dami et al. 2005), a handbook that he coauthored with Imed Dami and some other colleagues at Ohio State, as a good place to start. He also consults with growers and occasionally gets out and does some site visits, but he thinks that growers and prospective growers need to take advantage of the various available resources to educate themselves. There is often some misunderstanding on the part of owners about what state specialists can offer and how quickly. Ohio, Illinois, and Iowa are fortunate to have a few more resource specialists on growing grapes. Bruce Bordelon is it in Indiana. He shared his frustrations about those who have unrealistic expectations about what he can do for them:

> The problem is that with sixty-plus wineries now, and, I don't know, seventy-five, a hundred, a hundred fifty different grape growers out there in various stages of contacting me or not, I can't go see everybody, unfortunately. We do have great support in the counties through our county extension educators. Some of them are very knowledgeable about all the levels of agriculture production, and whether it be hogs to horses to corn and beans. They don't have a lot of experience in grapes and apples and stuff, but they *do* know *soils* and *drainage*

and *rules*, and they can be *very* helpful. So they are our first line of contact, the county guy, and have him see your site and talk about it. But also, I can advise. If you come to the training, if you read the book and come to our Hort Congress and our meetings, you should be able to gain enough knowledge to make those decisions for yourself without me acting as some sort of a consultant, and too many people want that. They want me to come see the site, give them some sort of blessing, and I've done that in various stages of, you know, "Wow, this is a great site. Good luck. I'm sure it's going to work great for you." And it might not work out very well because people don't do a very good job on the sites, to where you go out there and say, "No way I would ever plant grapes or fruit trees of any kind on this site." Too low-lying, too wet, flood-prone—I mean, you name it, everything's wrong with the site, and they go ahead and do it anyway. How do you want me to help you with that? So those are the sort of situations I try to avoid getting into, that me making some seal of approval. I want to teach *you* how to decide for yourself [his emphasis].

Having viticulturists dedicated to the state wine industries is very important given the north-south lengths of Ohio, Indiana, and Illinois and their geographical variation. A quick read of Bordelon's report "Growing Grapes in Indiana" (Bordelon 2001) will show you what I mean. The temperatures are generally higher in southern Indiana than in northern Indiana, and the risks there of early frosts in the fall or late frosts in the spring are lower. The number of frost-free days can vary between some parts of southern versus northern Indiana by as much as seventy days, or almost one-fifth of the year. That is a substantial difference. Winters are also milder in southern Indiana. How low temperatures go in the winter is also an important determinant of what grapes can be grown where, and low temperatures can range by as much as twenty-five degrees across the state. There are substantial variations in soil composition and terrain as well, which can affect water retention, drainage, susceptibility to frost, and other factors that matter to grapevines. Add the moderating temperature effects of lakes and rivers into the mix, and winery owners or people considering purchasing land for a vineyard are foolish if they don't take advantage of Bordelon's expertise and educate themselves.

Illinois and Ohio share some of the same range of temperatures, soils, and terrain. If you have never been in the southern parts of these states, you may be surprised to find hills and valleys where the glaciers stopped instead of the flat corn and soybean fields that are more prevalent in the central parts. Since these three states as well as Iowa are relatively flat to the north (except in the Mississippi River Valley and other river areas), and the northern parts are a couple to a few hundred miles closer to the Arctic than the southern parts depending on the state, they are occasionally exposed to incursions of Arctic air that force their way farther south than usual. In January 2014, almost all the *vinifera* grapes (Cabernet Franc, Cabernet Sauvignon, Chardonnay, Pinot Gris, Pinot Noir, and Riesling) as well as many vines were wiped out in Ohio all the way down to the Ohio River as the result of a cold wave caused by a polar vortex. Imed Dami has described it as "probably the worst grape damage on record in Ohio" (Ohio State University 2014). OARDC faculty and staff conducted workshops to help growers cope with the damage. Parts of Indiana and northeastern Illinois were also hit hard. Even the hybrid and native grape crops and vines suffered extensive damage, and harvests in the affected areas were generally much lower (ibid.).

There is a great deal of clay in large areas of the Midwest that does not drain well, especially if it is relatively flat. Grapevines do not like to stand in water for extended periods, so this often requires the installation of drainage tiles. The Midwest is also plagued by high humidity, a condition in which mold and mildew thrive. Grapevines are highly susceptible to these as well as a variety of pests, requiring vigilant monitoring and regular applications of fungicide and insecticide. I asked Bordelon if growing grapes organically in the Midwest was possible, and he said:

> If it's Norton or Steuben or Cayuga White, yeah, you know, those three varieties are probably tolerant enough of downy and powdery mildew that without the regular spray program, or the highly effective fungicides that we use, they would probably make it through and do reasonably well. The big challenge is going to be black rot, and that's what my colleague from Ohio State found. Okay, so what's the solution to black rot? Well, you can use organically approved fungicides like copper sulfate and a lot of the older mixtures of fixed coppers. That's a lot of copper. If you look at the number of applications you make a year, and the pounds of copper you apply, this is a problem that they're battling in Europe and have been for a number of years. We put *way* too much copper on out here, and now we have copper toxicity. I mean, our soils are full of copper, and copper is a heavy metal. In fact, of all the fungicides we use—and there's a whole long list that are available for us; we don't use but four or five, but there may be twenty-five that are in the spray guide—the only one that has a skull-and-crossbones *danger* signal warning on the label, you know, is copper sulfate. Yeah, the only one. The *only* one [his emphasis].

One issue with growing grapes shared by those in the Corn Belt of the U.S. is the possibility that a vineyard will be wiped out by the use of the herbicides 2,4-D or dicamba. These can easily drift in windy conditions for up to two days after application (Bordelon 2011). In 1964, 2,4-D was banned in five counties in Iowa with high concentrations of vineyards (Pirog 2002). The same herbicide destroyed the vineyards in Council Bluffs, Iowa, in the 1970s (Pinney 2005, 179) and continues to be a problem there today. In 2007, the Iowa Grape and Wine Development Commission funded a brochure that "promoted awareness of the harm some herbicides can have on grape vines" (Ovrom, n.d., 9). A couple of Illinois winery owners I interviewed specifically mentioned this as a problem collectively facing their industry. Purdue staff and extension specialists set up a voluntary registry, the DriftWatch Specialty Crop Site Registry (www.fieldwatch.com), where specialty crop growers in a number of Midwestern and Western states, as well as Saskatchewan, can map their locations to alert herbicide and pesticide applicators of potential drift problems.

Selecting the appropriate grape varieties for a particular location is essential to growing the highest-quality grapes possible to make the best wine the terroir will provide. Advances in grape hybridization have resulted in a range of cold-climate wine grapes that many owners and experts believe will produce high-quality wines. I think there are many white grape hybrids that make excellent wines, depending on the growing conditions: Chardonel, Seyval Blanc, Vidal, St. Pepin. The bigger challenge is in the production of dry red wines. Most cold-weather red grapes are quite low in tannins, chemical compounds that provide some of the dry, astringent qualities we associate with *vinifera*-based red wines such as Cabernet Sauvignon and Syrah/Shiraz. Primarily extracted from grape skins, they are also found in the seeds and pulp. Tannins contribute to "wine structure, mouthfeel, color stability and ageability" (Patterson 2011). Midwestern red wines made from hybrid grapes can seem light and thin, in part due to a lack of tannins. However, the Noiret grape, a cold-tolerant hybrid, is commonly quite high in tannins. If properly extracted and retained in the winemaking process, they can provide some astringency and a bit of bitterness that red wine drinkers associate with a well-structured wine (Patterson 2011; Spada 2015). Given my experience with drinking it, Noiret is especially beneficial to blends with other varieties low in tannins. Red hybrid varieties that are cold tolerant often have some problematic qualities, which blending can help counter. Tannins can also be imparted from oak barrels or simply added, but problems can be created when additives are used or when other winemaking techniques are employed to counter poor-quality fruit.

Quality is not just about getting good grapes, but also about having the knowledge and skill to get the most out of them. When I asked winery owners about their biggest concern regarding the growth of the industry in their respective states, they rarely mentioned the increasing competition but focused rather on the need to maintain and improve quality. They wanted their state governments to support educational programs for their industry to improve quality so that the entire industry would succeed and grow. And they were willing to assist. I consistently found winery owners across all four states talking about helping or being helped by other winery owners. They saw this as a necessity for the success of their state industries. Two newer Indiana winery owners told me that Oliver Winery had provided them with what was basically an unpaid internship, giving them the opportunity to learn about winemaking with the knowledge that they were going to become competitors. Another had interned with Chateau Thomas Winery. During my field research at Mallow Run, a young man who planned to open a winery in Sheridan, Indiana, picked and crushed grapes, pruned vines, and assisted with other aspects of grape growing and winemaking. There are also a growing number of people coming up through the industry who had jobs at other wineries before starting their own. Winemakers at newly opened wineries often consulted with their peers at other wineries—something you typically would not find among competitors in other industries. Mark Easley explained this willingness to help:

> I remember very clearly at one of the state meetings we had, and I forget who it was now, but the usual players were there—Jim Butler, Bill Oliver, Ted Huber—and somebody said, "Why do you guys come here and tell us all of your secrets?" And one of them got up, and I forget now who it was, and said, "If you make horrible wine, it reflects on all of us. We get known as the horrible wine state." You know, that is why we take time out of our busy calendar and come to this meeting. We go and help Purdue develop programs for extension and continuing education because [otherwise] you become the muddy water wine state. It really becomes a reflection of the area. The whole ship rises and all quality rises. So that's why we spend so much time on this continuing education aspect, and that's what's really changed the wine industry. You know, in the seventies it wasn't uncommon for you to go into Marsh [an Indiana grocery chain] and get a bad bottle of wine. Today, it's completely unacceptable.

Larry Satek shared with me how Jim Butler helped Satek Winery get off to a good start in the transition from vineyard to winery:

> We had taken our last two vintages and worked with Jim Butler at Butler Winery, who fermented them under his bond, and then when we became a bonded winery, we transferred the wine up here. And within thirty days of us becoming a bonded winery, we opened with one-to-two-year-old wines from our grapes, which was a huge selling point in terms of getting people to show up.

Illinois's state enologist, Bradley Beam, explained to me why winemaking can be such a challenge in the Midwest in comparison to California or other places with more consistent conditions for growing grapes, and related the kind of skill he thinks is essential for success:

> The big picture is figuring out how to be improvisational in the vineyard first and then in the winery. Because, I mean, you look at the last five years we've had, every year has been completely different than the next, and that affects every-thing—how you grow the grapes, when you pick the grapes, how you process the grapes. So, whereas if you're on the West Coast—I'm not trying to cast aspersions

on the West Coast, but they're a little more consistent. Like if you're in California, you know it's going to be dry. And we don't have that luxury of knowing what's around the corner. And that's a continental situation. You couple that with the fact that we're working with relatively understudied varieties for the most part. The Northern Grapes Project is doing a lot to correct that. They've done a lot of research on hybrids, especially extreme cold-hardy hybrids, in the past couple of years. It's kind of groundbreaking stuff. But, you know, there's so many variables that we have to try to manage that it makes it really challenging. So the big picture, though, I like to think of it as improvisation. You have to observe and react. All the time. You can't get formulaic with it. You really have to learn how to think behind it. And that's going to take some time, and it's certainly not for everybody. There are certainly much easier places to grow grapes and make wine than the Midwest.

Not only do climatic conditions vary in the Midwest from place to place and year to year, but different grape varieties have their own qualities and chemical properties, requiring different treatments to get the most out of them. Chris Lawlor-White observed, "You can put Cab in a barrel and taste it five years later, and it's a beautiful wine. You put a Foch in a barrel, and it could be vinegar in the next month. You better be tasting it every month."

One strategy Beam has used to improve quality is to hold twice-a-year roundtables where Illinois winemakers can bring samples of their wines at various stages of the process. Everyone tastes and critiques the wines, and Beam and the more experienced winemakers can help less experienced winemakers identify and resolve, and in the future avoid, problems. Some of the winemakers I interviewed specifically mentioned these roundtables as having been very helpful. Karen Hand, the head winemaker at Blue Sky Vineyard, said that some of the winemakers in southern Illinois were experiencing "cellar palate" and having difficulty tasting flaws in the flavor profiles of their Chambourcins. At one of Beam's roundtables, Lawlor-White identified the problem as a yeast, *Brettanomyces*, which commonly lives in oak barrels or in the winery. Collectively, Midwestern winemakers are still learning their craft, especially how to get the most out of French-American hybrid grapes. But they are seriously working on it and rapidly improving.

Quality Wine Initiatives in Ohio and Iowa

Ohio and Iowa have taken the push for quality to another level by starting programs that evaluate wine submitted by winemakers in those states and award quality seals that can be placed on the bottles and mentioned in advertising. Todd Steiner at the OARDC explained how the Ohio Quality Wine (OQW) program originated:

Figure 7.2. Christine Lawlor-White of Galena Cellars in Galena, Illinois, drawing a barrel sample, May 4, 2015. Photo by Greta Pennell.

We started kicking that off with industry interests back in the, oh, I would say, late 1990s. And something like that is not something that happens overnight. It's rather daunting trying to set that up. Really, nothing had been further established until about 2004. And then, through the Grape Industries program, the director at that time, and us at OSU and some key industry people, we did implement that. I shouldn't say implement, we started *really* kick-starting it, and getting the criteria developed for it. And we *started* it in 2007 with the annual Ohio Wine Competition [his emphasis]. And then we had different times throughout the years where we had different submittal times. But the most we've ever had is four times per year where wineries can submit. It's based on a twenty-point scale that we would see in most national and international competitions. The subcommittee decided to set the bar a little higher and go with fifteen points and higher, which is a silver, instead of like VQA [Vintner's Quality Alliance, a Canadian program], which would be more like a bronze standard, although everybody knows VQA and the success they've had there. Now, we're not legislative like VQA. So it is voluntary and it's gaining some support. And for those that have entered and receive the seal, we do some special marketing efforts through the Grape Industries Committee. So it's really a good thing, and the main goals are to basically have wines that can be recognized by both the media and consumers as being a quality product in the bottle. Something that, you know, if it has the seal, they can take it home and expect to have a good experience. And then the other thing would be to plant more grapes in the ground, which we need to keep up with our growing industry, and promote Ohio-grown grapes and product in the bottle.

The OQW program is only for Ohio-produced wines that are made with at least 90 percent Ohio-grown grapes. Wines submitted for evaluation are chemically tested and undergo a sensory analysis, much as would be done at a wine competition. There is no submission fee.

The Iowa Quality Wine Consortium program is somewhat similar to the Ohio program. It is a collaboration between the Iowa Wine Growers Association and the Midwest Grape and Wine Industry Institute. The MGWII conducts the chemical analysis and organizes panels for the sensory evaluation. There are three big differences between the Iowa and Ohio programs. First, wines that are eligible for the Iowa Quality Wine label need to contain a minimum of only 75 percent Iowa grapes. Second, the program also has a category for wines that are less than 75 percent Iowa grapes or fruit. Last, the minimum acceptable score is 13 out of 20 from three members of the five-member panel (Iowa Quality Wine Consortium 2015).

Getting to Quality

One of the biggest differences I noticed in quality across wineries was tied to the winemakers' years of experience. High-quality grape production and winemaking require a level of knowledge and skill that cannot be developed in only two or three years. Talented teachers, good sources of information, and some learning from experience are necessary to develop that knowledge and skill. Few Midwestern winemakers have enology degrees like Chris Lawlor-White or certificates like Mary Hofmann, although the VESTA and community college programs are starting to change this situation. But many of the really good winemakers have science backgrounds they can bring to bear, or they spent many years making wine before jumping into the business. Others took courses online and honed their skills in their basements, barns, or garages well before taking the big step into the commercial realm. The same goes for growing grapes. There is much one needs to know about grape varieties, soil, terrain, climate, microclimate, and care to bring in a good crop in three to five years. There is also much one needs to know about meeting government requirements and running a business.

The wine and grape specialists in all four states work hard to educate people who are considering opening a winery, emphasizing the seriousness of that undertaking. Christian Butzke, enologist for the Purdue Wine Grape Team, explained the problem from his perspective and what he and his colleagues try do about it:

There are a lot of those folks that as students we would call them "born-agains," who suddenly discover after an entire career that what they really want to do is become a winemaker because they had a few glasses of nice wine with their friends, or they traveled to Sonoma and had a good time. And that alone is not quite reason enough to change your career or get into this field, which is a very competitive, manual-labor-type environment. Again, that takes a lot of investment because you are dealing with a product that is difficult and expensive to produce. Many people here who are getting into grape growing come from corn and bean backgrounds, the kind of crops where you stick a seed in the ground in the spring and you come back in the fall to harvest it. I don't want to make fun of corn growers here, but it's a lot easier to do than grape growing. You have to be in the vineyard every single day of every single week [pounding the table for emphasis] and spray and look for insects. So even though a good amount of people have farmland and say, "Hey, why don't I just plant a vineyard? I hear you can make a few thousand dollars per acre there at growing grapes," it's very hard and it takes a lot of time. And if you want to make wine and run a winery at the same time, a lot of people might get in over their heads . . . People underestimate how much time it takes to run a winery, to man the tasting room, and to do all the paperwork you have to do to report to the federal government as to how much alcohol you produce [pounding the table for emphasis].

Butzke also talked about the financial obligations and cash flow problems that winery owners face after the grapes are out of the ground or purchased. Not only do they have to pay for the labor, bottles, and corks to produce the product, but it can sometimes take a year or two before the wine is finished and ready to sell. Butzke described how the Purdue Wine Grape Team attempts to help prospective winery owners better understand the commitment they will need to make with respect to both time and money:

That's why we often have meetings in here, in this very room [where I was interviewing him], with the Purdue Wine Grape Team to ask people who are interested in starting up wineries: "What do you know about the industry? What do you know about farming? How much money do you have? Have you ever written a business plan? Do you like wine?" And often the answer to those questions is no. People do not like wine, necessarily, that get into the wine industry. They have never run a business. They have never farmed anything. All they have is a patch of land somewhere and an idea and something they consider, you know, it's a cute retirement investment or hobby or profession, or people who obviously have lost their jobs. And so people have been getting into this business, and we have been trying to warn them as much as possible so that only people who really have some serious chances of surviving get into it.

Bradley Beam echoed Butzke's concerns about people getting into the business without sufficient capitalization or an adequate understanding of the work required and how this can affect quality:

> Time management really is the biggest thing. This is especially so for the small wineries. This is very common: They're trying to be the vineyard manager, trying to be the winemaker, they're trying to be the marketing director, they're trying to be tasting room staff and the entertainment people, sometimes even the caterers. The worry there is, you know, they're doing that because of the scale, the scale of production. So that's kind of the biggest issue. Where do we need to be in order to start making it a little easier on ourselves, especially when they get into the business when they're in their fifties and sixties? That's a good way to tire yourself out quickly and lose the spark that you once had. So trying to find ways, and I think the wineries that are most successful are either large enough that they can diversify and have a lot of employees, or they're highly specialized. They kind of have a well-thought-out mission statement: this is who we are, and this is *not* who we are [laughing, his emphasis], and not try to be everything for everybody. The problem with a destination winery is that you don't know who's going to walk through the door, especially in rural areas where there's a lot of nontraditional wine consumers. So you're not going to know what they're going to want. And so from a winemaking perspective, you see a lot of these small wineries trying to produce twelve to fifteen different wines. That's really challenging, too. Regardless of scale, if it's two hundred gallons or twenty thousand gallons, it's a lot of work. And to maintain the quality and keep your eye on the ball. Most of the faults that we see making it through to bottling are related to neglect. You know, a gasket leaked, and the lid fell, and there's oxygen getting in the wine. It starts to oxidize and get VA [volatile acidity]. Those are the big issues, and it's because people are working so hard. It's not because they're not paying attention, it's because they're working so hard that they get distracted.

Unfortunately, I heard many accounts about missteps and changes in plans. For example, Rudi and Mary Hofmann had planned to simply grow and sell grapes at White Oak Vineyards, but once they had a usable crop, they struggled to find a market for the first few years because a number of other vineyards had also begun selling grapes. Rudi described driving to St. Louis from the middle of Illinois to sell a load of grapes for "sixty or seventy cents a pound" while still having to "pay for the machinery, the spray, and maintaining and mowing and stuff. So we had to make a decision to either pull everything out or go the next step." The next step was to make wine. Mary shared those challenges with me:

> I think every winemaker does the same thing: they start out with the wine kits. And then they get a little more interested, and they're like, "Oh, so that was easy." Those wine kits make it look easy. You know, you pay a couple hundred dollars for the basic kit, and you have this wonderful success because, oh my gosh, it's

already pre-done for you. And you think you know so much after that. So we did a few kits and bottled in our son's bedroom one time. And we thought, yeah, we can do this. So then when the grapes started to actually produce, we started to *try* to make it on our own [her emphasis]. The first ones were not very good. We realized we were making a lot of mistakes, and wondered why we were making these mistakes, and that kind of thing.

To overcome the problems she was having, Mary took some online courses at the University of California, Davis, then went there for some classes. She found more support for making Midwestern wine at the University of Missouri, where she completed a certificate. I had the pleasure of sampling a nice assortment of her wines the day I interviewed her and Rudi. She had clearly made much progress in her winemaking journey.

Jeff Hill, the owner of Rettig Hill Winery, did his homework before jumping into the business. Hill developed a very clear plan of what he wanted to accomplish and how he would accomplish it. His goal was not to please everyone, but to make primarily dry wines using his own grapes or those sourced in his county, and to do it without a tasting room for direct sales—a combination I found nowhere else in any of the four states. He told me how important the Purdue Wine Grape Team had been to him:

Bottom line is, if Purdue didn't have that program, and I wasn't able to qualitatively or quantitatively tell what I was getting into, I would not have made the investment and taken the chance of just learning it on my own. So, it really lets a new winery decide if (a) they want to do it, and (b) is it possible, and (c) will it succeed or not? And that's why I have just the utmost respect for the older guys that have been in the business for a long time, because they didn't have that. You know, they just kind of went into it. Now, they're all smart guys and probably did enough research on their own, but they really took a lot of risk for a lot of the new guys like me.

On the flip side, Mark Easley loved to work in the vineyard and grow grapes, but he decided that the direction his winery needed to grow was in production and competing on grocery store shelves with the big guys. So he gave up the grape production. He still makes a variety of wines to sell out of the winery, but he does high volume with his sweet wines. He definitely has a plan. And as he stresses, sweet wines can also be of high quality.

There is no one way to be successful in the wine industry. Perhaps improving quality across the board with whatever style is produced will help Midwestern wineries with their identity problem. The industry in these states is still in the adolescent stage of maturation. There is a long way to go, but I have noticed substantial improvements in the Midwestern wines I have tasted from some wineries in the last ten years and a general improvement overall.

The moral to the story of this chapter and the previous one is that the support resources are there for those who are thinking about planting a vineyard or opening a winery in these states. But anyone considering this should take a deep breath, slow down, and draw on those resources sooner rather than in desperation later. Owning a winery is a full mind-and-body, all-in commitment. Unless you have the capital and wherewithal to hire the right people up front and spend a small fortune on equipment, you need to give yourself a chance to start working your way through the learning curve first.

In the final chapter, I consider the relationship of Midwestern wineries to the global industry and the fuzziness of the "local" label that many wineries use to distinguish themselves for marketing purposes. I also contemplate some possible directions in which Midwestern wineries could be headed as they respond to competition from both near and far.

8

Local Vino and *Mondovino*

Midwestern Wineries
in the Global Context

My friends and colleagues have joked numerous times that they would be happy to help me with my winery research. I explain that I'm writing about the Midwestern winery experience and the work of creating that experience, not just drinking wine. But of course, part of wine research is drinking wine, or at least in my mind I wouldn't be doing a good job with the research if I weren't also drinking and thinking about the product the wineries are producing. I have also been thinking about Midwestern wineries and wines in relation to what is going on nationally and globally. So I guess I have had to do double duty, checking on the local produce while also keeping my taste buds informed and my attention attuned to broader developments.

I intentionally used the title *Local Vino* for this book as a way to distinguish local production and distribution of wine from production for global distribution. Except for a few larger wineries or wineries near borders between states, most all wine that is produced by Midwestern wineries is available only in the state where the winery that makes it is located and is consumed mostly by residents in that state. As a result, many Midwestern winery owners have aligned their marketing with two somewhat different, although related, movements: (1) the "local food" movement, which promotes the consumption of food that has been grown nearby, and (2) the "buy local" movement, which advocates making purchases from locally owned businesses. The local food movement seeks to counter the environmental and, some would say, health costs of industrial food production, distribution, and consumption. The buy local movement seeks to counter the control that transnational corporations have over the many things we purchase, not just food. Buy local adherents think there are negative economic and political circumstances associated with this control. Large corporations tend to pull more money out of communities than they put in and are commonly able to shape political decisions to their benefit as a result of their deep pockets and organization. Wineries and the wine industry can also be considered along these two dimensions: (1) where they source their grapes and the other things they need to make and bottle wine, and (2) whether they are locally owned and operated. With regard to the latter, I would add how big a winery's reach is in terms of its distribution, since there may be a high-volume or elite-market winery located in a particular community whose residents are not the winery's target population.

Sourcing Grapes in the Midwest

When the 1971 law was written establishing the Indiana wine industry, it allowed grapes to be brought in from outside the state if sufficient supply was not available within the state. With the exception of a handful of wineries that can make all their wines from their own grapes, sufficient supply is not available and has never been available in all four of the states examined here; thus most Midwestern wineries must rely heavily on grapes or juice from other states, especially California and New York. Most winery owners are fairly pragmatic about this situation. Whether they are just starting or are growing their businesses, most need to make wine with fruit from other states, and they do that. But there are a range of views on this practice and what it means for moving the wine industry forward in their states.

In Indiana, Huber's Orchard, Winery and Vineyards is at one end of the spectrum, making all of its wine from fruit grown there, except perhaps in some very unusual circumstances. Other wineries aspire to be able to provide for their own needs in this way, or at least would like to use some mix of their own grapes and fruit from other vineyards nearby or in their state. Butler Winery, Rettig Hill Winery, and Turtle Run are good examples in Indiana. Turtle Run and Huber's benefit from their location in the Ohio River Valley, although they both are now part of the Indiana Uplands AVA, with a climate that supports some *vinifera* grapes such as Cabernet Sauvignon and Cabernet Franc. Rettig Hill is in the Ohio River Valley AVA and uses grapes either grown in its vineyard or sourced from within Ripley County, where it is located. Owner Jeff Hill explained his view on this:

> In a lot of research I did prior to getting into this endeavor, one has to define what a winemaker is. To me, and I think this is shared by a lot of other people in Indiana and outside of Indiana, part of being a winemaker is growing the grapes. In fact, I think that's about ninety percent of the work is growing the grapes. So, to complete that definition of winemaker, I thought it was imperative for me to grow my own grapes. I'm a winemaker from Indiana, so my opinion is I should be making wines from grapes grown in Indiana. And I even more narrowly define that as I just buy grapes from nearby vineyards that are four or five miles away. Nothing against people that buy grapes from California, because I think some years it's necessary because of supply issues. And it does address grape surplus

issues. You know, if they're having a huge surplus in California, instead of just letting the grapes rot on the vine, at least they get used for a productive use.

Butler Winery has been running radio advertisements for several years featuring Jim Butler talking about his wine. He stresses that his winery uses locally sourced grapes, either from his own vineyard or from nearby vineyards, and notes that he does not make "copycat wines" from California grapes. So during our interview in 2012, I asked if he would expand on that:

Well, it comes down to choice. Any winery in Indiana can buy Cabernet, and we can sell Cabernet to Cabernet people. But what does that do to help develop our own industry in the long run? And then you have the questions that, okay, I'm buying Cabernet from California. I can't produce it cheaper here than the people in California can, so how can I compete in the marketplace with [them]? When there are two hundred Chardonnays on the shelves in Bloomington, or wherever, where do you fit in that mix? And the more—and this is something that when we started up, that was kind of our philosophy—now it's timing well with the local food movement, because people do come in asking, and they have been for a couple of years, where do your grapes come from? They stand right in the middle of the vineyard and say, "Where do your grapes come from?" [laughing] Well, they've been to some of the other places, and they know in fact that is not what is really happening. There are a lot of wineries that have a showpiece spot that have maybe a half acre of grapes or an acre of grapes and they say, "Oh no, we have to pick these!"

And when the industry was starting out, there was no way we could start an industry with a rule that said everything had to come from Indiana. And some states have had that. Indiana's law, the Indiana Small Winery Law, actually said that you had to use Indiana fruit unless it wasn't available. For us, it wasn't available, which was, as we say, a loophole big enough to drive a tanker truck through. But that enabled the industry to really develop. And it was a huge investment, and so you need the cash flow. But as far as what we want to do, wine comes from the land, the whole idea of terroir. I didn't feel twenty years ago we could talk about terroir, but we are getting to that point now where we can see differences in the grapes that are grown, depending on where it may be, ten, fifteen miles away there could be a difference.

At the other end, the person most committed to only using grapes from California, Oregon, or Washington and using no locally sourced grapes is Charles Thomas. Dr. Thomas told me he believes the highest-quality grapes come from these areas, and that using Indiana grapes will always result in an inferior product. His goal is to make Old World–style wines, which by tradition require *vinifera* grapes, and these grapes require the long growing season found in those areas. As he put it to me, "I envision that we are a European winery in Indiana. And we used to have a slogan, it was three lines. It said, 'California grapes, Indiana winemakers, world-class results.'"

Dr. Thomas makes some very good wine, so perhaps he is on the right path. He told me he was strongly criticized by other owners at one time for using California grapes, but noted that now it is common among Indiana winemakers. He seemed to feel vindicated by this turn of events.

The big middle ground is occupied by those wineries that produce a range of wines with grapes or, quite commonly, juice sourced from whoever can provide dependable supplies. This is commonly Walker's Fruit Farms–Wine Juice LLC in Forestville, New York. Cabernet Sauvignon and other *vinifera* grapes often come from California. Winery owners recognize that wine drinkers are most familiar with varieties commonly associated with California, so they want to be able to offer those wines to make customers happy. Others like to test their abilities in comparison to the California wineries.

Mallow Run gets a fair amount of juice from Walker's, rhubarb juice for its most popular wine from Oregon, and Cabernet Sauvignon, Sangiovese, and Zinfandel grapes from California. When the estate-grown and bottled Chardonel is gone, Chardonel sourced from elsewhere in Indiana or from other states is still available. The need for those grapes from outside the state will be greater for the foreseeable future, since many of Mallow Run's Chardonel vines were wiped out by the low temperatures during the winter of 2013–14, and they did not replace most of the lost vines. They will likely try another white grape variety as an alternative or supplemental dry wine to the Chardonel. The largest winery in Indiana, Oliver Winery, has more than fifty acres planted in wine grapes, but over 90 percent of its wines are made from grapes or juice produced by someone else outside Indiana.

Some smaller wineries get their start using juice concentrate that requires adding water. I know of one winery owner who went in on a shipment of Chilean Syrah/Shiraz concentrate with a couple of other wineries, including one in Canada. Concentrated juice is available for purchase and relatively inexpensive due to the global wine industry. Can wineries make decent wine from concentrate? Certainly. I have occasionally had some, especially fruity semi-sweet white wines that I wouldn't have known were made from concentrate had I not been told. I'm guessing that even experts could sometimes be fooled. But this has been the exception for me more than the rule. More to the point, buying wine made from concentrate at a winery seems akin to going to a coffeehouse and getting instant coffee. Instant coffee has the caffeine and the warmth, and it is better than nothing if you want a cup of coffee. But it is processed, and so is juice concentrate. Sugar may have been added. Water of who knows what quality must be added. Concentrate may be fine for the home winemaker, but personally I expect more from professionals.

A practice that is even more extreme than using grapes, juice, or concentrate from other places is purchasing finished wine for bottling. In accordance with the TTB labeling requirements, if the label says "Bottled by," "Blended and Bottled by," or "Cellared and Bottled by," the wine was most likely not made by the winery. It may have been made locally, but it also may have been made in California or anywhere else. I can understand using small amounts in a blend to try to improve a troubled wine, but selling whole bottles of wine as one's own when they were in fact made elsewhere, with grapes from who knows where, strikes me as odd. I think this is a rather different situation from the Sateks' having taken their grapes to Butler Winery to make wine before they had their permit.

I found a similar range of practices and views across the four states I studied. I didn't find anyone as adamant as Charles Thomas about using only *vinifera* varietals that were grown on the West Coast, but there were plenty of winemakers, especially urban boutique winemakers, getting most or all their grapes, juice, or concentrate from distant places. Arnie Esterer, owner of Markko Vineyard, was just as committed to *vinifera* varietals as Dr. Thomas, viewing them as the only high-quality wine grapes, but the big difference was that he was growing and using only his own grapes. However, growing *vinifera* grapes is risky or impossible in much of the Midwest. Markko Vineyard benefits from its location near Lake Erie and the moderating effects bodies of water have on temperature.

In defense of those who use grapes from other places, there simply aren't enough local grapes being produced—not even close to enough. Bruce Bordelon told me that Indiana would need to grow three to four times the quantity of grapes it currently produces to create a truly Indiana product-based industry. The other states are in the same boat or worse. The number of wineries in Ohio and Iowa has grown substantially in the last few years, but the growth in the production of grapes is flat. Starting a vineyard, tending vines, spraying for diseases and pests, dealing with the risks posed by weather, harvesting, and waiting three to five years for a usable crop can easily dampen any initial enthusiasm that someone might have.

Despite this challenge, I agree with Jim Butler, Ted Huber, Chris Lawlor-White, and many other winery owners that for the Midwest's wine industries to thrive over the long term, they will need to develop identities more closely tied to locally sourced grapes—and for Lawlor-White and some other owners, other types of fruit. They will need to cultivate high-quality grapes that are well adapted and flavorful. Those grapes will then need to be turned into wines that have qualities people associate with the wines they like, including some fine wines that require more expensive treatment, or people will need to reeducate their taste buds and noses and expand their wine consciousness to include the different flavors. It will probably take a bit of both.

Developing a supply of Midwestern grapes is not just about identity and the importance of place or terroir to that identity. It could prove to be economically necessary for the industry's survival to put more effort into planting vines and encouraging the growth of a Midwestern grape supply. Just as many Midwestern wineries have survived and expanded by using grapes sourced from other areas, they may also go out of business if those supplies dry up or the price skyrockets. Midwestern wineries that rely on grapes from California have been fortunate that the supply from there has generally increased over the years. California grape prices have also gone up due to rising demand and shifts in the varieties grown, although the increase has been gradual overall, with some parts of California seeing a decrease depending on the varietal demand (Volpe et al. 2010). The 2015 California grape harvest was down overall from the bumper crops of 2012, 2013, and 2014. Prices on average also went down, in part due to excess supply from the previous three years (Wine Business.com 2016). So in the short run, Midwestern wineries dependent on California grapes will probably not have supply problems. But if supply continues to go down or demand increases in the next few years, prices might go up more than usual and/or some varieties might not be available. If so, then those Midwestern wineries with reliable local or regional suppliers would be less affected—unless those suppliers were still recovering from the vine losses suffered as a result of the 2014 polar vortex. Making a living off of an agricultural product is a roll of the dice despite the best-laid plans.

Some winery owners have already recognized the need to plan for more local sourcing. Mark Easley told me that his family's winery had begun contracting with growers both in and outside Indiana, and providing assistance with vineyard startups. Mark spent the summers of his youth raising grapes on his family's Cape Sandy property in Crawford County, along the Ohio River. Once heavily reliant on making wine from their own grapes, the Easleys sold the Cape Sandy property and began contracting with growers to focus on production. The winery released a Chambourcin in September 2013 made from grapes produced by two Indiana farm, and noted this contractual arrangement in the advertising.

Glancing through the *Indianapolis Star* one morning in August 2014, I noticed a Marsh supermarket advertisement offering Oliver Soft and Honey Wines and Easley Reggae Wines for $6.99, with the word "Local" appearing above the price. Local companies? Yes, in terms of central Indiana, where the *Star* distributes its papers. Fermented locally? Yes. Locally sourced grapes and honey? Mostly no. Clearly this regional grocery chain was trying to find a way to benefit from the "buy local" movement, but the wines they were promoting would not likely be considered "local food" because their ingredients aren't locally sourced. The companies are local for residents of central Indiana, but the wines they sell in large quantities are "local value added" and made with grapes from other states. These wineries are also the two biggest producers in the state and distribute to other states—in Oliver's case, many other states. Both wineries are starting to move into a different tier of distribution, and their target populations for the advertised wines are no longer the people walking through their winery doors but people beyond central Indiana. The wineries aren't local for those people. So the radio advertisements that Oliver ran in central Indiana in late 2015 about its "locally crafted wines" make sense only in that location. These two wineries are regional and growing, but they still barely register on the production scale of the international wine behemoths.

The Impact of Globalization on
Distribution in the Midwest

The title of this book is also a nod toward the 2004 documentary film *Mondovino*. Most Midwestern wineries are small, local operations, not *mondo*, or world sized (in Italian). That film got me thinking about the growing power of a few international wine conglomerates before I started exploring the topic in more depth. The story line hops from California and the Robert Mondavi company to France, where, according to the film, winery owners with a love for the old ways have been under attack by these huge conglomerates and their scientific wine consultants. One of those consultants, Michel Rolland, an enologist who has a lab in Bordeaux, is shown advising his clients to use a process he refers to as micro-oxygenation to soften wines and make them more palatable. The film then moves to Italy, where the same struggle is underway, and then to Argentina, where it is played out again. According to the film, the corporations and consultants cater to the tastes of the U.S. wine critic and rater Robert Parker, as well as to the average American drinker, who prefers predictable, fruit-forward, inoffensive wines that lack any relation to terroir. There are plenty of others who share this view of Parker. Colman, in his book *Wine Politics* (2008), observes: "[Parker] is the world's most influential wine critic. His notes and scores can send the fortunes of wineries around the world soaring or plummeting. Parker has been called the 'emperor of wine' and the 'dictator of taste.' Parker's influence is so great that many wineries have styled their wines into what he calls 'hedonistic fruit bombs' simply to please his palate" (2008, 2).

As Veseth (2011) suggests in *Wine Wars*, his book about the global wine market, the situation may not be as bad as the film claimed. The wines being produced by the global market for most of us who can't afford private jets, yachts, and top-end French or California wines are pretty darn cheap and of fairly high quality. The average stuff is much improved in comparison to the 1970s and 1980s. Veseth thinks there is a great likelihood that we will soon be limited to only a few options on what he refers to as the "wine wall"—the shelves at your place of purchase: (1) cheap stuff that isn't too offensive and matches our shrinking pocketbooks ("price sensitivity," as he puts it), (2) slightly better stuff such as the fruit bombs that line grocery store shelves and provide a pleasant enough experience to satisfy Americans' (and increasingly Chinese) Coca-Cola–trained taste buds, and (3) high-end (i.e., expensive) wines for the wealthy few that are an expression of the places in which they are produced. As Veseth (2011, 47–48) puts it, the problem with this situation is that we may end up with "nowhere" or "everywhere" wines that lack any qualities associated with place.

Veseth uses the term "terroirists," what seems to be a not too veiled play on the word "terrorists," to describe those who want to retain the qualities of wine associated with a particular place. (He doesn't mention this, but Todd Kliman used the term a year earlier, in his interesting book about the Norton grape, *The Wild Vine* [2010], although there it includes a hyphen: "terroir-ists.") In these times, with banks getting bailed out by the government while corporate CEOs sail off on their golden parachutes, and with the petroleum and healthcare industries raking in record profits while we watch gas prices and insurance costs shoot up (or in the case of gas prices, go up and back down), it's easy to be persuaded by stories about heartless corporate villains who want to control markets and manipulate our tastes and purchases for their profit. I won't go through Veseth's whole analysis, but one thing he claims that *Mondovino* leaves out is that the big French cooperatives that make more than half of France's wine tend to produce consistent, but mostly what he terms "mediocre," wine (2011, 169–76). He concludes that the concerns of the French terroirists are less about quality, or "tradition and terroir," than "about power and autonomy" and their fear of having to compete in the global market (176, 178). He notes that he is simplifying the story a bit (168), and I'm simplifying it even further in summary here. Whether the French terroirists are simply trying to protect themselves from global competition so they can go on making middling wines, or whether they are trying to protect the unique qualities of their winemaking and wines that are closely associated with place is not what interested me most about the film or the exploration it prompted for me. It was the direction the competition seemed to be headed.

From a U.S. perspective, there are two parts to what can be characterized as consolidation and concentration of ownership in the global wine industry. One is the concentration of distribution in the hands of fewer, bigger businesses. This is the group that many Midwestern winery owners perceive as the problem, since the wholesalers control access to retailers through the three-tier system in most states. I say "perceived" because there is a second part to consolidation, and that is on the production side, where wineries are being purchased by global corporations such as E. & J. Gallo, the Wine Group, and

Constellation. In 2013, those three companies controlled almost half of the U.S. wine market, with Gallo controlling almost as much as the other two combined, and they have a great deal of influence over the wholesale distributors. But let me first talk about the wholesale distributors in the United States, since that is the group most Midwest winery owners perceive as holding them down.

One reason the three-tier system was created by many state legislatures was to prevent producers from monopolizing the system. However, the unintended consequence is that it has resulted in what Pinney refers to as "monopoly conditions for the wholesalers" (2005, 347). There were more than ten thousand wholesale distributors in the 1960s. By 2012, those numbers were down to a few hundred, with the top ten wine and spirits wholesalers controlling over 60 percent of the market (Impact Newsletter 2012), and the top five over 50 percent (Thornton 2013). I think the more accurate term for describing the situation at this point is "oligopoly," or control by a few firms that make exclusive deals mostly with very large producers. The concentration of distribution ownership and restricted opportunities this poses for small Midwestern wineries is undeniable.

The other part of the story is that the wholesale distributors are organized nationally through the Wine and Spirits Wholesalers of America and have very deep pockets, whereas the small wine industries are primarily organized on the state level and, while booming, do not have the financial resources at their disposal to heavily support their efforts in the political game. An analysis funded by the Specialty Wine Retailers Association (2008), a California-based group of retailers that want to be able to purchase wines from wineries and distribute them to customers, found that from 2000 to 2006, more than $49 million was donated by wholesalers to state-level candidates across the United States. The report noted that more was spent by wholesalers in Ohio than by a long list of liberal and conservative interest groups combined.

The wholesale distributors are the most obvious obstacle to winery owners who want to expand into retail or ship to any state. But the transnational wine-producing conglomerates might be the bigger obstacle. When I asked Mark Easley about the issues or problems confronting winery owners, this was a big one for him. As he explained:

> I'd say the biggest one that regional wineries are facing is market access, without a doubt. The consolidation of the wholesaler tier is *really* becoming a problem [his emphasis]. With these wineries, we'll just never get market access. They will only be as good as what they can sell at their one location in their one spot in the state of Indiana, and that's kind of unfortunate because some of them are pretty darn good. But to me, market access is going to be a problem, and it's only getting worse. The large liquor companies in particular are really closing their grips on the mid-tier. The Diageos [an international beverage conglomerate] of

the world say, "I want my exclusive distributor; I do not want any other brands here." Gallo will say the same thing: "We are a Gallo house; we don't need any other wines." And you know, as small as Indiana is, with, what, three to five million people, you can only have so many wholesalers that can cover the whole state, and market access is going to be a real problem.

Gallo is not just a winery that produces the wine with that name on the label in Modesto, California. It is still run by the Gallo family, but it is a giant conglomerate that owns about sixty wine brands and additional beverage and spirit brands. It has products in ninety countries and both exports and imports wine (E. & J. Gallo Winery 2015). Gallo doesn't always indicate its ownership on the bottles of the wines it sells, so it would be easy to miss how often you might be purchasing the company's wines. It also sells a range of wines, from the bottom-shelf Carlo Rossi to the top-shelf Australian wines of Clarendon Hills. They have been the heavyweight at the bottom to mid-tier in price and quality, but they are expanding at the top. I get a daily news feed emailed from Wine Business.com, and the lead story is often about which winery is being purchased by which conglomerate. For example, the featured story on August 26, 2015, was a Gallo press release announcing that it was in the process of purchasing Talbott Vineyards, a high-end California winery in the Santa Lucia Highlands AVA. The purchase included the Talbott tasting room in Carmel Valley and a 525-acre vineyard (Wine Business.com 2015).

Gallo and the other big wine conglomerates have many wines that are highly desired by wholesalers because they can sell them in large quantities. For wholesalers to get a distribution deal with one of these major producer-suppliers, they typically have to agree to carry a wide variety of the wines in the producer-supplier's portfolio. Those wines crowd the shelves of retailers, and the wholesalers aren't particularly interested in bothering with a local winery that might move a few bottles of wine in a week.

It doesn't have to be this way. Alcohol production, distribution, retail sales, and direct shipping laws are state decisions. Ohio and Iowa allow wineries to distribute directly to retailers if they choose. I talked to owners of small wineries in both states who had their own sales personnel and self-distributed their wines to grocery and liquor stores. Jeff Quint estimated that his Cedar Ridge Winery, which is in eastern Iowa, distributes 60 percent of its wine to retail outlets. Two-tier distribution makes it economically feasible for small wineries to expand beyond their onsite sales if they make a quality product that attracts customer demand and are willing to put in the additional time and effort this requires. And they don't lose the 25 percent or so that distributors take. The distributor's cut may be worth it with higher-volume sales, but it can be tough to reach that level.

Local Dependence on the
Global Wine Industry

One of the things I was interested in exploring was to what extent the Mid-western wine industry is connected to or even dependent on the global wine industry. An in-depth analysis is beyond the scope of this particular book, but I thought it was worth sharing a brief summary of what I learned. Clearly the growing popularity of wine in the last forty years has been driven by the global industry. Wineries in the Midwest, along with those in the other states outside of California, wouldn't be doing as well as they are if Mondavi, Gallo, and a few others hadn't created the earlier demand for wine, and if the international conglomerates (including Gallo in its current form and Mondavi's owner, Constellation) hadn't built on that. On the other hand, the three-tier system foisted on the Midwestern wine industry by wholesalers and their political friends and fed by the large wine conglomerates has worked to keep all but a few wineries far from regional distribution, much less national or global.

The Midwest wine industry has benefited from the globalization of the wine industry in other ways. For example, there are no Midwestern producers of corks (natural, synthetic, or even screw caps). Real corks come mostly from Portugal and Spain. There are also no wine bottles made in the region anymore. The global behemoth O-I, formerly Owens-Illinois, no longer makes bottles in Illinois. It does produce bottles in California, one of its eighty plants in twenty-three countries (O-I, n.d.). Many of the wineries I visited used less expensive bottles that are produced in Mexico. The growth of the global wine industry has also resulted in a range of winemaking equipment that, while not inexpensive, has become readily available and more affordable.

French oak barrels are still commonly used for the flavors they provide, and I also saw Russian and Hungarian barrels. But there are a growing number of regional cooperages. I saw barrels made with oak from Kentucky, Indiana, Missouri, and Minnesota in the cellars I visited. Barrel choice is more a mat-ter of the flavors a winemaker seeks to impart. But there appears to be some movement toward more suppliers in the U.S. heartland rather than fewer.

Diversifying to Address Competition from
Craft Breweries and Distilleries

Perhaps the bigger immediate concern for local wineries is the new kids in the neighborhood who are experiencing their own boom: microbreweries, brewpubs, and distilleries. At the turn of the century, there were probably less than a dozen microbreweries in Indiana. Now there are more than one hundred, well surpassing the number of wineries. Some winery owners mentioned these as their biggest competitors. Jackie Trexel, owner of the urban winery Quail Crossing Cellars in Columbus Ohio, told me that in her attempt to get customers through the door, she wasn't competing so much with other wineries as with brewpubs and bars.

One of the real advantages of beer is that it takes much less time to ferment and get to the customer, so there is no need to wait the four to six months that it takes to produce simpler wines, let alone the year or two required for cask-aged wine. Ales can take as little as two weeks, and lagers up to two months. In contrast, if you are just starting a winery and want to use your own grapes, you must add the expense of the plants, the planting time and cost if you have help, a three-to-five-year wait, and a tremendous amount of tending to get your grapes ready for their first fermentation. Breweries also don't seem to have the same concern about sourcing their ingredients that wineries face in obtaining grapes. There is no TTB oversight regarding where the hops come from—no appellation of origin or AVA concerns. Sourcing of ingredients in terms of location is starting to become a topic, but the variety of hops or malted barley is more commonly mentioned at the brewpub unless one is getting very beer geeky about it. New York State did pass a farm brewery law in 2012 that provides tax breaks and allows onsite serving for breweries using New York ingredients (Jay 2015). So if there is a local sourcing trend, it is in its very early stages.

Some wineries have taken the old adage "If you can't beat them, join them" to heart and started their own breweries. In Ohio, Debonne Vineyards was the first to add a brewery, Cellar Rats. Valley Vineyards has Cellar Dweller Craft Beers. In Indiana, J & J Winery has Big Dawg Brewhaus, Simmons Winery has 450 North Brewery, and Cedar Creek Winery added "and Brew Co." to its name in 2015. Illinois and Iowa wineries haven't been as quick to make a move into brewing beer. Illinois has the Village Vintner Winery and Brewery in Algonquin. The winemaker at Jasper Winery in Des Moines, Iowa, Mason Groben, is also the brewmaster at Madhouse Brewing Company (and a graduate of the University of California, Davis's viticulture and enology program). The brewery and winery are not located at the same site. I wasn't able to identify another Iowa winery that produces beer, although wineries and breweries are promoted together by the Iowa Wine and Beer Promotion Board.

Micro-distilleries are also competing with wineries for customer attention. Two recently opened fifteen minutes from my home in an area that features six breweries and two wineries (one a meadery making honey-based wine). The first distillery in Indiana, Starlight Distillery, is located at Huber's Orchard, Winery and Vineyards. It was licensed in 2000, after Ted Huber pushed for legislation to make it possible for him to have both a winery and a distillery, and the first brandy was sold in 2004. Huber explained to me that a distillery

Figure 8.1. The still at Cedar Ridge Winery and Distillery, the first in Iowa since the repeal of Prohibition, May 6, 2015. Photo by Jim Pennell.

makes it possible to take the wine made in years when there are big crops and turn it into brandy, adding shelf life due to the higher alcohol level while reducing the volume of storage to one-tenth of what was needed for the wine. In addition to brandy and brandy-infused beverages, Starlight is producing vodka, gin, and bourbon.

In 2005, Jeff Quint added a distillery at Cedar Ridge Winery—the first distillery to open in the state of Iowa since Prohibition. Visitors can sample the rum, vodka, and whiskey produced there, but they cannot purchase drinks to consume on the premises as they can with wine because of legal restrictions. They can purchase up to two bottles per visit to take home. Quint told me he was hoping to have the law changed so that onsite consumption would be possible. I asked him if he was concerned that the winery and restaurant would become more like a bar and lose its laid-back vibe. He said he did have some concerns about it, but that they would continue to close early to avoid getting "that late bar crowd." He noted that if he were in an urban location, he would likely want to be open later. His distillery also promotes its local sourcing of corn for its whiskeys. Joel Kopsa of John Ernest Vineyard and Winery was also in the process of applying for a distillery permit when I spoke with him.

Do Midwestern Wineries Make "Good" Wine That Can Compete Internationally?

One question I often get from people I meet who are regular wine drinkers but are unfamiliar with Midwestern wines is, Are there Midwestern wines that are any good? "Good," of course, is a relative term; it depends upon the perceiver. Perhaps the more difficult question is, Are there Midwestern wines that a wine connoisseur would consider good? I think I can answer the first question fairly confidently, and that would be a resounding "yes." I'm not being a cheerleader here; there are some really good Midwestern wines.

Most of the wine drinkers who ask me whether there are any good Midwestern wines assume that the only wines being made are sweet wines. Some of the winemakers I talked to spent a fair amount of time explaining to me that sweet wines also have a range of qualities that a discriminating drinker can recognize. Although I don't usually go for them as my first choice, I can easily tell the difference between a well-made Niagara or Catawba and a poorly made one. Are there wines for the Cabernet Sauvignon, Merlot, and Pinot Noir drinkers on the red side, and Chardonnay, Sauvignon Blanc, and Pinot Grigio drinkers on the white side? Yes. There are actually some Cabernet Sauvignon, Chardonnay, and Pinot Noir grapes, and a larger quantity of Cabernet Franc grown in northeastern Ohio and the southern parts of Ohio, Indiana, and Illinois. Midwestern winemakers are making good wines from these familiar varieties, although their flavors can be a bit different from what most people are used to, and they are often a bit lighter than the heavy Syrahs and Cabernet Sauvignons from California.

I think the real promise is with French-American hybrid and American varieties that produce dry wines of complexity and character, such as Chardonel and Seyval Blanc on the white side, and Chambourcin and Norton on the red side. Some wineries are also making excellent red blends using varieties such as Chancellor, DeChaunac, Noiret, Corot Noir, and Leon Millot. On the white

Figure 8.2. Wine bottles of various Midwestern wineries. *From left to right*: Cedar Ridge Marechal Foch; Chateau Shamrock Apple Wine; Blue Sky Vineyard's 2012 Chambourcin Reserve; Markko 2012 Cabernet Sauvignon Reserve; Rettig Hill 2010 Ohio River Valley Belle Rouge; Butler 2013 Estate Vidal Blanc; Winery at Wolf Creek Summit County 2012 Cabernet Franc; Galena Cellars Frontenac Gris; Mallow Run Rosé of Corot Noir; Tassel Ridge 2013 Edelweiss; Henke 2012 Seyval; Alto Vineyards Saluki Dawg House Red.

side, Vignoles, Traminette, and Vidal can be made dry or semi-dry. There is much to enjoy about a well-made Vignoles that would please most white wine fans, and if not, then a good Chardonel will take care of many more. Mallow Run does a dry and a semi-sweet Traminette to address different taste preferences. In northeastern Ohio, as well as Michigan, you will also find Rieslings done in different styles. John Ernest's Morning Dew wine, a semi-dry made from the hybrid St. Pepin grape, was one of my "go-to" summer wines while I was working on this book—a little hint of a German style, but a wine that stood up well with the range of other white wines I drank.

But what about the wine connoisseur? Would Robert Parker find anything in the Midwest that he thought was worth drinking and recommending? I think so, but honestly, I don't know. So I will answer this question a little differently. Many of the Midwestern winemakers I talked to compared their wines to the wines of the world. Nick Ferrante, Ted Huber, Bill Oliver, Mark Easley, Jim Butler, Jeff Hill, Chris Lawlor-White, Karen Hand, and Jeff Quint all said in their own ways that in order for their wineries to do well, their wines have to compete with those that are distributed globally. Most of them talked about wine as an experience, but part of that experience is drinking good, not average, wine. When I drink Huber's Heritage wine, a Bordeaux-style blend of Cabernet Sauvignon, Cabernet Franc, and Petit Verdot, I think it compares with many of the finer wines I've had in my life. Blue Sky's Montage, a blend of Chambourcin, Noiret, and Norton, has much in common with fine Italian wines. One bit of fun I have with my wife is to pour her a glass of wine and have her guess what it is and where it is from. She plays this game pretty well usually, but she thought Montage was a European wine. The problem for Midwestern wines is that the connoisseurs who read *Wine Spectator* aren't going to read about Huber's Heritage or Blue Sky's Montage, and Robert Parker isn't going to rate it. Unless the connoisseurs go to Huber's, or go to the Louisville area and happen upon a restaurant that serves this fine wine, then behave uncharacteristically and take a chance on it, they will never know. Huber's isn't part of the corporate wine industry or the wine regions the industry has made famous. They also can't easily ship out of state to anywhere in the world.

The other problem is that our knowledge and palates have been biased, or perhaps the better word is trained, by the global wine industry and wine elites. People have a sense of what to expect from wine based on California Cabernet/Merlot/Pinot Noir training, or the usual whites. Chambourcin grapes can make an amazing wine, but people don't know what to expect because they usually haven't been educated about Chambourcin. Chambourcin is an interesting grape. Its lineage is a bit fuzzy, a French-American hybrid of nonspecific origins. I like to think of it as a "chameleon" wine that readily adapts to what nature provides it. It can vary substantially depending upon the year. All grapes do, but Chambourcin seems especially affected to me. It can range from a light, rich, cherry-flavored Pinot Noir–style wine to a darker, spicy Zinfandel. The winemaker's treatment of the grapes is also a factor. When I play the wine-guessing game with Greta, Chambourcin is often the stumper because it can seem similar to a range of other wines and can have excellent qualities whatever the style. Sometimes I find Chambourcins to be a bit musty or grassy. When I mentioned that I occasionally notice some mustiness in them, one winemaker said to me that maybe it wasn't the variety's fault, but that the grapes were a bit old or moldy. I learned that the grassiness probably comes from grapes that weren't quite ripe enough. Getting the best-quality grapes picked at just the right time can be a challenge, whether a winemaker is growing them or purchasing them. This is something the Midwest will need to improve on.

Midwestern wines tend to be lighter and less dense or concentrated, and the alcohol levels are often a percentage or two lower in comparison to the "big, intense, highly extracted wines" that Robert Parker is sometimes criticized for favoring (Veseth 2011, 123). However, the lighter Midwestern styles can often be more food friendly and provide more subtle flavors. I was never much of a fan of Cabernet Franc by itself, but I like the lighter style that is typical of these wines in the Midwest. Midwestern wines may also fare well if the move by some countries to once again lower the alcohol levels that define drunk driving catches hold and becomes law.

Often overlooked in discussions about the best wine regions or countries is that there are a lot of middling to poor wines from California, Australia, New Zealand, and France. I should throw in Italy and Spain. I know this too well. I occasionally take chances on unfamiliar low-priced wines hoping I will get lucky, and I have poured my share of those wines down the drain or doctored them and used them for meat marinade. Good and bad wines are made everywhere. The point about Midwestern wines is that there are many good ones that suit different taste preferences, and collectively they are generally improving. Some are stellar and reflect all the best qualities a winemaker can coax from the grapes, as wine competition judges regularly affirm.

Can Midwestern Wineries Become Global Players?

Assuming there are good Midwestern wines that people might like if they tried them, could the region's wineries end up being players in the global market? Will the newly created Loess Hills AVA, the Indiana Uplands AVA, the Shawnee Hills AVA, the very large Upper Mississippi Valley AVA, and the Ohio Valley AVA become recognizable players on the world, or at least the national, stage? It may seem like a pipe dream, but some winery owners are thinking that way, and in my view, rightly so. As wine historian Paul Lukacs notes in *The Great Wines of America: The Top Forty Vintners, Vineyards, and Vintages*, "Only a generation ago, a book about great American wine would have been regarded as a joke" (2005, 13). He is talking about perceptions of California wine prior to 1976, when two California wines beat out the French wines in the "Judgment of Paris" contest. For his list of "top forty" American wines, he includes a sparkling wine from Michigan, a Norton from Missouri, and a Viognier from Virginia, as well as two New York wines (a dry Riesling and a Merlot). A 2013 *Sunday New York Times* article on the success of the Virginia wine industry noted the inroads that the Virginia winery Barboursville Vineyards has made into the market in Brooklyn, New York, where its wines have become popular (Carter 2013).

That wineries in areas not known for wine could gain an international reputation may seem farfetched, but New Zealand went from unknown to a global exporter in a few decades. Chambourcin is grown on New Zealand's North Island, although not in sufficient quantities to be promoted internationally yet. Perhaps the surprise twist in the future will be the popularization of that grape variety by New Zealand wineries, thereby creating an opening and attracting attention to Midwest producers. Jeff Hill told me he thought Chambourcin is a grape variety that southern Indiana wineries could adopt as a signature red because it makes wines of very good quality and grows well there. Ditto for southern Illinois, where some of the best Chambourcins I have enjoyed have been sourced. Mallow Run grows Chambourcin grapes, but also often purchases additional Chambourcin from Illinois, and Bill Richardson commonly makes good wine from them. I say "commonly" because the crop of grapes every year is different, and different things can also happen in the winery that can affect what we taste.

Other French-American hybrids, and perhaps the American homegrown Norton grape, could become more internationally recognized and sought-after varieties. This would not play into the strengths of the major wine powers in Europe and the United States, so it would be a struggle. Still, Huber's 2012 Vignoles won the Wine of the Year award at the 2013 Indy International Wine Competition, selected as the best wine out of more than twenty-three hundred entries. Why wouldn't someone in Great Britain want to try a bottle of an expert-selected wine of the year that doesn't cost very much, even if only for the novelty? Part of the enjoyment of wine is in new discoveries and sharing them with your friends. The Noiret grape has tannins that make it a great blender, but I enjoyed the 100 percent Noiret of another Illinois winery, Sleepy Creek Vineyards. It was a medium-bodied red wine with a nice mouthfeel. I served it to guests, and they wanted to know what it was and where I got it. My discovery of the Marquette grape was a 2009 vintage produced by Tassel Ridge Winery in Iowa. I was very surprised that a grape created for cold climates at the University of Minnesota could produce such an intense, big-bodied red wine, so big that decanting was a good idea to give it some oxygen and soften it a bit.

The French are masters of blending to make good wine, and many Midwestern winemakers are adopting that strategy with good results. I already mentioned the blends produced by Huber's and Blue Sky, but I also tasted great blends at two Illinois wineries, Sleepy Creek Vineyards and Cameo Vineyards. At Rettig Hill I enjoyed a big red wine called Grande Noir, which that year was a blend of Villard Noir (once the most commonly grown grape in France until it was banned for its non-*vinifera* heritage) and Norton. According to winemaker Jeff Hill, however, its composition changes from year to year; in 2013, for example, it contained only Norton grapes. Again, giving a wine a fanciful name means that you don't have to change the label. The Marquette and Marechal Foch blend at White Oak Vineyards in Illinois was a wine that took advantage of the heavier quality of the first grape and the fruitier quality of the second. Massbach Ridge Winery's flagship red, Massbach Reserve, was also a nice surprise. It was a blend of mostly Frontenac with some Marechal Foch.

I really can't list all the interesting wines I had at wineries across the four states I studied. First, most of them will be different vintages by the time you read this, or they won't be making them, or they will be experimenting with different blends. I can talk about them, and I may drive you to this place or that, but that really isn't my intention here. Learning about them is really your assignment if you choose to accept it.

Contemplating the Future of Midwestern Wineries

My personal preference for dry wines or the preferences of the wine elite may not be where Midwestern wines find their way into the global market. Even if Europeans aren't interested, there is a long-standing and growing U.S. market for semi-dry and sweet wines (Thach and Chang 2015). As a number of the winemakers I interviewed explained, they can make the drier styles many of them and some of their customers prefer only if they also produce sweeter wines for the large number of customers who prefer those. Sweet, Concord-based wines are the top seller at many wineries. Mallow Run's top seller is a sweet but slightly tart rhubarb wine.

Mark Easley said that he was able to compete with the big wineries on the grocery store shelves because he made sweet wine people liked at a price they found reasonable, and the big wineries whose products are globally distributed weren't doing that so much. However, this is changing as the big producers respond to the growing U.S. demand. Easley also talked about a Chinese delegation that state officials brought to Indianapolis who were more interested in Indiana wines than many other products the state was trying to promote. Even Dr. Thomas admitted that, despite his reservations, when his production team pushed him to create a sweet wine, his Sweet Aubergine became a top seller. His winery also sells sweet wines in cute jugs with a historic Indiana cartoon character on the front—very "down home" coming from a self-professed European-style winemaker and wine lover. As he reminded me, though, the grapes in those jugs are *vinifera*. The recent Moscato craze, the popularity of wine coolers (a blend of wine, fruit juices, and flavor additives), and the earlier White Zinfandel boom were all a response to the demand for some sweetness in wines. They may not be wines that those with more developed palates find appealing, but they can have certain qualities that make them enjoyable and a good accompaniment to some foods.

It may also be that some Midwestern wineries become good at branding and promoting their brands, going for volume sales as opposed to producing and selling higher-priced, low-volume wines. Oliver and Easley have demonstrated some success with this. Meier's has been doing it for some time. Ferrante is the biggest single brand across Ohio and also distributes in Chicago

Figure 8.3. Chateau Thomas Winery's Blackberry Merlot label, featuring Abe Martin of Brown County, a historical cartoon figure created by humorist Kin Hubbard who was featured in U.S. newspapers in the first three decades of the twentieth century. Note the "For Sale in Indiana Only" statement, which allows the use of the Merlot varietal name. Label courtesy of Chateau Thomas Winery, Nashville, Indiana, used with permission.

and Florida. Of course, the more that Midwestern wineries focus on branding and volume, the more their products seem like the rest of the wines they are competing with on the grocery store shelves. But that may be precisely the point. They want to compete and win with what they can bring to the market, in some cases with flavors the global taste makers may be reluctant to produce.

I will note once again that most Midwestern wineries make a range of wines to suit customers' different tastes. Perhaps they can play both sides of the fence on this. Many people who drink wine that I casually talk to assume that Midwestern wineries primarily make sweet wines and offer little they would be interested in drinking. It is difficult to have more than one reputation, although I can hear the winemakers I talked to telling me they strive for quality in whatever they do, and that is what they are building their reputation on. Perhaps the sweet wine reputation will pay the bills, and the rest of us can then enjoy the other things they make in lower quantities. The problem is, you have to go to the wineries or catch them at a festival to find and learn about them, or have some knowledgeable friends. You aren't usually going to find these wines on the shelf at a grocery or liquor store, or if you do, it will be the higher-volume sweet varieties. I have noticed a little improvement with this situation at some of the local liquor stores in Indianapolis in the last few years, and I found even better circumstances in Ohio, Illinois, and Iowa. But without some experience with the wines or persuasive advertising, customers will reach for what they know.

It may seem somewhat absurd to think that small Midwestern wineries can compete with transnational wine corporations, but many winery owners talked to me about that. Some owners played down the competition and said the big transnational players had nothing to fear from them—that they *weren't* competing with them. These owners claimed they were primarily offering an experience of wine and place that the big dogs couldn't provide. No one wants to have a wedding at a liquor or grocery store. But the leaders in the state industries, those who have been doing it for a while and have a longer and perhaps broader view on the matter, talked about the need to expand market share relative to the Gallo and Constellation Brands portfolios. They know that the current legal arrangements are stacked against them, and it will require the states to create a more level playing field for them to successfully compete, given the current advantages the system provides to the big producers and distributors.

Beyond political changes, what might winemakers do to make potential customers better aware of the range of wines they produce? Given the diversity of terroir and the corresponding differences in the grapes that can be grown in Ohio, Indiana, and Illinois, I think wineries may need to create an image that captures that diversity. Or perhaps there is a need to create stronger local viticulture identities that center on commonalities of terroir, grapes, and wine styles in particular areas. Perhaps more AVAs can be created, or if not, some quasi-AVA marketing substitute such as small groups of wineries promoting their appellation of origin and emphasizing certain varietals and styles. There needs to be something that captures both specificity and diversity better than the label "Ohio Table Wine" or "Indiana Table Wine." As noted in chapter 7, Indiana Uplands AVA wineries have taken this step, in addition to organizing so they can act as a cooperative and attract USDA grants for research and marketing. This should help them further improve quality and continue to build a collective image as a premier winemaking region. The Grand River Valley AVA produces distinctive styles of *vinifera* wines and some hybrids in northeastern Ohio. Multiple wineries are located in close proximity in some parts of this area, making it look like a wine region. The Loess Hills area of western Iowa, which had a long history of producing grapes until they were wiped out by herbicides, recently attained AVA status. Perhaps the far northeastern part of Indiana could be the next. In some cases, it might make sense to reach across state lines to unite wineries with common terroir. The Ohio Valley and Upper Mississippi Valley AVAs are examples of this kind of collaboration, although perhaps they are too big for the purposes of building a common identity and facilitating tourism.

Although most owners thought that the number of wineries would continue to grow in the near future and that there was much room to increase the percentage of wine sales going to in-state wineries versus the global brands, a few sensed some new problems on the horizon. They were starting to notice the wineries that were closing, had gone up for sale, or had recently been sold. Some owners who started wineries in the last couple of decades as retirement ventures were reaching their absolute retirement age, when they couldn't really do the work anymore or simply wanted to do less. Some had prepared for a transition by creating multigenerational family ownership. Others were looking for buyers; still others were shutting down. Some wineries continue to limp along without the customer traffic and the capital necessary to move to the next level. Andy Troutman, who owns two wineries, one he started and another he bought, was concerned that despite the growth of wineries in the state, the Ohio industry could be entering a new period:

> Look at the number of wineries that are for sale in the Midwest, you know, people that have either openly said I'm trying to find a buyer or it's listed. Kinkead is for sale. There's one over by Youngstown. There's one in Loudonville that never opened, but the winery and vineyard are there. There was one up along the lake last year. People can't find buyers. And that's what concerns me is there's people building wineries all over the place, but the existing wineries that have clientele, or product, or equipment can't find buyers. So I don't know. I don't know if that trend will continue . . . There was a winery east of here on 224, on the other side of Akron, and it opened the same year this one [Wolf Creek] did. Beautiful winery. The family that started it, he was an architect, built this really nice winery, had all these vines growing right along the highway, and one son who was running it decided he didn't want to do it anymore, and they just closed up. They sold the property to a developer, and nothing has been done with it for—that was probably fifteen years ago.

Checking online, I found one other Ohio winery with a vineyard for sale beyond those Troutman mentioned. There are likely other owners who are thinking about it. Arnie Esterer was wondering what he was going to do when I spoke with him, since he is in his eighties. When I visited Rockside Vineyards in the quaint town of Lancaster, Ohio, in 2014, new owners were in the process of taking over the property from the retiring former owners. Kinkead Ridge Winery in Ripley, Ohio, was sold and is back in business, but its vineyard was wiped out by the 2014 polar vortex, and the new wines it has released were made from California grapes. So a premier winery that was primarily using its own grapes radically changed its approach to remain a viable business thanks to Mother Nature. Similarly, in Illinois, where growth has noticeably slowed in the last few years, I found two wineries advertised for sale online at the beginning of 2016.

The phenomenal growth of wineries in Iowa in the last decade has left the state with a mix of wildly successful, modestly successful, and struggling wineries with outcomes influenced heavily by whether they have a good location that can provide customer traffic and, as often goes hand in hand with that, the ability to invest in operations and improve quality. Jeff Quint's Cedar Ridge Winery has benefited from both. When I asked him what he thought about the number of wineries climbing each year in Iowa, he said:

> I think it's going to decline at some point. I actually would have guessed it would by now. If you look around at some of the other states that maybe had a head start on us, you're seeing some big guys kind of rise to the top, and then maybe not as many in total. And I think that is what you are going to see here. I don't know why you wouldn't. You know, by some wineries' standards we're tiny, but within the state we're in the top ten wineries. If you're going to do it as a business and try to make it your livelihood, you've got to get to a certain volume, and I'm not sure there's room for everybody to do that. It's just like anything else.

Quint is a long-time business professional in Cedar Rapids, so he understands what is common in competitive industries as they begin to mature. This doesn't mean there won't be room for small Midwestern wineries to start up; it will simply be more difficult to do it on a shoestring because there are a growing number of Midwestern wineries that are well run and making very good wine. There likely will be fewer niche opportunities, but they will remain. Economists Kym Anderson, David Norman, and Glyn Wittwer argue that this is happening at a global level, and although they weren't thinking of Midwestern wineries in their analysis, I think their observation still holds:

> Preference for heterogeneity on the demand side, and the infinite scope for experimentation by vignerons [i.e., grape cultivators] on the supply side, ensures that there will always be small and medium producers alongside the few large corporations in the wine industry. Undoubtedly the forces of globalization together with the boom in premium winegrape supplies will lead to more mergers, acquisitions, and other alliances among wineries within and across national

borders, but their success in the global marketplace is likely to continue to provide a slipstream in which astute smaller operators can also thrive. (2003, 677)

I think there is an important place and a promising future for small wineries, assuming that political circumstances improve or at least don't worsen. Successful local winery owners are contextually attuned to the potential and constraints of place. They are a part of the communities they serve in all but a few cases. They can try new things without getting permission from a board of directors and can get immediate feedback from customers. They can also capitalize on a little serendipitous luck they didn't foresee or expect. Big conglomerates find it difficult to capture these elements of creativity and sensitivity to a place and its people, and if they manage to do so, they are unable to maintain it for very long. A downturn sends them scurrying for products to cut or subsidiaries to sell.

Admittedly, local wineries may seem to be niche markets for older middle-class people and young upwardly mobile professionals compared to the markets for other products such as corn or toilet paper. They can be seen as elements of wealthy people's exclusive lifestyles that have attracted the discretionary income of the middle-class professional and well-paid working classes. Some of my sociologist and anthropologist peers make this argument in their analyses (e.g., Howland 2013). But if you visit a Midwestern winery, you won't find only the well-heeled drinking the wine. The class barrier that seemed to exist with wines prior to the 1970s was probably broken by the pop wines such as White Zinfandel. The divide today may be better understood as sweet versus dry. More likely it is cheaper versus more expensive. The local wines aren't on the cheap end of the scale, but winery owners know they aren't going to sell them if they aren't affordable. A bottle of wine, a little food, some friends, and perhaps some entertainment make for an inexpensive and enjoyable get-together. Hanging out with the Richardsons, Hofmanns, Creasaps, or Kopsas is not a lesson in pretentiousness, but a sharing of stories and love for the land and the amazing things it can produce with a little human ingenuity and investment. It's laid-back fun.

As a sociologist who has developed a deep appreciation for what small winery owners do, I am probably somewhat of a terroirist. (And I certainly hope those working in the National Security Administration can spell!) My heart is with the little guys who make commitments to people and the land and try to pursue those commitments in skilled, thoughtful ways. Yet I also know that corporations are good at creating standardized things as inexpensively as possible and that people benefit in many ways from the global system of production and distribution. Big corporations can produce quality products and satisfy basic human needs inexpensively. But they also are adept purveyors of generic goods that provide limited, momentary satisfactions. Perhaps it takes these minimally satisfactory experiences with mass-produced products to help people appreciate what happens at small wineries, and both will continue to coexist. As Veseth (2001, 219) suggests, having multiple choices is typically viewed by economists as better than having fewer options, so circumstances could be worse.

The worst almost happened for Indiana wineries in 2006, when the wholesale distributors nearly convinced the Indiana General Assembly to require every drop of wine produced in the state to go through their hands. Wiser heads prevailed, but it was pretty close. You would think that the job growth and other economic benefits provided by wineries would matter to conservative, moderate, and liberal legislators alike, who all seem to agree that jobs are the primary solution to our state and national problems. The problem for small wineries in the Midwest is that big corporations and their industry associations bring big money to the table and influence the political process. In my view, money shouldn't be equated with free political speech, but that is the current law of our land as a result of U.S. Supreme Court decisions. Although the small wineries are doing pretty well, they certainly aren't winning any big legislative battles. At best they are making incremental progress and hoping the big guys and their legislative buddies don't destroy them in this rather serious game.

Midwestern wineries have grown not just because of their products, but because they also fill another niche—the need for local places where people can gather—that mass-produced wines cannot satisfy. At a local winery, the place and product become tied together in customers' minds and produce experiences that cannot be matched by mass-produced wines created by large corporate entities, despite the latter's research and marketing efforts. Local wineries give people a place to come together and get to know other people in their communities, while reminding us that getting together and relying on each other for a good time can be more fun than surfing the internet or watching television. These qualities can also attract tourists, including to counties that have lost their factories and need the jobs that local wineries and complementary services provide.

Despite the many challenges posed by legal restrictions, and barring any sudden changes, I think that in terms of opportunities and rewards, the "cup" will continue to be more than half full for winery owners, even with the demands of their work. It is going to become more challenging for those seeking to start a winery because the quality and cost to successfully compete and meet customers' expectations has gone up. For those of us in the Midwest who are winery customers, I think the cup will also continue to be more than half full in terms of the further development of quality at our local wineries and the opportunity to visit interesting places and share in the conviviality of the people who gather there. We need to do this in a responsible manner and avoid drinking excessively and driving. We need to teach our children about the pleasures of sharing a bottle of wine while taking care of ourselves and others and enjoying our times together. There is much to learn, share, and enjoy about our local wineries. My account of the contributions of wineries to the lives of those who work there and their communities is hopefully just a beginning or stop along your way, but I hope you see the wineries in Midwestern states a little differently and value them for the blend of vision, hard work, and social and historical circumstances they represent. I also hope you enjoy their wines and learn more about them, whatever flavors and styles you prefer. They are gifts of tradition and culture that we almost lost in these United States.

References

Alcohol and Tobacco Tax and Trade Bureau, U.S. Department of the Treasury. 2008. "What You Should Know about Grape Wine Labels." http://www.ttb.gov/pdf/brochures/p51901 .pdf.

———. 2013. "Changes in Labeling and Formula Approval Bring Electronic Filing Options." Updated July 25, 2013. http://www.ttb.gov/labeling/label-formula-application -adjustment.shtml.

———. 2014. "Quick Reference Guide to Wine Excise Tax." Updated November 26, 2014. http://www.ttb.gov/tax_audit/taxguide.shtml.

———. 2015. "Wine Appellations of Origin." Updated October 16, 2015. http://www.ttb .gov/appellation/index.shtml#requirement.

Anderson, Kym, David Norman, and Glyn Wittwer. 2003. "Globalisation of the World's Wine Markets." *World Economy* 26 (5): 659–87.

Barr, Andrew. 1999. *Drink: A Social History of America*. New York: Carroll & Graf.

Baughman, Allyson, Alexandra Schroeder, and Dean Schroeder. 2011. "Oliver Winery and the Recipe for Values-Based Leadership: People, Product and Place." *Journal of Values Based Leadership* 4 (1). http://www.valuesbasedleadershipjournal.com/issues /vol4issue1/oliver_winery.php.

Bordelon, Bruce P. 2001. "Growing Grapes in Indiana." Purdue University Cooperative Extension Service. http://www.hort.purdue.edu/ext/HO-45.pdf.

———. 2010. "Traminette Vineyard Management: How to Grow Indiana's Signature Wine Grape." Purdue University Cooperative Extension Service. https://www.extension.purdue .edu/extmedia/FS/FS-60-W.pdf.

———. 2011. "Watch Out for: Grapes." Purdue University Cooperative Extension Service. https://www.extension.purdue.edu/extmedia/ho/dw-10-w.pdf.

Butler, James L., and John J. Butler. 2001. *Indiana Wine: A History*. Bloomington: Indiana University Press.

Caetano, Raul, Catherine L. Clark, and Tammy Tam. 1998. "Alcohol Consumption among Racial/Ethnic Minorities." *Alcohol, Health and Research World* 22 (4): 233–41.

Carter, Adrienne. 2013. "In the Old Dominion, a New Terroir." *New York Times*, July 7. http://www.nytimes.com/2013/07/07/business/virginia-wines-in-the-old-dominion -a-new-terroir.html.

Casas, Gloria. 2015. "St. Charles Horticulture Center Closing Due to State Budget Cuts." *Elgin Courier-News*, December 8. http://www.chicagotribune.com/suburbs/elgin-courier -news/news/ct-ecn-farm-research-center-closing-st-1208-20151207-story.html.

Cattell, Hudson. 2014. *Wines of Eastern North America: From Prohibition to the Present*. Ithaca, NY: Cornell University Press.

Colman, Tyler. 2008. *Wine Politics*. Berkeley: University of California Press.

Daley, Bill. 2011. "Remembering Fred Koehler, Pioneer Winemaker." *Chicago Tribune*, July 18. http://articles.chicagotribune.com/2011-07-18/features/chi-remembering-fred -koehler-winemaker_1_christina-anderson-heller-illinois-wines-wine-lovers.

Dami, Imed, Bruce Bordelon, David C. Ferree, Maurus Brown, Michael A. Ellis, Roger N. Williams, and Douglas Doohan. 2005. *Midwest Grape Production Guide*. Ohio State University Extension Bulletin 919. http://www.oardc.ohio-state.edu/fruitpathology /Bulletins/mw_grape_12aug05%20S.pdf.

E. & J. Gallo Winery. 2015. "Company Fact Sheet." http://gallo.com/press-room/fact-sheet /CompanyFactSheet.html. Accessed September 2, 2015.

Epstein, Aaron. 2015. "Shattering the (Wine) Glass Ceiling." *Edible San Diego*, March–April. http://www.ediblesandiego.com/issues/march-april-2015/shattering-the-wine-glass -ceiling.html.

Esterer, Arnie. n.d. "Markko Vineyard Trellis: Potential for Organic Winegrowers." http:// markko.com/markko-trellis-new. Accessed April 12, 2016.

Federation of Tax Administrators. 2015. "State Tax Rates on Wine." http://www.taxadmin .org. Accessed June 15, 2015.

Firelands Winery. 2016. "History of the Winery." http://www.firelandswinery.com/history .php. Accessed July 16, 2015.

Flannigan, Will. 2012. "Ohio's Wine Industry: The Movers, Shakers, and Growers of a Blossoming Trade." *Farm and Dairy*, June 25. http://www.farmanddairy.com/top-stories /ohio%E2%80%99s-wine-industry-the-movers-shakers-and-growers-of-a -blossoming-trade/38688.html.

Forman, Janet, with additional research from Kathleen Buckley. 2011. "Wine's Face Chang- ing: How Does an Increasingly Diverse U.S. Population Impact the Wine Industry?" *Wine Enthusiast*, April 19. http://www.winemag.com/Web-2011/Wine-rsquos-Face -Changing/.

Foulkes, Arthur E. 2007. "Hoosier Wineries, Wholesalers Locked in Legal, Legislative Bat- tle." *Terre Haute Tribune Star*, March 3. http://www.tribstar.com/news/local_news/hoosier -wineries-wholesalers-locked-in-legal-legislative-battle/article_4336d077–88ef -5af4-a037-dc00418c4f12.html.

Frank, Rimerman and Co. 2013. "The Economic Impact of Illinois Wine and Wine Grapes—2012." http://illinoiswine.com/wordpress/wp-content/uploads/2014/12 /Illinois-2012Wine-Economic-Impact-Report.pdf.

———. 2014a. "The Economic Impact of Ohio Wine and Wine Grapes—2012." http://www .tasteohiowines.com/wp-content/uploads/2016/01/Ohio-2012-Economic-Impact -Report_FINAL.pdf.

———. 2014b. "The Economic Impact of Iowa Wine and Wine Grapes—2012." https://www .traveliowa.com/UserDocs/Iowa_2012_EI_Report_Final.pdf.

Galena Cellars Vineyard & Winery. 2013. "The Lawlor Family." http://www.galenacellars
.com/about/family/. Accessed March 5, 2015.

Ganchiff, Mark. 2012. "Illinois Reduces Funding for Wine Industry." *Midwest Wine Press*,
June 2. http://midwestwinepress.com/2012/06/02/illinois-reduces-funding-for-wine
-industry/.

———. 2013. "Midwest Winery Rankings for 2013." *Midwest Wine Press*, April 24.
http://midwestwinepress.com/2013/04/24/Midwest-winery-rankings-2013/.

———. 2014. "Vintage Indiana 2014 Photos and Review." *Midwest Wine Press*, June 8. http://
midwestwinepress.com/2014/06/08/vintage-indiana-2014-photos/.

———. 2015. "2015 Midwest Winery Rankings." *Midwest Wine Press*, May 2. http://midwest
winepress.com/2015/05/02/2015-midwest-winery-rankings/.

Gary, Aaron R. 2010. "Treating All Grapes Equally: Interstate Alcohol Shipping after *Granholm*." *Wisconsin Lawyer* 83 (3). http://www.wisbar.org/NewsPublications/Wisconsin
Lawyer/Pages/Article.aspx?Volume=83&Issue=3&ArticleID=2037.

Gibson, Richard. 2003. "Franchise Fever." *Wall Street Journal*, December 15. http://www.wsj
.com/articles/SB107107079688571200.

Gilbert, Lucia Albino, and John Carl Gilbert. 2015. "Facts and Figures about California
Winemakers Who Are Women: A Summary from the Studies We Have Conducted."
Women Winemakers of California, Santa Clara University. http://webpages.scu.edu
/womenwinemakers/facts.php. Accessed July 4, 2015.

Goffman, Erving. 1959. *The Presentation of Self in Everyday Life*. Garden City, NY: Doubleday
Anchor.

Greenhouse, Linda. 2005. "Supreme Court Lifts Ban on Wine Shipping." *New York Times*,
May 17. http://www.nytimes.com/2005/05/17/politics/supreme-court-lifts-ban-on
-wine-shipping.html.

Gregory, Ted. 2003. "Illinois Wine Industry in Danger of Going Flat." *Chicago Tribune*,
July 12. http://articles.chicagotribune.com/2003-07-12/news/0307120123_1_wineries
-california-merlot-support-group.

Hargreaves, David. H. 1980. "A Sociological Critique of Individualism in Education."
British Journal of Educational Studies 28 (3): 187–98.

Hertz, Tom. 2006. "Understanding Mobility in America." Center for American Progress.
https://www.americanprogress.org/wp-content/uploads/kf/hertz_mobility_analysis.pdf.

"History of Baxter's Vineyards." n.d. http://www.nauvoowinery.com/baxters-history
.html. Accessed March 9, 2015.

Howland, Peter. 2013. "Distinction by Proxy: The Democratization of Fine Wine." *Journal
of Sociology* 49 (2–3): 325–40.

Illinois Department of Agriculture. 2005. "Gov. Blagojevich Announces *Opportunity Returns*
Grant Allocation for Illinois Wine Industry." News release, November 21. https://www
.agr.state.il.us/newsrels/r1121051.html.

Impact Newsletter. 2012. "Impact's Exclusive Ranking of the Top 10 U.S. Wine and
Spirits Wholesalers." http://www.commonwealthfoundation.org/docLib/20130517_
LiquorWholesalers.pdf.

Indiana Wine Grape Council. n.d. "Wineries of Indiana." http://www.indianawines.org
/wineries/. Accessed October 4, 2011, and December 30, 2015.

Indiana Wine Grape Market Development Council. 2014. "Bylaws." Revised April 21. https://ag.purdue.edu/foodsci/extension/winegrapeteam/Documents/WineGrape CouncilBylaws-Amended4-21-2014.pdf.

——. 2015. "Fall 2015 Council Meeting." https://ag.purdue.edu/foodsci/extension /winegrapeteam/Documents/11-12-2015%20Wine%20Grape%20Minutes-FinalDraft 03152016.pdf.

Iowa Code. 2009. "Chapter 175A: Grape and Wine Development." https://coolice.legis .iowa.gov/Cool-ICE/default.asp?category=billinfo&service=IowaCode&input=175A.

Iowa Legislative Fiscal Bureau. 2001. "FY 2001 Deappropriations Bills HF 399 and SF 267 Pass Appropriations Committees." Fiscal Update, February 26. Iowa Publications Online. http://publications.iowa.gov/8529/2/FU226B.docx.

Iowa Legislature. 2015. Iowa Alcoholic Beverage Control Act, Section 123.183: "Wine Gallonage Tax and Related Funds." https://coolice.legis.iowa.gov/cool-ice/default.asp ?category=billinfo&service=iowacode&input=123.

Iowa Quality Wine Consortium. 2015. "2015 Guidelines." http://www.extension.iastate.edu /wine/sites/www.extension.iastate.edu/files/wine/IQWC%20guidelines_Feb2015.pdf.

Iowa State University News Service. 2011. "Getting Wine from Grape to Glass Faster, Easier Is Focus of Grant to Wine Producing Group." News release, November 1. http://www.news .iastate.edu/news/2011/nov/winegrant.

Iowa Wine and Beer Promotion Board. 2013. "Meeting Minutes." Des Moines: Iowa Economic Development Authority. http://www.iowaeconomicdevelopment.com/UserDocs /documents/IEDA/60413IWBMinutes.pdf.

Iowa Wine Growers Association. n.d. "Funding Needs of the Iowa Wine and Grape Industry." https://www.legis.iowa.gov/docs/publications/SD/24781.pdf. Accessed June 16, 2015.

Jay, Ben. 2015. "Craft Breweries Multiply in the Finger Lakes." *New York Times*, September 24. http://www.nytimes.com/2015/09/27/travel/finger-lakes-craft-beer.html.

Jordan, Erin. 2014. "Iowa Wineries' Ag Designation Means Thousands in Tax Breaks." *The Gazette*, March 31. http://thegazette.com/2012/05/13/iowa-wineries-ag-designation -means-thousands-in-tax-breaks.

Kliman, Todd. 2010. *The Wild Vine: A Forgotten Grape and the Untold Story of American Wine.* New York: Clarkson Potter.

Krause, Rachel. 2016. "SIU Brews Up New Fermentation Science Degree." *WPSD Local 6*, March 24. http://www.wpsdlocal6.com/story/31561746/siu-brews-up-new-fermentation -science-degree.

Kushman, Rick, and Hank Beal. 2007. *A Moveable Thirst: Tales and Tastes from a Season in Napa Wine Country.* Hoboken, NJ: Wiley & Sons.

Lukacs, Paul. 2005. *The Great Wines of America: The Top Forty Vintners, Vineyards, and Vintages.* New York: Norton.

Lynfred Winery. 2014. "Founder: Fred Koehler, February 24, 1928–July 16, 2011." http://www .lynfredwinery.com/scripts/cpg.cfm/7. Accessed July 19, 2015.

Markell-Bani Fine Wines and Sparkling Beverages. 2016. "About Markell-Bani." http://www .markellbani.biz/_aboutus.html.

Marquis, Christopher, and Julie Battilana. 2007. "Acting Globally but Thinking Locally? The

Influence of Local Communities on Organizations." Harvard Business School Working Paper No. 08-034. http://hbswk.hbs.edu/item/acting-globally-but-thinking-locally -the-influence-of-local-communities-on-organizations.

Martinez, Michael. 2005. "Vintner Hopes Court Uncorks Wine Sales." *Chicago Tribune*, January 4. http://articles.chicagotribune.com/2005-01-04/news/0501040282_1_out -of-state-wineries-direct-shipment-wine-institute.

Meier's Wine Cellars. n.d. "History." http://meierswinecellars.com/about-us/history/. Accessed May 25, 2016.

Mid-American Wine Competition. 2015. "Competition Results." http://www.midamerican wine.org/2015medals/Pages/winery2015.aspx.

Newman, Katherine S. 1999. *Falling from Grace: Downward Mobility in the Age of Affluence*. Berkeley: University of California Press.

Ohio Revised Code. 2006. "924.51 Ohio Grape Industries Committee Created." http://law .justia.com/codes/ohio/2006/orc/jd_92451-46ff.html.

Ohio State University. 2014. "Most of Ohio's 2014 Wine Grape Crop Lost Due to Polar Vortex, Ohio State Survey Finds." News release, College of Food, Agricultural, and Environ mental Sciences, April 8. http://cfaes.osu.edu/news/articles/most-ohio%E2%80%99s -2014-wine-grape-crop-lost-due-polar-vortex-ohio-state-survey-finds.

O-I. n.d. "About O-I." http://www.o-i.com/About-O-I/Company-Facts/. Accessed May 25, 2016.

"Old Depot Gets Timely Face Lift." 2003. *Chicago Tribune*, November 30. http://articles .chicagotribune.com/2003-11-30/news/0311300397_1_stamp-monee-restoring.

Oldenburg, Ray. 1989. *The Great Good Place. Cafes, Coffee Shops, Community Centers, Beauty Parlors, General Stores, Bars, Hangouts, and How They Get You through the Day*. New York: Paragon House.

———. 1999. *The Great Good Place: Cafes, Coffee Shops, Bookstores, Bars, Hair Salons, and Other Hangouts at the Heart of a Community*. 2nd ed. Cambridge, MA: Da Capo Press.

———, ed. 2001. *Celebrating the Third Place: Inspiring Stories about the "Great Good Places" at the Heart of Our Communities*. New York: Marlowe & Co.

Osberg, James A. 2005. Comment regarding Notice No. 39: Proposed Establishment of Shawnee Hills Viticultural Area 20028–345P. May 25. Alcohol and Tobacco Tax and Trade Bureau, Notice of Proposed Rulemakings Comments. http://ttb.gov/nprm_comments /ttbnotice39/039004.pdf.

Ovrom, Paul. n.d. "Annual Report of the Iowa Grape and Wine Commission for Fiscal Year 2007." http://publications.iowa.gov/7636/1/GrapeWineCommFY07AnnualRpt.pdf.

Patterson, Tim. 2011. "Tannin Myths and Methods." *WineMaker*, October/November. https://winemakermag.com/1096-tannin-myths-and-methods.

Pinney, Thomas. 1989. *A History of Wine in America: From the Beginnings to Prohibition*. Berkeley: University of California Press.

———. 2005. *A History of Wine in America: From Prohibition to the Present*. Berkeley: University of California Press.

Pirog, Rich. 2002. "Grape Expectations: A Food System Perspective on Redeveloping the Iowa Grape Industry." Leopold Center for Sustainable Agriculture, Iowa State University. http://www.leopold.iastate.edu/pubs-and-papers/2002-08-grape-expectations.

Purdue University Research Foundation News. 2015. "Purdue-Related Startup to Help Wine Grape Growers Battle Drought." October 30. http://www.purdue.edu/newsroom/releases /2015/Q4/purdue-related-startup-to-help-wine-grape-growers-battle-drought.html.

Putnam, Robert D. 2000. *Bowling Alone: The Collapse and Revival of American Community.* New York: Simon & Schuster.

Rasmussen, Kristina. 2014. "Illinois Taxpayers Foot the Bill for Wine Industry." *Illinois Policy*, September 5. https://www.illinoispolicy.org/illinois-taxpayers-foot-the-bill-for -wine-industry/.

Real Beer. 2012. "Iowa Brewers Seek Support for Tourism Program." *Beer Therapy* (blog), March 16. http://www.realbeer.com/blog/?p=2409.

Scarborough Research. 2003. "A New Vintage of Wine Consumers Are Young and Ethnic According to Scarborough Research." http://www.businesswire.com/news/home /20030319005271/en/Vintage-Wine-Consumers-Young-Ethnic-Scarborough -Research.

Schor, Juliet B. 1998. *The Overspent American: Why We Want What We Don't Need.* New York: HarperCollins.

Smyth, Jeff. 2003. "Budget Cuts Eliminating Grape and Wine Council." *Southern Illinoisan,* November 18. http://thesouthern.com/news/budget-cuts-eliminating-grape-and -wine-council/article_947d1232-f950-5a14-8326-84ec58acc346.html.

———. 2004. "Illinois Wine Council Makes Final, Bittersweet Tour." *Southern Illinoisan,* June 28. http://thesouthern.com/news/illinois-wine-council-makes-final-bittersweet -tour/article_8e4a4507-ff6d-5c25-8c6a-02e2f4b1cbc2.html.

Spada, Piero. 2015. "Research on Hybrid Tannins Continues." *Midwest Wine Press*, May 2. http://midwestwinepress.com/2015/05/02/research-on-hybrid-tannins-continues/.

Specialty Wine Retailers Association. 2008. "Wholesale Protection: Alcohol Wholesalers' Control and Weakening of the American Wine Market through Its $50,000,000 in Campaign Contribution." January 8. http://nawr.org/wp-content/uploads/2013/02 /WholesaleProtection-2008.pdf.

Suttell, Scott. 2011. "Luxco Inc. of St. Louis Buys Paramount Distillers Inc." *Crain's Cleveland Business*, September 21. http://www.crainscleveland.com/article/20110921 /FREE/110929941/luxco-inc-of-st-louis-buys-paramount-distillers-inc.

Taber, George M. 2005. *Judgment of Paris: California vs. France and the Historic 1976 Paris Tasting That Revolutionized Wine.* New York: Scribner, 2005.

Teague, Lettie. 2015. "Women Vintners Chip Away at the Wineglass Ceiling." *Wall Street Journal*, May 1. http://www.wsj.com/articles/women-vintners-chip-away-at-the-wineglass -ceiling-1430496334.

Thach, Liz, and Kathryn Chang. 2015. "2015 Survey of American Wine Consumer Preferences." *Wine Business.com*, November 11. http://www.winebusiness.com/news/?go=get Article&dataid=160722.

Thornton, James. 2013. "The Tangled Economics of American Wine," *Wine-Searcher.com*, October 12. http://www.wine-searcher.com/m/2013/10/the-tangled-economics-of -american-wine.

Tiemann, Thomas K. 2008. "Grower-Only Farmers' Markets: Public Spaces and Third Places." *Journal of Popular Culture* 41 (3): 467–87.

Tordsen, Craig, Reg Clause, and Mary Holz-Clause. 2003. "General Iowa Statute and Regulatory Issues for Wine." June. Agricultural Marketing Resource Center, Iowa State University. http://www.agmrc.org/media/cms/iowawinestatutes_93304F9396EB6.pdf.

Trubek, Amy B. 2008. *The Taste of Place: A Cultural Journey into Terroir*. Berkeley: University of California Press.

Turkle, Sherry. 2011. *Alone Together: Why We Expect More from Technology and Less from Each Other*. New York: Basic Books.

U.S. Census Bureau. 2010. "Census Bureau's First Release of Comprehensive Data Shows Franchises Make Up More than 10 Percent of Employer Businesses." http://www.census.gov/newsroom/releases/archives/economic_census/cb10-141.html.

Veseth, Mike. 2011. *Wine Wars*. Lanham, MD: Rowman and Littlefield.

Volpe, Richard James, III, Richard Green, Dale Heien, and Richard Howitt. 2010. "Wine-Grape Production Trends Reflect Evolving Consumer Demand over 30 Years." *California Agriculture* 64 (1): 42–46. http://iv.ucdavis.edu/files/24512.pdf.

White, Michael L. 2012. "101 Iowa Grape & Wine Facts." Iowa State University Extension and Outreach. http://www.extension.iastate.edu/wine/sites/www.extension.iastate.edu/files/wine/062012%20101%20Facts%20About%20IA%20Grapes%20n%20Wine.pdf.

Wine Business.com. 2015. "E. & J. Gallo Announces Purchase of Talbott Vineyards." August 25. http://www.winebusiness.com/news/?go=getArticle&dataid=156776.

———. 2016. "A Few Takeaways from the Preliminary California Grape Crush Report," February 10. http://www.winebusiness.com/blog/?go=getBlogEntry&dataId=164672.

Wine Institute. 2015. "Number of California Wineries." Revised July 20. http://www.wineinstitute.org/resources/statistics/article124.

Wines and Vines. 2015. "Wine Industry Metrics—Winery Database." http://www.winesandvines.com/template.cfm?section=widc&widcDomain=wineries. Accessed January 9, 2016.

Woods, Timothy, and Matthew Ernst. 2011. "2011 Regional Winegrape Marketing and Price Outlook." http://www.uky.edu/Ag/NewCrops/winegrapesurvey11.pdf.

Index

JAMES R. PENNELL is a professor of sociology at the University of Indianapolis. He is also a lifelong musician and singer-songwriter who regularly performs in central Indiana.

Heartland Foodways

The University of Illinois Press
is a founding member of the
Association of American University Presses.

Text designed by Jim Proefrock
Composed in 11/13 Filosofia
at the University of Illinois Press
Cover designed by Jim Proefrock
Cover photo by Greta Eleen Pennell
Manufactured by Sheridan Books, Inc.

University of Illinois Press
1325 South Oak Street
Champaign, IL 61820-6903
www.press.uillinois.edu